Joseph F. Neussendorfer

GREAT LAKES BOOKS

THE
AMBASSADOR
BRIDGE

PHILIP P. MASON

THE AMBASSADOR BRIDGE

A MONUMENT TO PROGRESS

Wayne State University Press • Detroit 1987

Library of Congress Cataloging-in-Publication Data

Mason, Philip P. (Philip Parker), 1927–
   The Ambassador Bridge.

   (Great Lakes books)
   Includes index.
   1. Ambassador Bridge (Detroit, Mich. and Windsor,
Ont.)—History.   I. Title.   II. Series.
TG25.D5M37   1987   624'.55'0977434   87-18983
ISBN 0-8143-1839-8
ISBN 0-8143-1840-1 (pbk.)

Grateful acknowledgment is made to the Detroit International Bridge Company
for financial assistance in the publication of this volume.

To my father,
who first introduced me to
the importance of bridges

CONTENTS

Contents

12

Lancaster Takes Over: The 1960s

13

Changing with the Times: The 1970s

14

The Challenge of the Future: The Necklace of Lights

Appendix: Bridge Statistics

Notes
Index

ILLUSTRATIONS & MAPS

Illustrations
& Maps

13

Maps

ACKNOWLEDGMENTS

In my research on this book I have been assisted by many people who have extensive knowledge about the Ambassador Bridge, Detroit and Windsor, and the archival and library materials relating to the topic.

The Burton Historical Collection of the Detroit Public Library has extensive holdings relating to the bridge, the Detroit River, and surrounding communities. I am especially grateful for the assistance of Mrs. Alice Dalligan, chief of the Burton Historical Collection; Joseph Oldenburg, assistant director of the Detroit Public Library; Margaret Ward, Joan Gartland, and Janet Nelson of the Burton Historical Collection; and Mildred Hilton of the Business and Finance section, Detroit Public Library; and other library staff who were most helpful.

Mark Walsh, municipal archivist, Windsor, Ontario, helped me locate countless sources as I traced the Windsor connections to the bridge. The staff of the Local History Collections of the Windsor Public Library were also generous with their time and expertise. Jerry Malone, curator of

manuscripts at the University of Windsor, assisted my research, especially on Windsor history and in the voluminous papers of the Border Chamber of Commerce. I appreciate the assistance of Mary Jane Icely Handy, librarian of the *Windsor Star*, who located many interesting references, and photographs.

LeRoy Barnett, archivist at the State Archives of Michigan, made helpful suggestions and located important sources. The staffs of the Transportation Library at the University of Michigan, Michigan State Library, and the Ontario Provincial Archives graciously complied with my requests for material. Arthur M. Woodford, an authority on Detroit history, and Professor Larry Kulisek, of the University of Windsor, who is writing a history of Windsor, shared their expertise.

The staff of the Schwab Information Center at Bethlehem, Pennsylvania, shared their files. Jackson Durkee, an engineering consultant of Bethlehem, Pennsylvania, and Mrs. Jonathan Jones, widow of the one-time supervising engineer of the bridge, identified people and described engineering aspects of the bridge. Joseph Scherer, a partner of Mojeski and Masters, also assisted, by making the historical records of his company available.

I want to give special recognition to H. Hugh L. Pratley, consulting engineer, Montreal, who, with his father, Philip Louis Pratley, has been associated with the Ambassador Bridge since 1925. Mr. Pratley generously made available his records on the bridge, allowed me to accompany him on his annual inspection of the bridge in 1983, and gave me extensive interviews about his experiences as bridge inspector. He also read the manuscript in its entirety and made suggestions for its improvement.

David Glick, former vice-president of Greenfield Village and the Henry Ford Museum in Dearborn, Michigan, was helpful during my research on the early attempts to bridge the Detroit River. Charles J. Meyers, of Southfield, Michigan, also shared his information on the early bridges between Trenton, Grosse Ile, and Stony Island, Michigan.

At the Detroit Chamber of Commerce I received invaluable assistance from Louise Thomas, George Kiba, and Brenda Zimmerman. Joan Boram, library consultant and a local historian, shared her research material on the Detroit River. Kathryn Kozora, formerly with the Detroit Recreation Department, was most helpful.

In addition to the extensive archival material on the Ambassador Bridge, there are also available hundreds of photographs, posters, cartoons, films, and other pictorial records. They document the construction of the bridge and its history since the dedication and opening in 1929. Also represented are the individuals who were associated with plans to bridge the Detroit River since 1873.

In order to keep engineering consultants informed in New York, Pittsburgh, and Montreal, bridge officials hired photographers in Windsor and Detroit to photograph all stages of construction. These photographs are located at the Detroit International Bridge Company (D.I.B.) Archives; the Modjeski and Masters Engineering Company of Harrisburg, Pennsylvania; and in the personal files of H. Hugh L. Pratley of Montreal, Quebec, whose father, Philip L. Pratley, and his associate, Colonel C. N. Monsarrat, served as consultants to Joseph A. Bower.

The Burton Historical Collection of the Detroit Public Library also has a varied photographic collection relating to the bridge and the Detroit River. Especially valuable are the photographs given to the Burton Collection by the *Detroit News*. The *Windsor Star* and the *Detroit Free Press* also provided relevant photographs for use in the book, as did Ford Motor Company Archives, Detroit; the Detroit Institute of Arts; and Allen County Historical Museum of Lima, Ohio.

Richard Alwood of the American Commercial Photo Company gave permission for many excellent prints of the bridge, produced by Smith Brothers Photographers, to be included in the volume. Furthermore, Roy G. Lancaster provided access to his colorful slide collection which covered many aspects of the bridge's more recent history. Especially helpful were Helen Austin Sumner and H. Hugh L. Pratley, who loaned family photographs for the book.

Special thanks is given to John Sullivan of Aerial Associates in Ann Arbor, Michigan, whose views show better than wordy descriptions the extent of traffic congestion on the bridge and also delineate the proximity of interstate highways to the U.S. plaza of the bridge. In addition, we are indebted to Martha Smith, photographer from Bloomfield Hills, Michigan, for her beautiful color transparency of the necklace of lights used to illustrate the book's jacket.

I am most appreciative for the advice of my long-time friend and colleague, Dr. Stanley D. Solvick, of the Department of History at Wayne State University, who was always available for discussion. So, too, were George and Geneva Wiskemann of Lansing, Michigan, whose knowledge of Michigan history and related book sources is unmatched.

Special thanks go to Robert A. Bower of California, the son of Joseph A. Bower, for allowing me to interview him and making available some of his father's papers. I am also indebted to Helen Austin Sumner, of Lake San Marcos, California, the daughter of James W. Austin, who gave me a delightful account of her historic walk across the Detroit River footbridge in 1928. She also allowed me to review her father's personal papers relating to his tenure at the bridge. In addition, Jack Sumner, a friend of the Austin family, described the opening day festivities. Elmer Paquette, a bridge employee for more than thirty years, and other long-time bridge employees Dorothy Saull, John Hannan, and Frank Kefalis shared their experiences.

To Dorothy Rogalski, former secretary to the president of the bridge, I owe special gratitude. She showed me how to use the extensive archives of the Ambassador Bridge and located scores of documents which filled the gaps in my account of the earliest days of the bridge. Roy G. Lancaster, the president of the Ambassador Bridge since 1961, gave freely of his time and helped clarify many points of information. He also gave me lengthy interviews about his first-hand knowledge of the bridge's operation over the past twenty-five years, and identified related people and places in the border cities. He very kindly opened the bridge's archives and allowed me the freedom to complete my research at times convenient to me. Without his support and cooperation I could not have documented the book on many points of information.

Kathy Wildfong, of the Wayne State University Press, contributed greatly to the finished product. Her skill as an editor and her many thoughtful suggestions reveal themselves throughout the book.

Mark and Catherine Phillips were most competent as research assistants and spent many hours delving into newspapers and periodicals seeking references on the bridge. I am indebted to Susan Elaine Mason and Henrietta Dow Mason, who read and edited the manuscript. Estella L. Gleason, of the Archives staff, and John D. Fraser, of the McGregor Memorial Conference Center at Wayne State University, assisted me in a number of ways, made suggestions, and listened patiently to numerous research problems.

INTRODUCTION

The first known account of the Detroit River was written by Father Louis Hennepin, a Jesuit priest, on August 11, 1679, as he stood on the deck of the *Griffin*, the first ship to sail the Great Lakes. The *Griffin* was under the command of the noted French explorer Robert Chevalier de La Salle. Father Hennepin was deeply impressed with the beauty of the Detroit River, the vineyards, forests, and meadows which lined its banks, and its picturesque islands:

The islands are the finest in the world. They are covered with forests of nut and fruit trees, and with wild vines loaded with grapes. From these we made a large quantity of wine. The banks of the Strait [Detroit River] are vast meadows, and the prospect is terminated with some hills covered with vineyards, trees bearing good fruit; and the groves and forests so well arranged that one would think that Nature alone could not have laid out the grounds so effectively without the help of man, so charming was the prospect.

The country is well stocked with stags, wild goat, and bears, all of which furnish excellent food, and they are not at all fierce as in other countries. There are herds of buffaloes that trample down the flowers and grass as they rush around in their clumsy motion. There are great numbers of moose and elk, which in the size of their horns almost rival the branches of the great trees. Turkey cocks sweep along like clouds overhead.[1]

Sailing north, they entered a large body of water which they named "Lake Sainte Claire," the Lake St. Clair which we know today. At some point later in the voyage Father Hennepin left the ship and returned overland to civilization. The fate of the *Griffin* and the La Salle trip, however, is shrouded in mystery. It is believed that the ship foundered in a storm on its return voyage, for it disappeared without a trace. But Father Hennepin's historic description of the Detroit and Windsor area remains as a glimpse of an untouched river scene at the present site of the Ambassador Bridge.

The river that Father Hennepin so eloquently described winds north from the western end of Lake Erie for about twenty miles, passing two large islands and numerous small islands. It then turns in a northeasterly direction for eight miles until it reaches Lake St. Clair. Its average width is about two thousand feet and average depth about thirty-six feet. From Lake Erie to Lake Huron, the total distance of the Detroit River, including Lake St. Clair and the St. Clair River waterway, is approximately eighty-five miles.

From the earliest times, the Detroit River served as a major thoroughfare for Indian tribes from settlements located along the river on both sides. This water route facilitated travel by canoe between villages, movement of war parties, and trade between tribes to the east and west. Indeed, during the early seventeenth century, the

hostile Iroquois tribes of New York State sent war parties into Ontario, Michigan, and other areas adjacent to the Great Lakes via the Detroit River.

As French explorers probed the Midwest looking for a northwest passage to the Pacific Ocean, they seldom traveled the Detroit River route because of their fear of the warlike Iroquois. Instead, they reached the upper lakes, Superior, Huron, and Michigan, by following the Montreal River west to Lake Nippising. But as Iroquois hostilities waned, the river provided easy access to the north for fur traders who trapped and swapped their wares in wilderness outposts of the upper lakes.

Indeed, it was the northern route which Cadillac used when he brought an

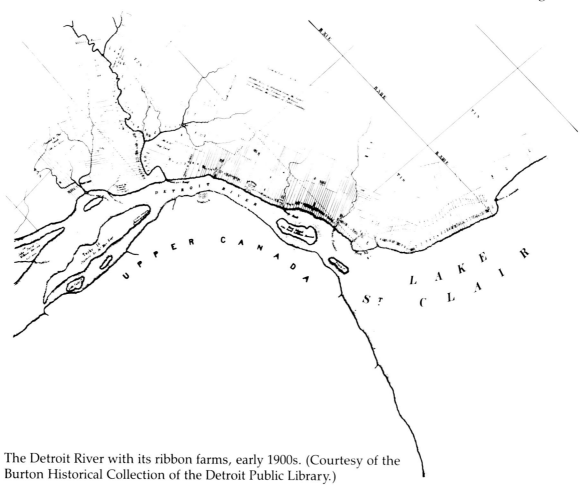

The Detroit River with its ribbon farms, early 1900s. (Courtesy of the Burton Historical Collection of the Detroit Public Library.)

expedition to what is now Detroit in July 1701. His purpose was to build a military post, fur trading center, and settlement, and his contingent included several hundred soldiers, *couriers du bois,* Indians, priests, and settlers. After selecting a site on the north side of the river, Cadillac built a stockaded village, which he named Fort Pontchartrain du Detroit. "Du Detroit" means "on the strait."

Detroit grew slowly during the eighteenth century. The fur trade dominated the interest of the fort's inhabitants, although some farmers settled and cultivated narrow "ribbon" farms on both the east and west sides of the fort. Farms were also established on the southern side of the river, from Fighting Island, opposite La Salle, Ontario, to Belle Isle. The settlement created was the oldest white settlement in the province of Ontario. Then in 1748 a Jesuit mission for Indians was founded on the Ontario side of the river. It served the thousands of Indians who were attracted to Detroit by the fur trade. Soon the French outpost at Detroit controlled the rich fur trade of the upper lakes, and it had become a military bastion, as well.

The strategic importance of Detroit and the waterway between Lake Erie and Lake Huron was recognized by the English as well as the French. During the continuous wars which marked the eighteenth century, Detroit became the key to the control of the fur trade on the lakes. Finally, in 1760 the English defeated the French and seized control of Detroit and the rest of North America.

Under the British, Detroit continued to occupy a dominant position in the power structure holding together the North American empire. In fact, Detroit was the main British outpost during the Revolutionary War, when it became the center for British raids upon American colonists in New York, Ohio, Indiana, and Illinois. Although the Treaty of Paris in 1783 provided for American control of Detroit and the rest of what is now Michigan, it was not until July 1796 that the British finally evacuated the fort and turned it over to American forces. Once the British departed, the Detroit River became more than an avenue of trade and commerce; it now served as the international border between the Province of Ontario, Canada, and the State of Michigan.

Settlement of Ontario and Michigan increased steadily during the nineteenth century. The building and improvement of roads, the completion of the Erie Canal in 1826 and the Welland Canal in 1829, and especially the construction of railroads in the latter half of the nineteenth century all facilitated the settlement process. Tens of thousands of settlers arrived in Detroit and Wayne County, Michigan, and in Walkerville, Sandwich, Amherstburg, and surrounding parts of Essex County, Ontario, to take up farming or to work in the towns. By mid-century, the Industrial Revolution and the resulting increase in factory production of goods attracted even greater numbers of new settlers and workers to the Detroit River area.

As the population and commerce needs increased, the Detroit River became even more significant as a trade waterway. Then, when other midwestern states opened for settlement, agricultural and urban centers evolved. For example, the opening of the vast iron and copper ranges in the Upper Peninsula of Michigan and in Minnesota, the white pine industry of Michigan and Wisconsin, and the rise of the cities of Chicago, Milwaukee, Duluth, and other ports all contributed dramatically to make the Detroit River a major link in commercial trade between the East and the West. By 1873, between April and December, navigation records showed that more than twenty-seven thousand vessels passed along the channel of the Detroit River. This

The Detroit River in 1836. Engraving by William James Bennett. (Courtesy of the Detroit Institute of Arts.)

The tugboat *Champion* with five schooners in tow at the head of Belle Isle on the Detroit River. From a painting by Seth Arca Whipple. (Courtesy of the Henry Ford Archives.)

number represented an estimated forty percent of the total coastal and foreign trade of the United States.

Detroit, Windsor, and Amherstburg also became railroad centers in the last half of the nineteenth century, with major lines connecting the east coast of Canada and the United States with Chicago and the agricultural and industrial centers of the Midwest. Railroad ferries were placed and operated between Windsor and Detroit to handle the steadily increasing railroad traffic, but were far from adequate even under the best conditions. During the busy navigational season, as well as the winter when severe storms and ice blocked the channel, thousands of railroad freight and passenger cars were stalled, sometimes waiting for days or longer to cross the river. The voices of merchants, business leaders, and farmers soon joined those of railroad officials in demanding and fighting for better ways to cross the river.

It soon became evident that the solution to the horrendous railroad bottleneck at Detroit and Windsor was either a railroad tunnel or a bridge. Both means were carefully considered by local business leaders, as well as by railroad company officials. In 1871, under the auspices of the Michigan Central Railroad Company, construction of a railroad tunnel was begun on both sides of the river. When this project failed and was abandoned in 1872, railroad officials turned their attention to plans for a railroad bridge. Two plans were proposed: one, to connect Trenton, Michigan, and Amherstburg, Ontario, via Grosse Ile and Stony Island; and a second, to connect downtown Detroit and Windsor, directly.

Unlike the tunnel project, the construction of a bridge across navigable, international waters required prior approval of the Canadian and United States governments. The public hearings called by the U.S. Corps of Engineers brought into the open the battle between two powerful interests, the railroads and the shippers. Both insisted that the cargoes which they carried were essential to the economic well-being of the United States and Canada. The railroad interests wanted to span the Detroit River, leaving space between piers for vessels to pass; the vessel interests insisted that no piers be placed in the river. Business groups, boards of commerce, and governments of Great Lakes port cities all took sides in the growing controversy. For example, resolutions were passed by local government and shipping organizations in Buffalo, Cleveland, Toledo, Minneapolis, and Milwaukee opposing the construction of a bridge across the Detroit River.

The bridge proposal was defeated by the vessel interests in 1873 and continuously over the next half century, whenever a proposal was made to the U.S. Corps of Engineers. Although additional ferries, designed to withstand ice floes, were put into operation, they were unable to keep pace with the large volume of freight traffic between Detroit and Windsor, especially after the opening of new railroad lines. Even the construction and opening of a railroad tunnel between Detroit and Windsor in 1909 did not solve the problem. The tunnel was adequate for the immediate needs of the Michigan Central Railroad, which had constructed it, but not for the other railroad companies. Furthermore, by 1910 a new economic force, the automobile industry, had appeared on the scene, and with it motorists, who demanded a quick way to cross the river.

New technology was to become a consideration in other ways. For example, by 1910 new engineering developments in the design and construction of long span bridges answered the complaints of vessel owners and their powerful organization, the Lake Carriers Association. It would be just a matter of time before a bridge would

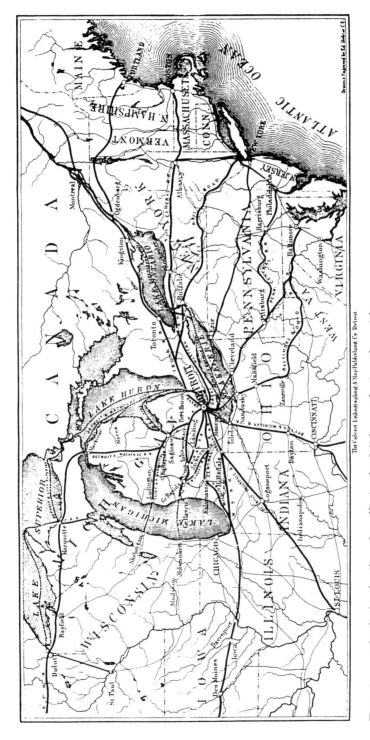

Detroit was the hub of railroad traffic in the Midwest during the mid-nineteenth century. (Courtesy of the Burton Historical Collection of the Detroit Public Library.)

be built across the river. By the end of World War I, it was more a question of whether the structure would be publicly or privately owned, who would provide the leadership to build it, and where it would be located. These problems were finally resolved during the 1920s with the construction and opening of the Ambassador Bridge.

The Ambassador Bridge will describe in some detail the various attempts from the 1870s to the 1920s to build a bridge across the Detroit River, and will define the role of individuals who proposed and campaigned for the structure, including railroad officials, businessmen, and bridge engineers. Another part of the book will detail the design and construction of the span, documented by a superb collection of photographs taken at each stage of construction. Still another important segment relates to the operation of the Ambassador Bridge during its first fifty-eight years, including the impact of the Great Depression, World War II, and numerous economic and political crises. The men who guided the fortunes of the bridge will also be highlighted: James F. Joy, Gustav Lindenthal, Charles Evan Fowler, James W. Austin, Joseph A. Bower, R. Bryson McDougald, Charles P. McTague, C. Clinton Campbell, Robert A. Bower, and Roy G. Lancaster.

The Ambassador Bridge never attained the international reputation of the Niagara suspension bridge or the Golden Gate Bridge, nor was it considered the architectural marvel the Brooklyn Bridge was. Even

so, it holds a significant place in the history of suspension bridges. For a few years, it held the distinction of being the longest suspension bridge in the world; and it has always been the longest suspension bridge over international waters.

Furthermore, despite its fifty-eight years, it is in excellent condition and promises to carry more automobiles and commercial trucks than ever before. It also represents one of the first spans built exclusively for vehicular traffic and one which has successfully competed with railroads for tonnage of cargo crossings. To citizens of western Ontario and southeastern Michigan, it has become a beautiful and permanent part of the architecture and skyline of the region. And since 1981, when the "necklace of lights" was installed on the main cables, its presence is even more striking to residents and motorists.

More than two hundred years ago, Father Louis Hennepin described for posterity the Detroit River and the beautiful scenery on its banks. No longer are there wild forests, rich vineyards, vast meadows, or wild animals in abundance. Skyscrapers, factories, forges, steel mills, and office buildings of various sizes and shapes stand in their places. What was once a verdant wilderness has become the industrial heartland of North America—all because of the Detroit River. The Ambassador Bridge, which crosses that river, serves as a monument which links two nations which shared their origins more than three hundred years ago.

CHAPTER 1

Early Attempts to Bridge the River
1870–1909

By the end of the Civil War, Detroit had already become a major United States railroad center. Railroad lines reached into the rich lumber and mining regions of northern Michigan and spiked westward into the fertile farming center of the nation. The Michigan Central Railroad, which reached Chicago in 1854, became one of the main arteries of transportation to send grain and meat products to eastern markets.

Across the Detroit River in Windsor, the Great Western Railroad, whose lines from Niagara to Detroit had opened in 1854, made connections with the New York Central, piercing eastward toward the Atlantic. Although lake vessels competed aggressively with the railroads during the summer and fall months, ice closed lake transportation from December 1 to at least April 1 every year. Winters of the Midwest provided a virtual monopoly to the railroads.[1]

At the Detroit River, ferries operated continuously, carrying railroad passengers and freight to waiting trains on the opposite shore. At first, railroad cars had to be unloaded and passengers and freight carried across the river. In 1867 the *Great Western* became the first in a series of railroad ferries to be equipped to carry railroad freight cars intact. At the terminals on both sides of the river, tracks were built "which could be lowered or raised to admit the cars passing directly from the boats to the railroads."[2] The capacity of the railroad ferries differed. The *Great Western* carried fourteen railroad cars; among the other well known nineteenth-century ferries, the *Transit* carried ten; the *Michigan*, sixteen; the *Transfer*, eighteen; the *Transport*, twenty-one; and the *Trenton*, eight.[3]

Despite the railroad ferry facilities at Detroit and Windsor, a troublesome bottleneck developed, especially during the busy seasons. There were seemingly endless delays on both sides of the river. Even before winter set in and ice floes created additional hazards to navigation, railroad traffic frequently was delayed. At times there were as many as seven hundred to one thousand cars waiting to cross at each side of the river.[4] Passenger service was also disrupted by the inadequate ferry service. By 1870 ferries handled fifteen thousand passenger cars and four hundred thousand freight cars.[5] According to railroad officials, that was only a small percentage of the potential market.

Disruption in railroad service caused by the inadequate ferry service had serious economic repercussions. Each year Chicago and other lake ports were forced to put millions of bushels of grain into storage because they could not be shipped to eastern markets. Manufactured and other goods, including imports from Europe, were also held up for long periods in the East, awaiting clearance for westward transport. As a result of these delays, prices of all agricultural produce, as well as beef and pork, remained high. Farmers and merchants looked to the railroads for a solution.[6]

James F. Joy, the president of the Michigan Central Railroad and one of the nation's leading railroad promoters, responded to the challenge. Since the early 1840s, shortly after he migrated to Detroit from New England, Joy had thrown himself with a fervor into railroad development. He was active in legal and financial circles in Michigan and soon became recognized nationally as a railroad builder and financier. After taking control of the Michigan Central Railroad, he completed the line from Kalamazoo to Chicago and made it one of the most profitable railways in the country. Joy's close connections with numerous other railroads and a close friendship with Cornelius Vanderbilt facilitated his rise as a railroad magnate.[7]

In the years following the end of the Civil War, Joy recognized the inherent inadequacy of the ferry service across the Detroit River. Unless a more effective and reliable means of transporting passengers and cars could be found, the Michigan and Ontario railroads would lose out to competing

James F. Joy. (Courtesy of the Burton Historical Collection of the Detroit Public Library.)

southern lines. In 1869 Joy, acting with the knowledge and support of the leaders of the Great Western Railroad, developed a plan to build a railroad tunnel under the Detroit River. This was not a new idea. Several successful railroad tunnels had been built earlier, including one under the Thames in England. Nevertheless, tunnel engineering was in its infancy, and Joy knew it.

Joy hired E. S. Chesbrough of Chicago, who had built the extensive sewer system under that city, to conduct a feasibility study for a tunnel between Detroit and Windsor. In the fall of 1868, Chesbrough tested the velocity and direction of the river currents and made borings in both sides of the river to determine the nature of the subsoil and depth to bedrock. In January 1869 Chesbrough presented his findings to Joy and recommended the construction of a railroad tunnel running from the foot of St. Antoine Street in Detroit to Parent Avenue in Windsor. His plans called for twin, single-track tunnels, eighty-six hundred feet long and fifteen feet in diameter, surrounded by solid walls of masonry. Chesbrough's analysis of the river borings indicated a simple and relatively inexpensive engineering project. Limestone bedrock was found at 110 feet below the surface of the river, covered by successive layers of hardpan with boulders, hard blue clay, laminated clay, and, finally, the soft blue clay of the river bottom.[8]

Joy accepted Chesbrough's report and immediately began to implement his recommendations. Because of the widespread prejudice against railroads, Joy organized the Detroit River Railroad Tunnel Company under Michigan state law.[9] In May 1871 the company sought approval for the tunnel project from the Detroit Common Council and the Windsor City Council. Despite some opposition to the involvement of the railroad companies, the project was approved by Windsor and Detroit authorities.[10] Chesbrough's final engineering plans were reviewed and approved and construction contracts were awarded. D. D. McBean of Chicago was selected as superintendent of the project.

On September 14, 1871, ground breaking ceremonies were held and work started simultaneously in Detroit and Windsor with the sinking of vertical shafts, 3,275 feet apart. When the proper depth was reached, horizontal tunnels, or drifts, were dug toward opposite shores. Following Chesbrough's plan, drainage tunnels, each about five feet in diameter and covered with masonry, would be built first. Later, the larger tunnels would be built parallel to the drifts.

Work on the tunnels proceeded slowly. Relatively crude tools impeded progress. Steel tunnel shields, powerful ventilating equipment, and efficient excavating equipment apparatus so common in twentieth-century engineering projects had not yet been developed. Labor disputes erupted when Canadian workers went on strike over payment of wages in American money, which at that time was worth considerably less than Canadian currency. The workers finally settled for $.25 more a day, amounting to $2.50 for an eight-hour shift.[11] Inadequate soil information also caused problems. Instead of the blue clay predicted, the workers hit hardpan and huge boulders on both sides of the river. Sulfurous gases plagued the laborers, causing discomfort and frequent work stoppages.

Eleven hundred eighty feet of the tunnel from the American shore had been excavated when the ventilating equipment failed in 1872. Before the huge fans were repaired, two workers inspecting a reported leak in the tunnel face were overcome by poisonous gases and died before they could be rescued. After the accident, workers continued to excavate an additional 40 feet before the work was abandoned. Although work on the Canadian side continued for a few weeks thereafter, it, too, was abandoned when the contractors asked to be relieved of "further obligations." The excavation had extended only 380 feet from the Canadian shore.[12]

Chesbrough and McBean were enraged at the closing of the tunnel construction, charging that James Joy and other backers lacked faith in the venture. Joy, on the other hand, cited the time delays and the cost overruns, reporting to his railroad's board of directors that the obstacles to completion were "so great as to force upon our minds the conviction that if practicable at all, the railroad tunnel would be too expensive for a private company to undertake its construction."[13] A similar explanation for abandonment of the tunnel was presented to the shareholders of the Great Western Railway Company in London, Ontario, on April 7, 1873.[14]

The agitation for better railroad crossings at the Detroit River did not end with the failure of the tunnel project. In late 1872 and early 1873, a devastating Michigan winter—the worst of the century—brought the river crossing issue to a head again, drawing public authorities into the picture. For four solid months, ice jammed the riverway, forcing the curtailment of ferry service and all river operations. For about two months the ice was so thick that no ferries could operate. At one time, more than twelve hundred freight cars were stalled in the railroad yards in Detroit, awaiting passage across the river to Buffalo and eastern cities. Freight transport from Chicago, Milwaukee, Minneapolis, and other western cities stopped completely, causing prices of grain and other goods to soar. Hundreds of passengers were stranded, unable to complete their journeys. The Michican Central and Great Western railroads lost more than $1 million during the crisis.[15]

Merchants, railroad operators, and other businessmen in the Detroit and Windsor areas clamored for action. On January 28, 1873, the Detroit Board of Trade called a special public meeting to discuss what might be done. The board appointed a special committee to assess the feasibility of completing the tunnel project or, as an alternative, to determine the "practicality of bridging the River."[16]

Within a week, the committee reported that the tunnel was "doomed to failure." Even if the project could be resurrected, the committee concluded, it would take at least five years to complete. The board of trade unanimously resolved: "That this Board earnestly petition Congress to pass a bill authorizing the construction of a bridge across the Detroit River at such a point near the city as may be found most desirable, and by its provisions, guarding the interests of commerce."[17] The board urged the Parliament of Canada to endorse

similar plans for a bridge at Windsor. The *Detroit Free Press* reacted, endorsing the bridge proposal on its editorial pages. The *Free Press* prophesied correctly, however, that the bridge would face strong opposition by powerful "vessel owning interests."[18]

The board of trade leaders, including James F. Joy, immediately contacted congressional leaders and sought support for the bridge, which under federal law required an investigation and approval by the United States War Department. On March 3, 1873, Congress acted, directing the secretary of war to appoint the U.S. Corps of Engineers to

> inquire into the practicality of bridging, consistently with the interests of navigation, the channel between Lake Huron and Lake Erie at such points as may be needed for the passing of railroad trains across said channel . . . and further to inquire into the number and character of the vessels navigating said channel and the number of trips by each; and if said bridging is practicable, to report what extent of span or space and elevation above the water, will be required in the construction of such bridge or bridges, so as not seriously to injure the navigation of said channel.[19]

The secretary of war appointed a special board of engineers, chaired by Major General G. K. Warren, to conduct the investigation. Public hearings commenced in Detroit on May 12, 1873. Detailed records of the various arguments for and against the bridge proposal were kept, from which the board was able to determine the nature and extent of commerce on the Detroit River, as well as the character of railroad service in Michigan and Ontario.[20]

Leading the lobby in favor of a railroad bridge, not surprisingly, was James Joy. At the public hearings, Joy attacked the issue on multiple fronts. He reviewed the long-

Michigan Central Railroad ferry docking in Detroit. (Courtesy of Wayne State University, Archives of Labor History and Urban Affairs.)

standing problems of railroads in getting passengers and produce across the river. He cited the harsh winter of 1872 to 1873, holding it responsible for the million-dollar revenue loss suffered by the railroads and the sharp rise in grain and other foodstuff prices. But he did not allow the weather to be the scapegoat for the inherent inadequacy of the ferry service. Joy maintained, persuasively, that long before ice developed on the river, the ferries were unable to meet the demands of crossing traffic.

Joy's most compelling arguments were economic. The railroads, he argued, had more than $150 million invested in Detroit and Windsor, compared to only $50 million by shipping interests. A railroad bridge, said Joy, could increase the railroads' investment tenfold. Moreover, the impact on the marketplace would be staggering. According to Joy, uninterrupted train service across the Detroit River would be "felt upon every farm, and by every businessman, in fact, by every inhabitant of the great Northwest, and through all arteries and channels

Car ferry bucking ice. (Courtesy of the Allen County Museum.)

through which business of any kind moves and money circulates throughout the whole western country."[21]

Others joined Joy in supporting the bridge. Officials of other railroad companies and prominent Detroit merchants and business leaders lent their support. They described, from personal experience, the railroad bottleneck existing on both sides of the Detroit River, the inadequacy of the ferry service, and the "deleterious effects" of these conditions upon the business climate of Detroit. A railroad bridge connecting downtown Detroit and Windsor, they argued, was essential to continued growth of Michigan's and Detroit's economies.[22]

The bridge was not without its opponents, however. Forceful testimony presented during the public hearings described the prospective dangers of the bridge, attacked the monopolistic nature of the railroads, and claimed that a railroad bridge would be far more detrimental to commerce than was the status quo. The major argument of those opposed to the bridge centered upon the overwhelming importance of Great Lakes shipping on the Detroit River to the economy of the United States. The shipping interests claimed that a bridge would raise the prices of transportation and endorsed the existing ferry service as an adequate means of river crossing. "Such a bridge," one petitioner stated, "would not relieve or expedite the business of railroads, while it would be a serious hindrance to the much larger shipping interests of the lakes, and thus raise the cost of transportation, to the injury of the people."[23]

Shipowners, joined by some merchants, reminded the board that shipping, too, was a valuable asset to the city of Detroit. Opponents of the bridge argued that ships carried more freight than railroads "at lower prices."[24] Ship captains rallied to the opposition's cause. They dramatically described the swift and treacherous current of the Detroit River, the difficulties of towing vessels through the narrow sections of the river, and the losses surely to be suffered from accidents. Any bridge which would locate piers in the river would be a potential hazard to shipping and "must be blocked . . . at all costs."[25]

Another argument presented by bridge opponents was that a railroad bridge would benefit only passengers, especially wealthy travelers, whereas the shipping prices on grains and other foodstuffs would rise.[26] The "monopolistic practices of railroads" were cited often during the hearings with the implication that the bridge would enhance the power of the railroad barons and allow them arbitrarily to raise rates. Vessel owners and operators, on the other hand, were depicted by bridge opponents as the veritable backbone of the American free enterprise system. Finally, adding to the diversity of opinions and positions on the bridge were those who continued to favor a tunnel as the answer to the river crossing problem.[27]

In addition to testimony on the need for a railroad bridge from Detroit to Windsor, the board of engineers considered three specific bridge plans—a high bridge with headway of 150 feet over the center of the channel, a low drawbridge 12 feet above the water, and a "winter bridge" also 12 feet high, with two spans of 400 feet each which would be removed during the shipping season. Each bridge was designed to run at direct right angles to the current, from the foot of Second Avenue in Detroit to downtown Windsor. Detailed testimony was presented on each type of bridge—including cost estimates, traffic projections, and the bridge's impact upon river commerce. Each design had its proponents and detractors.[28]

The most impressive and expansive of the proposed structures, the "high bridge," consisted of six spans of 420 feet each and one span of 130 feet, giving it a total length

The ferry *Victoria* docking at the foot of Ouelette Avenue, Windsor, in the 1880s. (Courtesy of the Burton Historical Collection of the Detroit Public Library.)

Goods unloaded from a Detroit-Windsor ferry at the foot of Woodward Avenue, Detroit, in the 1880s. (Courtesy of the Burton Historical Collection of the Detroit Public Library.)

of 2,650 feet. The bridge would be 50 feet wide and accommodate two railroad tracks. Two piers constructed on land and six located in the channel would support the iron superstructure 150 feet above the surface of the river at the center of the span. The cost of the high bridge was estimated at $8,947,000, the length of time for construction at three years.

The second plan called for a low bridge 12 feet above the water, with two long fixed spans, each about 200 feet long, connecting to two pivot draw spans which, when opened, would allow four passages for vessels, each 168 feet wide. The bridge itself, 32 feet wide, would accommodate two railroad tracks. Iron trusses 28 feet high, rising to 38 feet in the center, would give an impressive appearance to the international bridge. Backers estimated that the drawbridge would take a year and a half to construct at a cost of $2,451,000.

The proposed "winter bridge" would be similar in design to the drawbridge. In its center there would be three spans resting upon temporary, movable liaison piers. These spans, 700 feet in length, would be removed each year from April 1 to December 1. Ferry service would return for eight months each year to transport railroad cars across the river. The cost estimate for this structure was $1,966,500. The time for construction was projected to be one and one-half years.

The railroad companies favored the low drawbridge design. According to James Joy, the drawbridge could be "closed three times a day for a space of ten minutes each, thus giving time for the transfer of all their trains. . . ." Joy cited the use of the railroad drawbridge in Chicago under which 43,735 vessels passed during the navigation season of 1868 without any serious interruption of shipping. He predicted that by careful planning of sailing schedules, the drawbridge would not significantly inter-fere with shipping on the Detroit River.[29]

Testifying on behalf of the bridge proposal, Russell A. Alger, a prominent Michigan lumberman, reported his experience towing huge rafts of white pine timber down through the Detroit River each year to mills in Detroit, Wyandotte, Ecorse, Toledo, Sandusky, Buffalo, Tonawanda, and other Lake Erie ports. The rafts, each of which averaged a load of nearly one million board feet, were approximately 100 feet wide and from 1,500 to 2,000 feet long. According to Alger, his tug captains had no trouble navigating the Detroit River, and a drawbridge with 200-foot openings, he predicted, would pose no obstacle to navigation.[30]

Joy and his railroad associates opposed the high bridge plan because of the long approaches which, in turn, would require that the terminal be located a mile and a half from the river. They criticized the winter bridge because it provided river crossing only four months a year. Despite initial dissatisfaction with the winter bridge plan, however, the railroads later altered their position and endorsed it. They pragmatically realized that a winter bridge might be just the compromise that would sell the bridge proposal.[31]

The vessel interests were adamantly opposed to each bridge proposal, taking the position that *any* bridge which involved the placement of piers in the river was unacceptable. To buttress their arguments against the bridge the shipowners, ship captains, and ferry operators testified about the potential danger of bridge piers, abutments, and the bridge spans. Even clear passages of 700 feet between piers would be dangerous in high winds, they argued, especially to tugs with six to ten vessels in tow.[32]

The drawbridge plan was opposed with equal vigor. It was estimated by the shipowners that about nine thousand vessels a year would be delayed waiting for the drawbridge to open and that an additional thirty-five hundred sailing vessels would be forced to anchor and wait for tug boats to tow them safely by the bridge piers. The losses to be suffered from such delays were projected to be millions of dollars.

After three days of acrimonious debate, the board of engineers adjourned its public hearings to solicit additional information on the potential impact of the bridge. It arranged to gather accurate data on the number, types, and capacity of vessels that passed different points along the Detroit River, such as Stony Island, Fort Wayne, and St. Clair Flats. The board gathered information on the actual number of vessels of each class—side wheel steamers, propellers, steam barges, tugs, barks, brigs, two- and three-masted ships, and rafts—which passed the St. Clair Flats in 1873. It collected the measurements of each raft of logs and the length of each tow per vessel. Data on railroad, freight and passengers, destinations, and value of grain and produce was also obtained from the various railroad companies which had connections in Detroit or Windsor. The operations of ferry boats across the river were also carefully documented, providing information on the number of trips per month, time of running, loading, unloading, and lying idle. At the same time, the board invited and received numerous written statements from interested parties.[33]

On November 14, 1873, the board of engineers reconvened in Detroit and listened to several days of final arguments. It adjourned on November 19. Little more than a month later, on December 24, 1873, the board issued its final report. Its conclusions were as follows:[34]

1st. That a bridge giving a clear headway of 150 feet, and clear spans of 400 feet, would not seriously injure navigation, but would be very expensive, involving long and in some places inconvenient approaches.

2d. That no bridge giving passage to vessels by draws alone, with draw spans at present practicable, can be permitted without serious injury to navigation.

3d. That a bridge giving a clear opening of 700 feet from April 1 to December 1, with two draw-openings 100 feet in the clear, and with the permanent foundations of its moveable piers 18 feet below lowest stage of water, will not be a serious obstacle to navigation.

4th. For the reasons heretofore given, although the question has not been directly referred to it, the Board deem the crossing of the river by tunnel as the only unobjectionable method; and from all the information they have obtained, think a tunnel at Detroit or Stony Island is by no minds impracticable, at a cost not so great as to debar its construction.

Finally, the Board would remark that at no place between Lakes Huron and Erie should a bridge be permitted which would give less facilities to navigation than the one already discussed, having 700 feet clear opening; that no construction should be commenced without prior approval of the plan and location by the Secretary of War; that under his direction the construction should be so carried on as during its progress to give least obstacle to navigation; that the opening of 700 feet should be kept clear to navigation from April 1 to December 1 of each year under severe penalty; that as a portion of the opening might be in Canadian waters, to control this portion so far as the interests of American commerce are concerned the United States should reserve the right at any time to stop the running of trains across the American portion of the bridge.[35]

Despite the discouraging rulings of the United States Department of Army Board of Engineers, agitation for the bridge continued. Backed by the Detroit Board of Trade, an influential organization of merchants and industrialists from all parts of southern Michigan, a series of public meetings were held to discuss the need for a railroad crossing over the Detroit River.

At one such meeting, on April 7, 1874, several hundred citizens met in Detroit to consider the bridge proposal. Even in the face of spirited opposition by vessel owners in the audience, who accused bridge proponents of being "lackeys" of the railroad companies, the audience, mostly merchants and railroad officials, endorsed plans for a railroad bridge. Not to be outdone, the vessel owners met a week later at Young Men's Hall in Detroit and recommended the construction of a tunnel under the Detroit River near Belle Isle.[36]

The proposal for a bridge connecting Detroit and Ontario was not the only proposal presented. The Michigan, Midland and Canada Railway Company sought the financial backing of a bridge to cross the St. Clair River, just below the city of St. Clair, about forty miles north of Detroit.[37]

Another bridge site was located south of Detroit and was to connect Trenton, Michigan, and Amherstburg, Ontario. This plan, introduced in 1872, was backed by a conglomerate of railroads, including the Canada Southern, the Chicago Canada, the Chicago, the Canada and Southern, and the Cincinnati, Dayton and Michigan railroad companies. The proposed bridge spans extending 6,640 feet over the waterways would connect Trenton and Grosse Ile, thence to Stony Island, and the third section would cross to the shore of Ontario near Amherstburg. Although the total bridge project was not completed, the first two sections connecting Grosse Ile with Trenton and Stony Island were finished in 1873.[38] Because of the opposition of vessel owners, the final span over the main shipping channel was never completed. In 1874 the sponsoring railroad companies built docks on Stony Island and the Ontario mainland to accommodate railroad car ferries.[39]

Several attempts were also made in the 1870s to tunnel under the Detroit River between Stony Island and the Ontario shore. These plans, backed by Cornelius Vanderbilt of New York City, the railroad baron who controlled the Michigan Central and Canada Southern railroads, were finally abandoned in 1879 because of the treacherous river currents in the vicinity of the Detroit River called the "Lime Kilns" and because of the prohibitive costs of excavating the limestone and removing the large boulders on the river bottom.

The Stony Island and St. Clair River proposals, however, only encouraged Detroit merchants and industrialists to renew their attempts to build a bridge between downtown Detroit and Windsor. Working through the Detroit Board of Trade, they lobbied the Michigan state legislature to support a Detroit-Windsor bridge plan.[40] As a result of such efforts, in 1880 the state legislature authorized the city of Detroit to open negotiations with Canadian authorities for the construction of a bridge or tunnel connecting Belle Isle and the Canadian shore and simultaneously authorized the city to issue bonds of $500,000 for these projects.[41]

The legislature's actions were challenged on constitutional grounds because of the prohibition on the use of local funds for internal improvements. The issue of the propriety of the legislature's actions was placed on the ballot in November 1880 but lost by a vote of 58,040 to 37,340.[42] Although a bridge was ultimately built connecting Detroit and Belle Isle, the Canadian connection was not pursued further, in large part because powerful business interests in Detroit and Windsor considered the Belle Isle site too far from the downtown area.[43]

At nearly the same time that the state

legislature was making efforts to facilitate the construction of a railroad river crossing from Detroit to Windsor, the Congress of the United States on June 20, 1879, authorized the secretary of war

> to inquire into and report whether, for railroad purposes, the river Detroit can be bridged or tunneled at the City of Detroit, or within one mile above or below said City, in such manner as to accomodate the large trade and commerce crossing the river at that point and without material or undue injury to the navigation of said river, a good and sufficient tug being always kept by bridge owners to assist any craft when required.[44]

On October 14, 1879, a United States War Department Board of Inquiry conducted hearings in Detroit lasting for five days. Railroad officials led by James Joy, merchants, vessel owners, ship captains, and citizens testified and presented arguments similar to those advanced in 1873. In addition, outside groups were involved. The governor of Minnesota and the city governments of St. Paul, Minneapolis, Cleveland, Buffalo, and other Great Lakes localities submitted resolutions opposing the construction of the bridge across the Detroit River.[45]

A substantial portion of the testimony taken by the board addressed the volume of commerce at Detroit. For the fiscal year ending June 30, 1879, 22,150 vessels had passed the Fort Gratiot Lighthouse. During the 1878 calendar year, railroad commerce at Detroit consisted of 129,133 passengers, 12,258 passenger cars, 3,873 baggage cars, and 104,359 freight cars.[46]

The board of inquiry issued the official report of its investigation on December 8, 1879. It ruled that the bridge should be located a "considerable distance above or below the business portion of the City, so that its use will not be interfered with by the local traffic in front of the City. . . ." The

lower end of Belle Isle and a site near the foot of 24th Street in Detroit were recommended as locations for the bridge.

Noting the advances in bridge building during the decade prior to its current inquiry, the board approved the drawbridge concept, with the provision that the draw section have "openings of 300 feet on each side of a pivot pier, and of 400 feet between the two pivot piers." It was proposed further that the fixed spans should have a headway of at least 60 feet.[47] Neither the railroads nor the vessel interests embraced the decisions of the board of inquiry. The officials of the Lake Carriers Association claimed that the bridge, as approved by the board of inquiry, "would be a menace to navigation" on the Detroit River and seriously disrupt the economy of the Midwest. They argued further that there was no need for a bridge, regardless of type, and that "the building of a tunnel was both feasible and practicable. . . ."[48]

The railroad companies and Detroit merchants were similarly dissatisfied with the findings and recommendations of the board of inquiry. Not only was the cost of the proposed bridge, with its complicated movable spans prohibitive, but the provision that the bridge be kept open for the exclusive convenience of the vessel owners during the navigation season was unacceptable to them. As a result, no bridge plan was developed and no action was taken by the railroad companies.

James Joy, Cornelius Vanderbilt, and other railroad officials were greatly annoyed at the decision of the board of inquiry, but it was the vessel owners whom they held largely responsible. Joy summarized the sentiments of railroad leaders in March 1879 when he charged that "the vessel men know that by creating diversions they may postpone its considerations and they are industrious and active, and cunning to accomplish the end aimed at." By supporting a Detroit-Windsor tunnel, he alleged, "they will drive railroads into combinations which in turn will drive them from Detroit."[49]

The railroad interests did, however, make a major decision which greatly benefited Detroit and Windsor when the Canada Southern Railway, in 1883, built a line from Essex Junction to Windsor. Up until that time, the Canada Southern line ran directly to the Detroit River at the village of Gordon about two miles above Amherstburg. The new rail route made Windsor the terminus of the major Ontario railroad lines, and, as a direct result, its economy prospered and the future role of Amherstburg as the site of a railroad bridge or tunnel was diminished.[50]

Meanwhile, the need for a railroad crossing at Detroit continued in the 1880s. In the fiscal year ending June 30, 1887, 389,239 railroad cars had been ferried across the Detroit River—an average of more than a thousand cars per day. Hundreds more waited for days on each side of the river because of inadequate ferry service. In winter months, ice clogged the ferry landing slips, causing even further delays. Agitation for a bridge continued in the state legislature and in the United States Congress.[51]

On February 1, 1889, the United States Senate Committee on Commerce called upon the secretary of war and the Corps of Engineers to again investigate the feasibility of a bridge across the Detroit River. Brigadier General Orlando M. Poe, who had distinguished himself in the Civil War, was placed in charge of the investigation.[52] As in previous years, the board scheduled public meetings to collect information on the bridge proposal. The hearings, which began on May 1, 1889, solicited statistics on railroad and vessel traffic, took testimony from city officials and residents along the lakes, and considered the arguments of railroad representatives and shipowners.

In addition, the board invited bridge and tunnel engineers to present their ideas for a bridge and tunnel. Luther Beecher, a Detroit engineer, presented a definite plan for the construction of a tunnel under the Detroit River, to be constructed within two years at a cost not to exceed $4 million, exclusive of the cost of approaches.[53] The board also investigated the ferry service operating between Detroit and Windsor and found it inadequate despite the fact that a new ferry boat, designed to break ice jams, had been recently constructed and put into use by the Michigan Central Railroad.[54]

The board focused its attention upon proposals for the construction of a bridge across the Detroit River. In contrast to earlier board hearings, no consideration was given to "low" or drawbridges, which were, by then, considered quite "inadmissible" by General Poe and his fellow Army Corps of Engineers officers.[55] On the other hand, the idea of a winter bridge, with spans that could be removed during the open navigation season, was given special attention. Three plans were presented to the board, each with clear openings of 1,000 feet and with fixed spans ranging in length from 150 to 200 feet. Each such plan provided for piers above and below the surface of the river.[56]

Also of special interest to the board was the proposal of Gustav Lindenthal of Pittsburgh, who presented plans for a "continuous girder bridge consisting of a central span of 1,000 feet clear opening, with two side spans of 750 feet in the clear, the bottom chord being at a clear height of 140 feet above the water at the center of the long span." The Lindenthal plan called for the construction of two piers in the river. In order to provide a gentle slope to the bridge, approaches of one and one-half miles inland on each side of the river were recommended.[57]

Lindenthal not only presented a detailed plan for the bridge, but also set forth for board review detailed cost estimates. Exclusive of approaches, the structure would cost about $6 million according to Lindenthal. "Capitalists could build the bridge and throw it open to the use of all railroads at a charge of sixty-two cents per railroad car for passage," and still "receive a fair return for their investment."[58] Finally, Lindenthal stated that his bridge "would permit passage of trains at any ordinary speed."[59] This declaration was an obvious reference to the Niagara Falls railroad suspension bridge which restricted locomotive speeds to three miles an hour.

Strangely, the Lindenthal plan was attacked by the railroad representatives as well as by the shipping interests, and provided the only point of agreement between these historical adversaries during the course of the hearings of the board of inquiry. Vessel owners claimed that the two piers—one of which would be located in the main channel of the river—"would present so serious an obstruction to navigation that it ought not to be built."[60] They also objected to the "proposed height of the bottom chord as not sufficient to permit the passage of all vessels now navigating the lakes."[61]

The railroad representatives, on the other hand, found other deficiencies in Lindenthal's proposal. The projected cost was prohibitive, they claimed, and the length and grade of approaches were unacceptable. Detroit merchants raised concerns about the location of the railroad terminus a substantial distance from the downtown business district and the existing railroad terminals.[62]

On July 10, 1889, the board issued a report of its findings. It concluded first that it was feasible to build a bridge across the Detroit River at Detroit. Second, it found that the high bridge "proposed by Mr. Lindenthal, is the least objectionable and the most conservative of the shipping interests and

therefore the best plan." The board did not consider the height of the bridge, its location, or the use of two piers to be serious obstacles to shipping. The third recommendation of the board endorsed the proposal for a winter bridge, with removable spans, providing for clear openings of 1,000, 750, and 200 feet, respectively.[63]

The board postponed its decision on a tunnel until the following year when it held hearings and reviewed several tunnel plans. The board took special interest in the single-track railroad tunnel then under construction below the St. Clair River in Port Huron, and other tunnels already completed in England and under the Hudson River in New York. The board approved the single-track tunnel concept for Detroit but recognized that the projected cost of the plan, $3.5 million exclusive of "land damages," might be too high for the railroads to bear.[64] No action followed the report of the board of inquiry. The Lake Carriers Association continued to fight every bridge proposal even though the Lindenthal plan had been a major improvement over the earlier drawbridge and low span bridge proposals.[65]

In retrospect, it is clear that the 1889 hearings encapsulated a history of bridge development. This record served to highlight the need for a bridge over the Detroit River. The success of other railroad bridges—such as the Eads Bridge over the Mississippi at St. Louis opened in 1874 and the Brooklyn Bridge in 1883—and the use of new bridge building techniques, such as the introduction of steel wire for suspension cables, acted to validate the railroad bridge concept for use at Detroit and to eliminate many of the reservations advanced against a railroad bridge in the past.

In addition, bridge successes elsewhere had developed the expertise of Gustav Lindenthal from which Detroit was able to benefit. By 1889 Lindenthal was already one of the most influential and emminent bridge designers of the nineteenth century. He had won national acclaim for two of his bridge projects—the replacement of Roebling's railway bridge over the Monongahela River and the new Seventh Avenue Bridge over the Allegheny River in Pittsburgh. In 1888 Lindenthal had submitted his design for a 3,100-foot span over the Hudson River, for rail lines as well as carriage lines. Although the plan lay dormant until after World War I, with the Pennsylvania Railroad deciding instead to tunnel under the Hudson River, it did provide the basis for Lindenthal's proposal for the Detroit River bridge.[66]

Still, it would be years before the plans for a bridge over the Detroit River took wing. In the years following the third major review by the board of inquiry in 1889, there were continuous attempts to develop support for and approval of a bridge across the Detroit River. Windsor and Detroit merchants and United States and Canadian railroad officials were joined by engineers, designers, and bridge construction companies in presenting plans for a bridge connecting Michigan and Ontario.

In 1895 Senator James McMillan and Congressman John B. Corliss of Detroit introduced legislation authorizing the construction of a bridge across the Detroit River, 142 feet high with a single pier in the center of the river. The cost of the structure, estimated at $4 million, was to be financed by the newly incorporated Michigan Central Bridge Company of Detroit. Among the leading backers of the new company were Cornelius Vanderbilt, Chauncey Depew, and C. F. Fox, of New York, and Ashley Pond, Henry N. Campbell, H. B. Ledyard, and Henry Russell, of Detroit.[67]

As in previous debates about the feasibility of a bridge, railroad and local business interests endorsed the Corliss proposal, citing the significant economic advantages to the Northwest and especially to Michigan and the Detroit area. The proposal was endorsed and supported by Michigan governor John T. Rich, Detroit mayor Hazen Pingree, Russell A. Alger, Joseph H. Dickinson, and H. B. Ledyard, all prominent Michigan business leaders.[68]

Not to be outdone, representatives of the Lake Carriers Association from Cleveland, Buffalo, and Chicago attacked the bridge proposal and questioned the motives of its sponsors, urged on by vessel owners and ship captains. Mayor George Swift of Chicago and Illinois congressman E. P. Cooke, as well as members of the Illinois and Ohio congressional delegations, protested against the bridge proposal.[69]

Angered by the "obstructive tactics of the Lake Carriers Association," the *Detroit News* characterized the association's stand against the span as "mean and petty selfishness."[70] Regardless of the tenor of the debate, the position of the Lake Carriers Association prevailed; the legislation was soundly defeated in Congress.[71]

The turn of the twentieth century witnessed a new surge of interest in bridging the Detroit River. J. H. Walker of Walkerville, Ontario, and other Canadian and Detroit merchants incorporated as the Pere Marquette International Bridge Company with plans to cross the Detroit River near Amherstburg.[72] A more serious plan was presented in 1901 for a bridge between Detroit and Windsor. Officials of the Grand Trunk Railroad and the Michigan Central Railroad, along with other railway companies, joined the Detroit Board of Commerce to fight for a railroad bridge.[73]

Based upon the design of a Windsor engineer, George S. Morrison, a cantilever bridge of a sufficient height to satisfy the Lake Carriers Association was proposed. The cost was estimated at about $10 million and was to be borne primarily by the railroads, especially the Michigan Central, and by city of Detroit revenue bonds. To authorize issue of the bonds, the Detroit City Council requested the Michigan legislature to act, approving such bonds to "construct and maintain an additional bridge or bridges over the American channel of the Detroit River."[74]

Unfortunately, the latest proposal for a bridge became entangled in the internal politics of Detroit city government. Because of the need for long approaches to maintain a sufficiently low grade for passage of the heavy locomotives, it was necessary to build new terminals about one and one-half miles from the river bank. This, in turn, required the construction of railroad tracks across several major city streets, including Michigan Avenue, Grand River Avenue, and 12th Street, or Jefferson and Gratiot Avenues, depending on which of the two routes was chosen.

The railroad companies' proposal called for grade separation, that is, a height differential between the approach and the street, of six feet. This plan was approved by the Grade Separation Committee of the Detroit City Council in 1901, but in 1903 the committee reversed its position and insisted upon a separation of six and one-half feet.[75] A major controversy erupted between the city council and the railroads, with neither side willing to compromise. By 1904 the bridge plan was again dead in the water.

It is difficult to determine, even with the assistance of newspaper records, common council minutes, and other archival sources, the reasons for the breakdown in negotiations between the two sides. Railroad officials appear to have insisted that a grade separation of greater than six feet would be ruinous to them as well as to local businesses along the route of the tracks. It is possible that the dissatisfaction was fed by a growing interest in a railroad tunnel. Recent successes of electric trains eliminated the danger of gaseous asphyxiation accidents in such underground structures. Both the New York Central and the Canadian Pacific railroads had been successful in running electric trains through tunnels. The lower cost of a tunnel might also have buoyed the railroads' interest.

For whatever reasons, in 1905 officials of the Michigan Central Railroad organized the Detroit River Tunnel Company, and in October 1906 work had begun on the tunnel approaches in Detroit and Windsor. Trenches were dug sixty feet below the surface of the river, and airtight concrete tubes, floated downriver from Lake St. Clair where they were built, were lowered into the trenches. The tube sections, each 268 feet long and 64.6 feet wide, were tipped into place and fastened together. The tunnel was completed in September 1909 and opened to traffic in June 1910.[76]

The completion of the Detroit River railroad tunnel in 1910 ended nearly a half century of agitation by railroads and Detroit and Windsor merchants for a Detroit River railroad crossing. Scores of resolutions calling for a bridge or tunnel are found throughout city, state, and federal government records. Three boards of inquiry had been appointed by the secretary of war to evaluate the need for and feasibility of a bridge across, or, in the alternative, a tunnel under the Detroit River. Lobbying efforts on both sides of the river captured public and legislative attention and at least once the issue of a railroad river crossing was placed as a public referendum on the Michigan statewide ballot.

The long and often spirited battle pitted two powerful groups against each other—the railroads and the shipping interests. The shipping interests, under the auspices of the Lake Carriers Association, fought to protect the economic interests of

Railroad car ferries, 1910. (Courtesy of the Allen County Museum.)

The Detroit portal of the Michigan Central Railroad tunnel, November 1910. (Courtesy of the Allen County Museum.)

the hundreds of vessel owners whose ships had for decades traveled the river encumbered only by natural obstacles. From the beginning, they opposed any bridge which required the construction of piers in the river or whose spans would sweep low over the water. Even though many sections of the Detroit River allowed navigation widths of only four hundred feet, the shipowners adamantly opposed the construction of a bridge allowing clearances of one thousand feet. In 1909, when the Detroit River tunnel was nearly completed, a spokesman for the Lake Carriers Association remarked proudly, "now that the long struggle has ended, we feel sure if the railroad interests would give a free expression of their feelings they could without dissenting voice admit that they were more than glad that their propositions for a bridge had been defeated. . . ."[77]

Such an admission was not forthcoming. Railroad officials were left to look back silently upon a long series of failures, despite the backing and endorsements for a railroad bridge by the United States Army Corps of Engineers and other governmental bodies. The skillful, often hostile, campaign waged by the Lake Carriers Association was a major obstacle to the railroads' efforts, but the failure of the railroads to unite behind a single proposal and route for a bridge crossing was equally significant.

The Michigan Central and Great Western railroads favored the Detroit-Windsor route, but the Canada Southern and Dayton-Michigan lines preferred a bridge connecting Amherstburg and Trenton. Other railroad companies preferred a route across the St. Clair River nearly forty miles north of Detroit. The conservative management of the Great Western Railroad was often cited by James F. Joy as an obstacle to the bridge plans. Furthermore, the widespread hostility toward railroads in Michigan, especially on the part of farmers who believed that railroads were monopolistic and freight prices were excessive, continuously eroded support for the bridge proposals. The small population of Windsor could do little to motivate a groundswell of international support for the bridge.

George Catlin, one of Detroit's influential historians and chroniclers, had yet another explanation. He cited the "extreme conservatism" of Detroit businessmen and property owners who refused to accept any "modernizing alternatives" in their business operations. To many Detroit business leaders who considered modern plumbing and elevators "an innovation of pure laziness and degeneracy," wrote Catlin, a railroad bridge over the Detroit River must have seemed a frivolous idea indeed.[78]

The new century was to bring about profound changes in the economy and business leadership of Detroit and Michigan and the southwestern Ontario region. Whereas railroads dominated the nineteenth century, the automobile would become the major economic force of the twentieth century. The demands of automobile owners and the new trucking industry created powerful economic forces which would usher in a new age of vehicular bridges in the United States and Canada.

CHAPTER 2

The Fowler Plan: Too Much, Too Soon

The Detroit-Windsor railroad tunnel met the immediate needs of the Michigan Central, Great Western, and other railroads which operated between Ontario and Michigan. Nevertheless, it was obvious to railroad officials as well as to other business leaders that another means of crossing the Detroit River would be needed to meet the increasing demand for river commerce facilities. With the rise of Detroit and Windsor as automobile capitals of the United States and Canada, improved transportation facilities were essential. Furthermore, it was increasingly evident that the Detroit-Windsor and the Detroit-Walkerville ferries were totally inadequate.

This new demand for an automobile crossing over the Detroit River, combined with major engineering advances in bridging wide expanses of water, turned eyes again to a bridge over the Detroit River. It was only a matter of time before the tunnel would have to be supplemented by another major means of moving vehicular traffic across the Detroit River.

Although there was a proposal in 1912 to build an international bridge between Detroit and Windsor commemorating a century of peace between the United States and Canada, World War I forced the postponement of any definite plans for a bridge.[1] Later, following the entry of Canada and the United States into the war, proposals surfaced to build a memorial bridge to the "youth of Canada and the United States who served in the Great War." This proposal won the endorsement of Mayor E. Blake Winter of Windsor and James Couzens, the mayor of Detroit, in 1919.[2] In fact, each mayor had begun independently to make plans to build a bridge. Mayor Winter, acting on the advice of city engineer Waddell of Windsor, proposed a suspension bridge, 2,500 feet in length, 120 feet above the river at the center, and 80 feet above the ground at the harbor lines. The bridge was designed to connect Park Street and Ouellette Avenue in Windsor and Randolph and Bates streets in Detroit.[3]

In order to avoid placing the terminal a mile away from downtown Detroit, Waddell envisioned a spiral entrance and elevators to carry passengers 80 feet high to meet buses at the upper level. Mayor Winter approached the Canadian government for funds to build the bridge, but his plan was rejected by Premier Robert L. Borden because "Dominion finances would not permit its consideration at this time."[4]

Meanwhile, James Couzens, ruling out a plan for a tunnel, proposed a high bridge between Detroit and Windsor. Although he presented no formal plans, he indicated his preference for a span connecting Belle Isle and Walkerville. Couzens sought and received the endorsement of the Lake Carriers Association for the high bridge.[5] The Couzens and Winter proposals were endorsed by business groups and local newspapers.[6]

At the time these bridge plans were receiving public attention, two New York engineers, Charles Evan Fowler and Gustav Lindenthal, became interested in a Detroit River bridge. It is not known whether they were invited to develop a bridge plan by Detroit civic or business leaders or devised a plan on their own initiative. Whatever drew them to Detroit, they arrived in August 1919 with the purpose of investigating the feasibility of a bridge across the Detroit River.

Gustav Lindenthal was no stranger to the Detroit River and its needs for a bridge, having made an elaborate presentation for such a span in 1889. Since that time, Lindenthal had continued his professional rise to become one of the foremost bridge engineers in the world and, in fact, by 1920 was widely recognized as the "Dean of American bridge engineering."[7]

By 1920 Lindenthal had already been involved in major bridge projects in the United States. In 1902 he was appointed bridge commissioner for New York, and under his supervision the Williamsburg Bridge over the East River in New York was completed in 1903. He helped plan and design the Queensboro and Manhattan bridges between 1907 and 1909, and in 1917 Lindenthal built the famous Hell Gate Bridge over the East River. The two-span, continuous truss railroad bridge built over the Ohio River near Sciotoville, Ohio, between 1914 and 1917 and called "perhaps the boldest continuous bridge in existence," was also among Lindenthal's achievements. Further, he was involved in developing a plan to remodel John A. Roebling's historic Brooklyn Bridge.[8]

In addition to his experience as a bridge designer, Lindenthal was recognized for his influence over and training of several brilliant young bridge engineers. Two of these were Othmar Ammann and David Steinman, who were associated with Lindenthal during the formative periods of their careers. Steinman was later recognized in Michigan for his design and construction of the Mackinac Bridge, which opened in 1958.[9]

Charles Evan Fowler did not have the international reputation of Lindenthal but was highly respected for his bridge designs and construction. Fowler had built the Youngstown Bridge over the Ohio River and bridges in White Pass, Alaska, and Sydney, Australia. He had built a twenty-four-mile causeway over Lake Pontchartrain at New Orleans and had completed a design for a cantilever bridge between San Francisco and Oakland. Before coming to Detroit, Fowler had completed the rebuilding of the Niagara River Parkway arch bridge.[10]

Fowler also had experience in local government and business affairs. He served as president of the Seattle, Washington, Park Board and for ten years was a trustee of the Seattle Chamber of Commerce. He had taught at the University of Washington and was the author of numerous books on bridge design and construction.

Unlike many bridge designers and engineers who preferred the drawing board and construction work, Lindenthal and Fowler were consummate promoters and salesmen. Their forceful and magnetic personalities, knowledge of community and local government institutions, and public relations experience made them ideal for the task of "selling" a bridge to Detroit and Windsor in 1919. They were not discouraged by past failures of efforts to build a bridge nor by the competition from the Detroit-Windsor railroad tunnel.

From funds to be raised, Fowler was to receive five hundred dollars a month for expenses, starting in November 1919. He would not receive a salary "until such time as the project is put in definite shape and financed." The original contractual provisions settled on prior to Lindenthal's withdrawal provided that if the project was fully funded, Fowler and Lindenthal "shall be entitled to a joint fee . . . of 2 percent on the entire cost of the project. . . ."[11]

Sometime in the spring of 1920 Lindenthal withdrew from the project, leaving Fowler in sole charge. The reason for the split was never publicly announced, although some years later Fowler reported that he and Lindenthal differed on the design of the bridge proposed for Detroit.[12] In addition, Lindenthal had interests in the New York area which he wished to pursue. Since 1888, when he first proposed a bridge across the Hudson River, Lindenthal had made this span his lifelong goal. The construction of a tunnel under the Hudson River in 1904 had postponed any action on a bridge, but in the 1920s Lindenthal carried on an active campaign for such a Hudson River crossing. Finally, age may have been a factor in Lindenthal's decision to withdraw from the Detroit River venture; he was sixty-nine years old when he came to Detroit in 1919.

After Lindenthal withdrew from the project, Fowler hired David Steinman, who

Charles Evan Fowler in 1920.

had recently cut his ties with the Lindenthal firm, as chief assistant. Steinman never took an active part in the Detroit-Windsor bridge promotion and indeed may have been hired only to lend prestige to the engineering side of the overall plan.[13] Fowler was completely in charge, with headquarters in the Detroit Chamber of Commerce building.[14]

His first priority was to gather traffic data on actual and potential river crossings in the Detroit-Windsor area. He investigated the Detroit-Windsor ferries and interviewed tourists and commuters who traveled daily between Windsor and Detroit. In addition to a preliminary traffic survey conducted in the fall of 1919, Fowler commissioned more elaborate traffic studies between January and June of 1920.[15]

According to Fowler, the traffic surveys of 1920 indicated that approximately 10,585,000 passengers, 521,950 automobiles, 73,000 trucks, and 16,060 teams crossed the Detroit River each year. From data furnished by the Grand Trunk, Canadian Pacific, Pere Marquette, Wabash and Pennsylvanian railroads, it was determined that 628,000 railroad cars crossed the Detroit River in 1919. Fowler made estimates of the future use of the bridge based upon the survey data and the traffic across the bay between San Francisco and Oakland, Alameda, and Berkeley, California. He predicted that 20 million people per year would cross the Detroit River by 1925, including 10 million passengers, 2,628,000 automobiles, 600,000 trucks, and 1,050,000 railroad cars. Of the total crossings, Fowler predicted that 70 percent would use the Detroit-Windsor bridge.[16]

The proposed toll rates for the new bridge varied according to the method of crossing the bridge and the number of passengers. An automobile with two persons would cost thirty cents, additional passengers two and a half cents each, pedestrians five cents, trucks up to two tons fifty cents and twenty-five cents for each additional ton, and railroad freight cars two dollars each. On the basis of these tolls, Fowler estimated that the bridge income in 1925 would range from a minimum of $2,440,000 to a high of $3,725,000.[17]

After ruling out a tunnel as too costly, Fowler gave careful attention to the various types of bridges which could be built, specifically the cantilever, arch, and suspension designs. A major consideration was the length of the proposed bridge—in excess of eighteen hundred feet, which would make it one of the longest bridges in the world. Fowler was also aware from his meetings with officials of the Lake Carriers Association and the Dominion Marine Association that the bridge had to be "at least 110 feet high at the center, nor less than 100

feet at the pier headlines" so that Great Lakes vessels could pass under it.[18]

The cantilever bridge, similar to the one in Quebec over the St. Lawrence River and to Fowler's design for a bridge between San Francisco and Oakland, was ruled out because it "would not permit the necessary curvature of the American approach." The arch bridge, similar to the Hell Gate Bridge designed by Gustav Lindenthal, was also considered. Fowler recognized its "artistic" elements and other advantages but finally decided that a suspension bridge would be best suited for the Detroit River, based on both cost and artistic considerations.[19]

Fowler's plan called for a combination railroad and vehicular bridge, constructed on two levels. The lower deck was designed to carry four standard-gauge railroad tracks with trains electrically operated. Telephone and telegraph wires, pipes, and other utilities would be placed in the center of the span. The upper deck would consist of two twenty-eight-foot roadways, each accommodating three lanes of automobile traffic. Tramway tracks for electrically operated trolleys were to be placed in the center. All grades were less than 1.5 percent. Two massive towers held the cables aloft over the river. The plan also provided that lower and upper decks could be constructed separately if funds were limited.[20]

Three sites were considered by Fowler: one connecting Belle Isle and Walkerville, a second connecting Woodward Avenue and Ouellette Avenue, and a third starting at 21st Street in Detroit and crossing the Detroit River at right angles. The Belle Isle site was rejected because of the high cost required to build the American approach over the inside channel and its distance from downtown Windsor. The Woodward Avenue site had many natural advantages, but its cost would be so high—an estimated $60 million—that it was deemed impractical. The 21st Street location was chosen as the best site. Although it was some distance from the downtown centers of Detroit and Windsor, it had much to offer according to Fowler. It was from five to eight minutes from the Detroit and Windsor post offices and near the major railroad terminals. The "extensive factory district of west Detroit" was adjacent to the proposed American terminal and near the planned industrial center in Ojibway and Sandwich. Furthermore, the cost of the property needed for the approaches and terminals was far less than the Woodward Avenue site. Fowler estimated that the combined railroad and highway bridge would cost $28,125,000; the latter alone, $11,500,000.[21]

Even before final designs were ready,

Fowler had established a corporation to build the bridge. On April 1, 1920, the American Transit Company was formed under the laws of the state of Nevada. On April 8, 1921, the Canadian Transit Company was established with the approval of the House of Commons in Ottawa.[22] On June 6, 1921, the two companies "entered into an agreement for the united construction and financing of the Detroit and Windsor Bridge." Among the directors listed in the incorporation proceedings were W. A. Mara and J. H. Cullen of Detroit, and William J. Pulling, E. Blake Winter, Wallace R. Campbell, and Charles Stanley King of the Windsor area. Later, other prominent business leaders were elected to the boards of

The original Fowler plan for a Detroit-Windsor bridge.

INCORPORATED UNDER THE LAWS OF THE STATE OF NEVADA. AUTHORIZED IN MICHIGAN.

Number
1

Shares
$100.00

American Transit Company

CAPITAL STOCK $5,000,000.

FULLY PAID   NON ASSESSABLE

This Certifies that ———— Charles E. Fowler ———— is the owner of
Ten (10) Shares of the Capital Stock of
American Transit Company
transferable only on the books of this Corporation in person or by Attorney upon
surrender of this Certificate properly endorsed.

IN WITNESS WHEREOF, the said Corporation has caused this Certificate to be signed by
its duly authorized officers and its Corporate Seal to be hereunto affixed
this 29th day of December A. D. 1921.

G. E. Ehrenberg
ASSISTANT SECRETARY.

W. B. Gregory
PRESIDENT.

SHARES $ 100 EACH

Charles Evan Fowler purchased the first hundred shares of American
Transit Company stock. (Courtesy of the D.I.B. Archives.)

directors of the American and Canadian transit companies, including William B. Gregory, Hiram H. Walker, J. W. Austin, Allan Templeton, A. F. Healy, Charles Van Dusen, J. O. Reaume, and J. O. Murfin.[23]

After detailed bridge engineering plans were prepared in 1921, Fowler established a special board of consulting engineers to review the plans, the location, the traffic surveys, and the financing. The five member board included Professor C. R. Young of the University of Toronto, Colonel C. N. Monsarrat, noted Montreal bridge engineer and builder of the Quebec Bridge, George H. Pegram, chief engineer of the Interboro Transit Company of New York City, and Professor William H. Burr of New York

City and member of the boards of engineers of the Panama Canal and the East River Bridge Company. The board of consulting engineers completed its investigation in August 1921 and unanimously endorsed the general design of the bridge and the safety features of the plan.[24]

Approval of the design and location of the Detroit-Windsor bridge was essential in order to obtain financial backing for the venture. Fowler recognized that a major promotional campaign was necessary to win the support of the business and financial community. Strong support of the major railroad companies operating in the Detroit and Windsor area was likewise essential to the success of the project.

As a matter of fact, Fowler gave winning the support of Detroit and Windsor business and community leaders the highest priority. In the fall of 1919 and 1920 these promoters had met with officials of the Detroit and Windsor boards of commerce and requested their support and financial backing. They received endorsements from both chambers of commerce and additional assistance from Allan A. Templeton, president of the Detroit board. Templeton arranged for Fowler to have office space in the board headquarters on Lafayette Boulevard and also provided free telephone service and supplies for the bridge campaign. In addition, Templeton raised funds for gathering "data as to traffic, tenants, right-of-way, franchises" and surveying, mapping, and preliminary engineering work. For each three hundred dollars contributed, the donors were to receive preferred stock in the American or Canadian transit company and the option of buying additional preferred stock from one thousand dollars to five thousand dollars.[25]

With strong support from Templeton, from his successor as president of the Detroit Board of Commerce, John A. Russell, and from Harvey J. Campbell, the secretary of the board, Fowler was able to wage a vigorous promotional campaign. He contacted leaders of business and trade organizations in the Detroit and Windsor area, and met with civic and local government leaders of communities to be affected by the bridge. He accepted invitations to speak at public meetings and requested to be put on the programs of group meetings.

In his public presentations, Fowler stressed the needs of an international bridge, the merits of his own engineering designs for the bridge, and the benefits of such a structure. He received loud applause each time he cited the inadequate ferry service between Michigan and Ontario cities—especially from the thousands of daily commuters who spent increasing amounts of time in line waiting for ferry service.

As a result of such efforts, a special and important endorsement was given to Fowler on July 15, 1920, when the Detroit Board of Commerce hosted a meeting of twenty-five leading "capitalists" from Detroit and Windsor. After reviewing Fowler's proposals, they unanimously endorsed the bridge and pledged financial support for Fowler's work. Later, the Detroit Board of Commerce formally endorsed the bridge proposal.[26]

Tourist organizations and real estate groups were also targeted by Fowler for special attention. Fowler argued persuasively that the proposed bridge would create "an extensive suburban movement from heavily populated Detroit to the Windsor area as much desirable property will be brought within a few minutes ride" from Detroit. He also predicted that the bridge "should bring the border cities a population of not less than 200,000 persons."[27]

Fowler's message had great appeal to the business community and other potential bridge users. He was a dynamic, forceful, and persuasive speaker who attracted increasingly large audiences. The local press gave widespread coverage to his presentations and the various interviews and press conferences in which he participated. Endorsements soon followed. Trade and merchant associations, tourist organizations, and real estate groups formally endorsed Fowler's bridge proposal.[28]

Railroad support, in particular financial support, was also essential to the success of the original Fowler proposal. Fowler proposed that the railroads servicing the Detroit and Windsor area "guarantee the principal and interest on bonds for the full cost of the structure, or in the amount of $28 million."[29] This type of support was vital to a comprehensive fundraising effort.

In pursuit of such commitments, Fowler arranged meetings with leading railroad officials in the winter of 1919 to 1920, including Howard G. Kelly, president of the Grand Trunk Railway, Edward W. Beatty and J. M. R. Fairbain, president and chief engineer, respectively, of the Canadian Pacific Railroad, W. H. Williams, chairman of the board of directors of the Wabash Railroad, Samuel Rea, president of the Pennsylvania Railroad, and F. H. Alfred, president of the Pere Marquette Railroad. Officials of the Michigan Central Railroad were also contacted, but they were satisfied that the Detroit-Windsor railroad tunnel, which they built and operated, would meet their international transportation needs until after 1925.[30]

In his negotiations with railroad officials, Fowler offered a guarantee of a minimum of 1,050,000 railroad car crossings per year. He also maintained that toll rates for railroad cars would not surpass those currently charged by ferry companies. In the event that the "total car movement over the bridge amounts to 1,580,000 cars per annum," Fowler promised that the crossing rate per car would be reduced to $1.67.[31]

Location of the bridge terminals was of special interest to the railroad companies and undoubtedly influenced their support for the bridge. Officials of the Wabash, Pennsylvania, and Pere Marquette lines and the Canadian Pacific Railroad Company were pleased at the proposed bridge location. On the other hand, the Grand Trunk Railroad officials objected to the location of the bridge. Fowler responded that the proposed location would be less costly "than the present ferry service even in good weather."[32]

Despite theoretical support for various aspects of the bridge proposal and Fowler's aggressive promotional techniques, the railroad companies, unlike other business groups, did not immediately endorse the Fowler plan nor did they commit any funds

to the bridge project. The economic recession of 1921 had a particularly severe impact on the railroads and no doubt influenced the railroad leaders.

Fowler was not slow to recognize that he would not get financial support for the bridge from the railroad companies at that time. He immediately shifted his emphasis and eliminated plans for the railroad tier of the bridge. He did make provisions in his plans for the later addition of railroad facilities. With this change in plans, the projected cost of the bridge dropped in half to $15 million.

Approval by federal and local governmental agencies in Canada and the United States was also necessary for all aspects of the bridge project, including bridge design, sale of bonds, purchase of property, bridge location, and toll rates. Location of the bridge over international and navigable waters required special approval from Ottawa and Washington. These endorsements came in 1921 with passage of legislation in both houses of Congress and approval by President Woodrow Wilson on March 4, 1921. The Canadian Parliament approved a similar measure on April 4, 1921, after a bill had been introduced by W. C. Kennedy, a Parliament member from Ontario. Both bills provided that construction of the bridge "must begin within three years after the bill became law, and that it must be completed within seven years."[33]

Canadian government highway and railroad officials were also contacted by Fowler. At the time the Canadian government was building a major trunk highway from Montreal to Windsor. It did not take much persuading for them to acknowledge the great importance of an international bridge connecting Ontario and Michigan and the populous Midwest. Sir Robert Borden, prime minister of Canada, and Dr. John D. Reid, the Canadian minister of railways, advised Fowler that they had "great sympathy with the project." Fowler in turn responded that he hoped that they "might be expected to lend their influence to have one half of the financing taken care of in Canada or through Canadian financiers."[34]

Fowler's final coup in the area of prominent endorsements was received in November 1921, from President Warren Harding. In a letter to Fowler dated November 5, Harding wrote, "I have been impressed that the various projects for the construction of great bridges across the boundary waters between the United States and Canada are particularly deserving of public interest in both countries, because they invariably are calculated to bring into yet more intimate relations two countries between which more than a century of unbroken peace has been recorded." The Detroit-Windsor bridge would be another step "toward further cementing these relations," concluded the president. Fowler did not hesitate to publicize this prestigious endorsement.[35]

Once bridge designs and specifications were prepared and approved by the board of engineers and endorsements received from government, civic, and business groups, Fowler and his board turned their attention to the monumental task of raising $15 million through the sale of stocks and bonds. Under the terms of the Fowler plan, the bridge would be "built and financed solely for the public benefit without profits accruing to the promoters further than a reasonable compensation to the directors for their three to four years tenure of office."[36]

To raise the necessary funds, Fowler selected the Russell T. Scott Company of Toronto. A former Windsor resident, Russell Scott won a place in Canadian financial circles as a "skillful and energetic" fundraiser and was widely recognized for "his unusual ability to develop and create 100 percent efficient sales organizations having directed and trained over 10,000 security salesmen."[37] After the Michigan Public Securities Commission had approved the bond issue, Scott opened offices in Windsor and Detroit and hired forty salesmen to work exclusively on the sale of bridge securities. Public meetings were held to promote the sale of bonds and local newspapers carried a series of full page advertisements extolling the investment possibilities.[38]

It was not long before Scott found himself in difficulty. His "high pressure" tactics in selling bridge securities aroused strong opposition from government and business groups in Toronto and Windsor. Fowler recognized the problem and became alarmed about Scott's lack of success.

The situation came to a head in April 1922, when A. F. Healy, a prominent Essex County financier, president of the National Finance Corporation and member of the Canadian Transit Company board of directors, conducted his own investigation of Russell Scott's operation. He was appalled at discovering not only unethical business practices but Scott's virtual failure to raise any substantial funds. Only $400,000 in stock had been sold by April 1922, hopelessly short of the needed funds. Scott was removed and the fundraising was taken over by Albert Healy.[39]

By then, however, the damage had been done. Accounts of Scott's unethical practices had circulated throughout financial circles in the United States and Canada. The momentum and goodwill built up by Charles Evan Fowler was lost. The bridge project was dead.

Meanwhile, Scott's career took a tragic turn. His own losses were estimated by some in financial circles to be in excess of $2 million, and he was forced into bankruptcy. Shortly afterwards, he moved to Chicago and there ran afoul of the law. He was arrested for defrauding a landlord, charged with petty larceny and vagrancy, and finally was arrested and convicted for the murder of a drugstore clerk during a robbery. Scott committed suicide in a Cook County jail cell in October 1927, after several reprieves from a death sentence.[40]

The selection of Russell Scott to head the fundraising for Fowler's bridge project did irreparable harm to the project and ended, for the moment, plans for the construction of a international bridge between Detroit and Windsor. Despite the Scott episode, however, it its doubtful that the Fowler plan could have won the necessary financial support. The recession of 1920 to 1922 and the shortage of investment capital in Detroit and Windsor made the task of fundraising extremely difficult, if not impossible, even with the most established and financially secure investment bankers. Furthermore, Fowler lacked the financial experience needed for the fundraising effort and made a basic error in not recognizing earlier that the railroad companies would not underwrite the total cost of the bridge. He also underestimated the opposition of some Detroit real estate interests and merchants who opposed the location of the bridge.

In a larger sense, Fowler underestimated the opposition to a privately owned, international bridge. For more than a decade, the issue of municipal ownership of the street railway and other transportation facilities had been a hotly debated and hard-fought political issue in Detroit. The election of James Couzens as mayor of Detroit in 1919 was based largely upon his pledge to end the private streetcar monopoly in Detroit. In 1922 the voters backed Couzens in supporting municipal ownership of the street railway companies. Although ownership of transportation facilities was not a heated political issue in Windsor and adjacent communities, the idea had its vocal supporters, including the mayor of Windsor, Frank Mitchell. The failure of Fowler to deal with the issue contributed to his failure to raise necessary funds for the bridge.[41]

The Fowler plan was an important chapter in the history of the Ambassador Bridge and indeed a vital link in the development of an international bridge between Detroit and Windsor. Future promoters who took over the project used Fowler's organizations—the Canadian and American transit companies—revised his specifications for a suspension bridge, adopted the identical location for the bridge and its terminals proposed by Fowler, and used the modest funds collected to renew the project. Charles Evan Fowler deserves important credit for his contributions to the Ambassador Bridge.[42]

CHAPTER 3

Joseph Bower Takes Command

By the end of 1923, failure of the Fowler plan was manifest and the entire bridge project was near collapse. Of the $12 million needed, only $420,000 had been raised by the sale of bonds. Even Fowler became discouraged and returned to his New York headquarters to pursue more promising engineering projects.

It was at this juncture that James W. Austin took over the leadership of the bridge project and tried to salvage the international bridge plan. A successful and enterprising businessman, Austin had been associated with the Canadian and American transit companies as treasurer and director. For the previous twenty years, Austin had been involved in the paint business, serving for most of that time as purchasing agent for the Acme Lead Color Works. In 1920 he resigned this job to become secretary and treasurer of the Detroit Graphite Company. In this capacity, he became a strong advocate for an international bridge and joined Fowler in his business endeavors.[1]

The failure of the bond campaign dis-

James W. Austin. (Courtesy of the D.I.B. Archives.)

couraged most of the bridge's active supporters, but not James Austin. He recognized that it was not Russell Scott who should bear sole blame for the failure of the bridge project, nor was it prevailing economic conditions. Austin realized that there was insufficient investment capital in Detroit and Windsor to finance the bridge, even if potential investors had been fully committed to the project. Outside help would be necessary and Austin set out to find it.

During the winter of 1923 to 1924, Austin arranged to meet C. D. Marshall, partner in the prestigious firm of McClintic-Marshall of Pennsylvania and New York, the largest independent steel fabricator in the United States. The company had extensive experience in design and construction of railroad and automobile bridges over major rivers in the United States and the lock gates of the Panama Canal. McClintic-Marshall had also built office buildings, factories, and steel mills, including the Packard and Ford Rouge River plants in Detroit.

Following Austin's initial contact with C. D. Marshall and H. H. McClintic, they met several times to review the plans of the American and Canadian transit companies to build a Detroit-Windsor bridge. Marshall became excited about the Detroit-Windsor project and was anxious to direct the construction. His company, however, did not have the necessary funds at that time to underwrite the cost of the bridge. So Marshall arranged for Austin to seek the help of Joseph A. Bower, a highly respected New York financier, who was vice-president of the New York Trust Company. The initial meeting between Bower and Austin was held in New York City in April 1924.[2]

Joseph A. Bower was well known in financial and business circles throughout the United States. In 1914 he had joined the financial firm of Hale and Kilburn in Philadelphia as president, and three years later he was elected vice-president of the Liberty National Bank of New York, one of the powerful J. P. Morgan banks which later merged with the New York Trust Company. Bower was a recognized expert in rescuing and reorganizing declining or mismanaged companies.[3]

Austin discovered that Bower also had excellent Detroit connections and was familiar with the Detroit and Windsor areas, having been a resident of Detroit for more than twenty years. Joseph Bower's roots in Detroit dated back to 1882, when, at the age of two, he moved with his parents from Colorado to Detroit. When he was only ten years old, his father died, and Bower worked at odd jobs to help his mother bring up the family. At one time, he later recalled, he held three jobs at once—one as an office boy for Judge Willard W. Lillibridge; a second as clerk at a sporting goods store; and a third, at night, at the Detroit Police Department recording incoming messages from police call boxes. After such a difficult beginning, he went on to graduate from Detroit Business College and studied law in the offices of Judge Lillibridge.[4]

At the same time, Bower pursued other interests. In 1902 the *Detroit News Tribune* featured a long article by Bower on the art of palmistry. According to the account, Bower, who described himself as an expert on the subject, had aided the Detroit Police Department by "reading the hands of over fifty dead people especially the victims of murder or accident . . ." as well as the hands of criminals. By reading the "fate lines" on the hands of subjects, Bower claimed he was able to determine whether they were destined for crime or success in business.[5]

Bower must have lost interest in this unusual pursuit, for there is no reference to it in records of his later career. There is evidence, however, that he was soon attracted to the world of finance. In 1908 he joined

Joseph A. Bower and J. W. Austin. (Courtesy of the D.I.B. Archives.)

the staff of the Detroit Trust Company and soon rose from a position of junior clerk to vice-president. He also developed an expertise in managing industrial corporations in which the Trust Company had a financial interest, especially those companies with financial or management problems. Bower also served as managing director of the firm of Pingree and Wilkins Brothers of Detroit.[6]

Bower's success in financial and business circles in Detroit soon attracted the attention of eastern financiers associated with J. Pierpont Morgan and Company. In August 1915 they persuaded him to leave his position in Detroit to join them as "representative of a group of New York banking houses in which the management of the in-

dustrial corporations with which they are associated need assistance."[7] In announcing his departure from Detroit, the *Free Press* paid tribute to the young man's business acumen:

> He won his first spurs in the financial world putting apparently insolvent corporations on their feet. He found out where the trouble lay, and the rest was easy. Some men are content to know what happens when a corporation gets into financial straits. Joseph A. Bower insists on knowing why it happened, what it means, and where the trouble is to be remedied.[8]

James Austin and his colleagues on the boards of directors of the American and Canadian transit companies were convinced immediately that Joseph Bower was the ideal person to rescue their ailing bridge enterprise. When he was approached by the Detroit-Windsor group, Bower responded enthusiastically for a number of reasons. He liked the challenge of trying to salvage the bridge, and he saw a privately owned international toll bridge as an excellent investment venture for his family and close business associates. Furthermore, Bower was impressed by the unselfish motives of Austin and bridge promoters, for Austin had been candid about his own special interests from the first meeting with Bower in April 1924. According to Bower, "Austin told me he would give me the contract to build the bridge, if he could have the contract to paint the bridge once it was built." "That's all he wanted out of it," Bower later recalled.[9]

As the initial meeting with Austin and Marshall ended, Bower "agreed to make some initial investigations to determine the possibility of being of service in financing the project."[10] In the months that followed, it became clear what Bower meant by "initial investigations" and how he dissected a business problem. He first hired the engineering firm of McClintic-Marshall to study the Charles Evan Fowler design, specifications, and construction costs. This assignment did not require extensive study because the firm was already familiar with the bridge project; indeed, it had earlier negotiated with Fowler to construct the Detroit-Windsor bridge. Bower, however, had decided to eliminate the railroad feature of the Fowler design and to concentrate solely on a vehicular bridge. A new bridge design, therefore, would be needed.[11]

Bower's next action was to hire the firm of Coverdale and Colpitts of New York and Montreal to conduct a traffic survey of the Detroit and Windsor area. Although Fowler had completed similar surveys in 1919 and 1922, Bower wanted more extensive and current data on which to project revenues from toll charges.[12]

Bower also visited Detroit often in the summer of 1924 to meet the directors of the American and Canadian transit companies and to study the fundraising plan of Russell T. Scott and his successor, A. F. Healy, president of the American Bond Corporation. Bower also wanted to make his own evaluation of public sentiment in Michigan and Ontario for a privately owned international toll bridge. He was already familiar with the earlier public controversy over municipal ownership of street railways, which had divided politicians and citizens of Detroit. Finally, in the fall of 1924, Bower visited and made a "thorough study of bridges on the American continent and in Europe."[13]

Although complete traffic surveys could not be finished until the summer vacation months of 1925, Bower had gathered enough data to decide upon a plan of action. McClintic-Marshall informed him that, based upon their engineering studies, "a bridge of adequate capacity to handle the traffic can be completed under present costs of labor and materials, at a cost of approximately $12,000,000."[14]

Bower decided to proceed with the bridge, albeit cautiously. On April 25, 1925, one year after he had first met with Austin and Marshall, Bower signed an option agreement with the American and Canadian transit companies "to acquire the entire property and assets of the Transit Companies and to construct the bridge." In return, Bower agreed to pay the sum of $420,000 "to reimburse all subscribers for, and holders of, the bonds on the Company," and to pay liabilities to those investors in the earlier project. The latter included the American Bond Company, formerly R. T. Scott Company, $120,000; Fowler Engineering Company, $5,490.47; A. C. Kingston, Canadian Transit Company counsel, $8,134.77; Sherman D. Callender, American Transit Company counsel, $9,181.25; and George H. Pegram, C. N. Monsarrat, William H. Burr, and C. R. Young, Board of consulting engineers, $7,500 each. He also agreed to pay Charles Evan Fowler $25,000 per year for three years for his work as consulting engineer. On their parts, the transit companies agreed "to procure a guarantee by the government of the Dominion of Canada or by the Premier of Ontario of the First Mortgage bonds." On June 1, 1925, Bower exercised his option and purchased all rights to the American Transit Company.[15]

As soon as the option agreement was signed, Bower announced his plan to finance the cost of the bridge. He ruled out any stock selling arrangement. Instead, he stated, "I propose to organize a company of a few friends. We would subscribe a million dollars, raise an additional $6,000,000 by a bond issue and leave the County of Essex, Ontario, which is primarily interested in the project, to back a bond issue for the remaining $5,000,000."[16]

Bower justified the "guaranty provision" on the grounds that Essex County and especially the "Border Cities of Walkerville, Windsor, Sandwich, Tecumseh, Ford City, Kingsville, and LaSalle have more to gain from the construction of a bridge than Detroit."[17] He might have added that his legal counsel in Detroit had advised him that a similar guaranty proposal from Detroit would have violated the Constitution of the state of Michigan and the Detroit City Charter.[18]

Although Bower's guaranty proposal for the bridge was innovative, there were precedents for it. Similar guaranties had been given by the Province of Quebec and the Dominion of Canada for the construction of bridges over the St. Lawrence River at Montreal and Quebec.[19] Bower planned to lobby for provincial and national government financial support, but he decided to attempt first to get such a guaranty from the local governments of Essex County, since these communities would most directly benefit from a Detroit-Windsor bridge.

From the beginning, Bower recognized the difficulties of securing guaranty of $5 million from Essex County voters, especially in view of the fact that Detroit was not providing a similar guaranty. Nevertheless, he believed that he could win the support and, furthermore, that the endorsement of Essex County communities would facilitate the sale of bridge bonds.[20]

With the assistance of influential businessmen and directors of the Canadian Transit Company, such as Charles Mc-Tague, Hiram Walker, A. F. Healy, and Wallace Campbell, Joseph Bower organized a countywide campaign to round up support for the bridge guaranty. Accompanied by his business colleagues and usually by DeWitt Smith, a consulting bridge engineer from New York City, Bower met with key public officials in most Essex County communities and with leaders of business, merchant, real estate, and tourist groups, as well as with educational leaders. He solic-

ited and accepted invitations to talk about his bridge plans to local organizations and clubs, and he met often with editors of local newspapers and kept them informed of his plans. Indeed, Bower used the news media extensively to spread the story of the bridge and its great benefits to the communities and citizens of Essex County.[21]

Public meetings usually followed the same format. In his introductory remarks, Bower stressed the economic advantages of the bridge: prospective real estate developments, an increase in property values and tax revenues, a rise in tourism, an influx of American dollars into Canada, and the great industrial development of Essex County. Thousands of new jobs would be created for Canadian citizens as a result of the bridge, he claimed. Bower also appealed to the thousands of Canadians who commuted daily to work in Detroit. Frequent delays in ferry service were a detriment to such individuals and were cited by Bower in support of the bridge proposal.[22]

Bower explained in his remarks the proposed financing of the bridge and the need for the guaranty from the local, provincial and national levels of government. He noted that he was personally investing $1 million in the venture. Despite his carefully planned remarks, however, Bower had to respond continually to the question: How would the Canadian bond issues fare if the bridge did not prove a financial success? "In that event," he replied on numerous occasions, "they would not be badly off . . . for myself and fellow stockholders who subscribed the $1,000,000, would be the first to fade from the picture. . . ."[23] Any further losses would be spread over the county, he explained, and "in the end the bond holders would have the bridge, which would be one of the greatest assets imaginable."[24]

In the midst of his campaign to win support for the guaranty, Bower and other bridge supporters were faced with another, more serious challenge—the announcement of plans to build a tunnel between the downtown section of Windsor and Detroit. Led by F. G. Engholm, a Toronto engineer, and a group of financiers from Toronto and Ottawa, backers of the tunnel outlined their proposal in June 1925. During the months that followed, Engholm not only campaigned on behalf of a Detroit-Windsor tunnel, but he also attacked the proposed bridge plan, charging that the bridge, to be located several miles from downtown Windsor, would discourage tourists from visiting Windsor. Furthermore, he labeled the bridge a "purely American enterprise," whereas the tunnel, he noted, would be a Canadian project.[25] Another tunnel supporter, a Windsor alderman, strongly criticized Bower and his plan because, he stated, "a bridge makes for slums."[26]

During the campaign, Engholm centered his criticism on Bower's proposal for a government guaranty and, at the same time, attacked Bower's personal integrity. "If Mr. Bower is a man of his word," he challenged, "I think he should go ahead and construct a bridge on his own."[27] Later, he insisted that "Bower will get all of his money back and rate payers will be left holding the bag. The bridge," concluded Engholm, "is a white elephant."[28]

Even without Engholm's verbal counterattacks, the prospect of a tunnel connecting convenient downtown areas of Detroit and Windsor made Bower's task more formidable. To his credit, Bower refused to become embroiled in the tunnel-versus-bridge controversy, nor did he ever raise the question of the safety of tunnel travel. "If I thought the tunnel was a better proposition," Bower declared before a large public meeting in Windsor, "I would have built it."[29]

Another serious obstacle facing Bower was winning the support of Frank Mitchell,

the popular mayor of Windsor. Mitchell was highly regarded in political circles in communities outside of Windsor, as well as within the city. Mitchell not only had reservations about Bower's plans to finance the bridge with a guaranty from Essex County, but he favored construction of a municipally owned bridge between Windsor and Detroit. He had won a popular following as a result of his criticism of ferry and utility company rate schedules and he predicted that a private bridge company would also arbitrarily establish rates.[30]

In his effort to gain support for a municipally owned and operated bridge, Mitchell met often in May and June of 1925 with mayors and public officials of neighboring Essex County towns, in order to obtain their reactions to his idea. Moreover, on several occasions, he met with Mayor John Smith of Detroit and sought Smith's support for this cooperative venture.[31]

On May 29, 1925, Mitchell appointed an Essex County Bridge Committee, made up of leading politicians of the surrounding communities, and directed them to investigate the merits of a municipal, as compared to a private, bridge.[32] The mayor was shrewd enough as a politician to recognize that Bower was winning support from prominent business and community leaders in Essex County. For example, Wallace Campbell, vice-president and treasurer of the Ford Motor Company of Canada, had endorsed the Bower proposal and had extended his support by recruiting support from other Canadian businessmen. Furthermore, as previously noted, A. F. Healy, a respected businessman from north Essex, was campaigning vigorously for the Bower plan.[33]

Mitchell was soon to realize that his plan for a municipal bridge would require a very substantial tax hike for county taxpayers. In some respects, the threat of possible financial liability posed by failure of

Bower's bridge proposal was more palatable to the taxpayers than the certainty of tax hikes necessitated by a municipally owned bridge.[34]

In June 1925 Mayor Mitchell sent a delegation of business leaders to Ottawa to lobby for enabling legislation to allow Essex County to guarantee $5 million in bonds for either a private or a municipal bridge.[35] In July 1925 Mitchell accepted an invitation from Bower to travel to New York and meet with officials of the New York Trust Company and engineers of the McClintic-Marshall Company. Accompanied by Edward A. Bryon, city engineer of Windsor, Mitchell received red carpet treatment from Joseph Bower as they toured together bridge operations in the New York area.[36]

By the end of his New York visit, Mitchell was impressed by Bower and his business colleagues, but before he would endorse Bower's proposal, he wanted assurances from Bower that Canadian taxpayers would have control over the toll rates, especially in the event of a deficit or default. Mitchell also insisted that Bower make available to Essex County business leaders and public officials final bridge designs and plans within sixty days. Bower agreed to Mitchell's requests.[37]

On August 6, 1925, Mayor Mitchell and the Essex County Bridge Committee endorsed Bower's plan for a private bridge across the Detroit River. The committee also urged Bower to proceed with development of a new bridge design and to authorize a traffic survey. Finally, the committee recommended that the issue of a bond guaranty be placed on the ballot in Windsor municipal elections during the winter of 1925 to 1926.[38] On August 10, 1925, the Windsor City Council also endorsed the Bower plan by an eight-to-three vote, contingent upon approval of the voters.[39] In the weeks that followed, most other Essex County municipalities gave similar endorsements.[40] These

actions represented a major victory for Bower.

With authorization of Windsor authorities, Bower called in Coverdale and Colpitts to survey all of the vehicular traffic, including tourist and commercial use "on all of the main highways in Ontario west of Toronto and leading to the Border Cities and . . . in Michigan leading to Detroit and Port Huron."[41] During August and September 1925, periodic checks were made of the traffic movement on inner-city Detroit streets and of the ferry service on the St. Clair and Detroit rivers.

All large manufacturing firms in Detroit and Windsor were contacted to determine the extent of current operations, transportation needs, future plans, and the potential use of an international bridge in Windsor and Detroit. Of special interest to Coverdale and Colpitts was the transportation of new automobiles destined for delivery to dealerships from plants in Ontario and Michigan. Data was secured also on the railroad freight crossing the river through tunnels and via ferries between Detroit and Windsor and between Port Huron and Sarnia.

In addition, information was collected on population trends, automobile registration, building construction, and manufacturing production in selected cities near Windsor and Detroit. Traffic statistics of three Niagara River bridges were accumulated to provide comparative information and to help project future use of the Detroit-Windsor bridge.

The results of the Coverdale and Colpitts survey supported Bower's optimism over the need for a bridge. During 1925, according to the survey, 1,148,000 automobiles and an estimated 14,965,000 passengers crossed the Detroit River on the Walkerville and Windsor ferries. On Labor Day 1925, the old record set by the Detroit-Windsor ferry of a daily crossing of 2,300 automobiles was broken when 4,300 cars were carried across.[42] Automobile tourist permits reached 24,021 by October 1, 1925, more than double the record high of 10,000 during the same period in 1924.[43] Frequent traffic delays in crossing the Detroit River were also documented. On Labor Day 1925, for example, the unusually heavy auto traffic kept the ferries running until 1:45 A.M. At one time during the evening, more than 600 cars were waiting in line at the Windsor ferry docks.[44]

Based upon the data collected, Coverdale and Colpitts estimated that during the first year of operation, approximately 2,750,000 vehicles would use the bridge. With toll rates set at eighty percent of existing ferry rates, the bridge would produce a gross revenue of $1.5 million, of which $1.1 million would be available for bond interest and taxes. The findings of the survey were widely publicized.[45]

At the same time that the traffic survey was being conducted, the staff of McClintic-Marshall was making its engineering studies. Test borings were made in Sandwich, Ontario, at the end of Huron Line Road near Assumption College, and in Detroit, near the intersection of Jefferson Avenue and 24th Street. The findings indicated the depth and type of soil and bedrock essential for the piers and anchorages and also provided useful data for construction cost estimates.[46] Meanwhile, Bower hired real estate firms in Windsor and Detroit to procure options on land needed for the bridge approaches and terminal areas.[47]

With the information obtained from the preliminary surveys in August and September and the soil test borings, engineers at McClintic-Marshall developed preliminary plans for the bridge. In their deliberations, they carefully considered three types of bridge spans, the arch, cantilever, and suspension designs. The arch was eliminated early in the talks because the depth

of the bedrock identified by the best borings "rendered the foundation work impracticable." On the other hand, not only was the cantilever design feasible, but the anchor pier requirements gave it an advantage over the other types.[48]

The suspension design was also found to be suitable for the Detroit River crossing. Since the construction of the Niagara suspension bridge across the Niagara River in 1855, and the one across the Ohio River at Cincinnati in 1867, there had been a continuous series of improvements and engineering innovations in every stage of suspension bridge construction. The introduction of erection machinery had facilitated the construction of high bridge towers, and new devices and procedures to protect workers deep below the surface of the river had lessened the danger of bends and asphyxiation. Elimination of expansion joints in bridge trusses, replacement of massive stone towers with slender steel towers, elimination of top bracing and substitution of fixed saddles for roller-mount saddles on top of the towers were innovations available to the McClintic-Marshall engineers. Improvements in the quality of cable wire and the demonstrated feasibility of using only two, rather than four, suspension cables to hold up the roadway were other factors considered. Finally, the aesthetic appearance of a suspension bridge, with its high towers reaching skyward, its slender cable lines, and its striking appearance for miles up and down the Detroit river, influenced the bridge designers to choose this type of bridge.[49]

The location of the bridge was also carefully reviewed by McClintic-Marshall engineers. The Belle Isle site was ruled out immediately as too costly, and prohibitive property values in downtown Detroit and Windsor caused the rejection of the Woodward Avenue-Ouellette Avenue site. As Fowler had decided earlier, the best location was the narrowest point of the Detroit River, near Huron Line Road in Sandwich and 19th Street in Detroit.[50]

The original Fowler plan for a double tier bridge with railroad tracks on one level, was scrapped in favor of a single level, automobile span with a forty-seven-foot roadway and a single sidewalk for pedestrians. Bus travel was included, but there was no design allowance for electric streetcars. According to the engineers, 120,000 vehicles could be handled each day "at a mean speed of ten miles per hour."[51] McClintic-Marshall proposed to construct the bridge superstructure and subcontract the substructures and anchorages to other experienced bridge firms.

As provided by his agreement with the Windsor City Council, Bower made the bridge designs and plans available in late October 1925 to city officials and community leaders in Detroit and Windsor. The projected cost of the bridge had risen from the earlier estimate of $12 million to $16,499,400. Of the total, $837,000 was for construction, $1,968,000 was designated for engineering services and overhead, $1.8 million would go to real estate costs, $945,000 had been earmarked for costs, legal fees, and commitments to Fowler and his colleagues associated with the earlier bridge project, $2,461,000 was required for financing and interest on bonds, and $488,000 was to be held in reserves.[52]

In promulgating the bridge plans, Joseph Bower explained, "I have planned a stronger and heavier bridge to adequately serve the demands of future traffic, providing more roadway and greater terminal facilities."[53] In justifying the sharp increase in the cost of the bridge, Bower noted that it had become necessary "to acquire more land on both sides of the river than originally planned."[54]

In order to finance the bridge, Bower proposed to issue first mortgage bonds of $8 million; sinking fund debentures of $6 million; preferred stock of $1 million; and common stock of $1 million—a total of $16 million. The common voting stock "will be purchased by me," Bower announced.[55] The $6 million in debentures on which he requested a county guarantee was "to be paid off over the first twenty years in order that the entire financing may be accomplished on a conservative basis and at a low cost," which, he stated, "would permit lower tolls and a greater volume of business."[56]

Public response to the bridge design and plans was favorable throughout Essex County, Ontario. Even the cost estimates drew relatively little criticism. Some opposition remained, however. The location of the bridge several miles from the center of the business and hotel district of Windsor was the subject of criticism, as were some budget items. Structural provisions and the safety of the suspension design were the center of attacks by opponents of the bridge plan.[57]

Bower did not underestimate the concerns of the opposition, especially on the safety issue. At his suggestion, Wallace R. Campbell, vice-president and treasurer of the Ford Motor Company of Canada and an active proponent of the bridge, immediately called together a group of the leading businessmen of Essex County to form the Essex County Transportation Committee to review the bridge design, specifications, and budget. At its organizational meeting on October 20, 1925, Campbell was elected chairman, Herbert W. Wilson, former mayor of Windsor, was elected treasurer, and George Hanrahan, vice-chairman of the Essex Border Utilities Commission, was elected secretary.[58]

With funds pledged by business firms of Essex County, the committee hired Colonel C. N. Monsarrat, prominent Montreal bridge engineer, to review the bridge plans, the traffic survey, and the financial proposal. The selection of Monsarrat was a shrewd move. Not only was he a distinguished and highly respected Canadian engineer, but he also had considerable experience in bridge construction. He was chief engineer of bridges for the Canadian Pacific Railway for a number of years. In 1911 the Dominion government appointed him chairman and chief engineer of the board of engineers for the Quebec Bridge. Upon its completion, he was appointed general consulting engineer to the Dominion government in 1918. He entered private practice in 1921 and was appointed consulting engineer to the Canadian National Railways.[59]

Furthermore, although the public announcements of his appointment by the Essex County Transportation Committee did not specify this fact, Monsarrat was already familiar with the Detroit-Windsor bridge project. In 1922, he had served on the board of engineers to review the Charles Evan Fowler bridge plan.

Another key decision of the Essex County committee was to call for a plebiscite—a vote on the Bower bridge proposal—at the upcoming municipal elections held in Essex County communities in December 1925 and January 1926. Although the vote did not obligate the communities to any form of financial support or guaranty, it would be, according to Campbell, "an informal expression of their desire for immediate better cross river transportation."[60]

Colonel Monsarrat spent about two weeks reviewing the Coverdale and Colpitts traffic survey and its findings. He also conducted an on-site survey of his own. He studied the bridge design, location, and construction plans. On November 5, 1925, he presented his findings to the Campbell committee. He endorsed the McClintic-Marshall plan, stating, "I am of the opinion, therefore, that both the type and ca-

pacity are satisfactory from topographical, technical and economic viewpoints, and are well chosen to meet the demands of the situation." The findings of the traffic study, the projected earnings from tolls, and the new budget were also approved by Monsarrat.[61]

The Monsarrat report was immediately published in booklet form and distributed throughout Essex County. The news media also gave widespread publicity to the re-

Report

of

Col. C. N. MONSARRAT

on the proposed

DETROIT RIVER BRIDGE

ISSUED BY THE
Better Transportation Committee
of Essex County

Title page of the Monsarrat report, which won support for the bridge in the Essex County election. (Courtesy of the D.I.B. Archives.)

port. It helped combat criticism of the bridge design and danger potential as well as criticism of cost factors and projected profits. The fact that Monsarrat was a distinguished Canadian engineer also helped to diffuse the anti-American sentiment against the Bower project.[62]

With the Monsarrat endorsement, Joseph Bower stepped up his campaign to win voter approval of the bridge at the upcoming Essex County municipal elections. Accompanied by engineers and leading Essex County business leaders, Bower visited every municipality in November and December 1925. The meetings often became controversial, with charges leveled at Bower and the bridge promoters that a "yes" vote on the plebiscite would result in additional levies on taxpayers in Essex County. Bower successfully challenged this claim, arguing that the plan did not call for taxes nor even a guaranty. The vote was to convince the provincial and national governments "that the citizens of Essex County want a Bridge." Bower also promised that construction of the bridge, if approved by the voters, could begin in the spring of 1926.[63]

By December 1, 1925, even before any election was run, Bower and the bridge supporters had received recommendations for a "yes" vote from leading businessmen, community leaders, and public officials of Essex County. In addition to the Better Transportation Committee, Bower won endorsements from local business and community leaders, including Hiram Walker; Herbert Wilson; E. Blake Winter, former mayor of Windsor; M. G. Campbell, vice-president of Kelsey Wheel Company; George Duck, president of the Border Chamber of Commerce; Right Reverend M. F. Fallon, bishop of London, Ontario; U. G. Reaume; Lieutenant Colonel George H. Wilkinson; James Scofield; Edmond Odette; and B. Ross McKenzie. *The Border*

Cities Star endorsed the project under the headline "Build the Bridge and Build It with the Least Possible Delay."[64]

By the first week in January 1926, the municipal elections were completed and the bridge plebiscite had won a clear majority of the votes with 13,874 in favor and 8,794 against. In Windsor, the vote was 4,983 "yes," 1,368 "no"; Sandwich, 1,556 to 104; Ford, 1043 to 320; Riverside, 789 to 314; Amherstburg, 613 to 97; and, La Salle, 248 to 32. Only in the outlying county communities away from the Detroit River, such as Tilbury, Rochester, Maidstone, Mersea, and Anderton, did the plebiscite lose.[65]

The bridge plebiscite was heralded as a great victory for Joseph Bower and his colleagues. After the vote was officially certified, Bower and Charles McTague made frequent trips to Toronto and Ottawa to meet with government officials. Business and government leaders from Windsor and neighboring cities also lobbied for a government subsidy for the bridge.[66] Bower admitted candidly in March 1926, after an extensive visit to Ottawa and Toronto, "I am working all of the time to get the construction of the Border Cities Bridge started this summer. I have never worked so hard on anything in my life."[67]

Despite the efforts of Bower and bridge supporters, little was accomplished in winning a government subsidy either on the provincial or national level. A heated national election scheduled for September 1926 dominated the public scene and the energies of public elected officials.[68] There were, of course, precedents for a government subsidy of bridge construction, such as the span then being built in Quebec, but also there was widespread and vocal opposition to the allocation of government funds or any form of guaranty to a privately owned and operated bridge company. The final blow came in January 1927, when G. Howard Ferguson, the premier of Ontario, announced that the British North America Act "would not permit the Province to guarantee bonds for the bridge."[69]

Although the announcement set back Bower's strategy for financing the Detroit-Windsor Bridge, it did not come as a complete surprise. His frequent meetings with government officials in Ottawa and Toronto, as well as the advice of Charles McTague and other astute politicians, had prepared him for the strong opposition to any form of government guaranty or subsidy. Furthermore, as early as the fall of 1925, Bower began developing a contingency plan to finance the bridge entirely from private sources without any governmental guaranty or subsidy.[70] Such a plan would be more expensive, raising the total cost to about $20 million and would also involve more speculation in the sale of bridge securities.

At the same time, Bower had to face other serious deadlines which threatened the entire bridge project. The United States Congress had renewed the franchise of the American Transit Company in May 1926 until May 13, 1927, with the provision that construction of the bridge had to commence on or before that date and had to be completed within five years. The Canadian Transit Company operated under a similar franchise granted by the Canadian House of Commons, although it had an extra year, until March of 1928, to start construction and an additional five years for completion.

The announcement in February 1927 that the Canadian government had granted the Windsor Subway Company permission to build a tunnel under the Detroit River between the downtown sections of Windsor and Detroit created an even greater sense of urgency for Bower and his business associates. With these new obstacles, it would have been simple for Joseph Bower to withdraw from the bridge project, as he had been advised to do by some of his colleagues. This course of action he refused to take. The bridge had now become a personal challenge. On March 14, 1927, he announced that he would go ahead on the Detroit-Windsor bridge without a government subsidy or guaranty.[71]

CHAPTER 4

The Detroit Campaign:
Fighting the Deadline

Joseph Bower's announcement that construction of a Detroit-Windsor bridge would proceed was widely acclaimed in the Windsor and Detroit areas. Enthusiastic public support for the venture was summed up in an editorial, "A Bridge at Last," published in the *Detroit Free Press* on March 11, 1927:

> The prospect ahead is cause for rejoicing. A bridge such as the one projected will be a logical extension of the system of spans joining nation to nation that at present is composed of the bridges at Montreal, Fort Erie and Niagara. At no place along the border is such a connecting link needed more than it is needed here. At no point can one be more useful or more used. Once erected, a bridge will be so much of a convenience to scores of thousands of people and so much of a help to business that it soon will be looked upon as common necessity, and the public will wonder how this part of the world ever got along without it.

The need to start actual construction of the Detroit-Windsor bridge by May 13 required the constant attention of Joseph Bower and his associates. His first priority was securing the approval of the preliminary bridge design and plans by the Canadian and United States governments. In March, these documents were submitted to the Dominion Railway Board of Canada, the United States Department of War, and the United States and Canada Joint Waterways Commission.[1] The last action proved unnecessary when the U.S. State Department ruled that only the approval of the two governmental agencies were required.[2]

The endorsement of the plans by the United States and Canadian governments proved to be more complicated than expected. Public hearings were scheduled in Detroit by the United States War Department on March 15 and March 27, and invitations were sent to interested organizations and business groups. Although there was some opposition to the proposed bridge by tunnel interests, the real controversy centered upon the height of the bridge over the Detroit River channel, just as it had in the 1870s and in subsequent years.[3]

Controversy over the height issue of the McClintic-Marshall plans came as a surprise to Joseph Bower and his assistants. The new designs followed in general the Charles Evan Fowler proposal, which had been endorsed by the powerful Lake Carriers Association in 1919. Indeed, McClintic-Marshall designers had actually increased Fowler's clearances to heights of 135 feet above high water at the center of the span and 120 feet at the pier head lines. Representatives of the shipping companies, veteran Great Lakes ship captains and navigators, and other organizations sharply criticized these heights as a "menace to navigation."[4] They argued that the masts and radio antennae of many ships operating on the Great Lakes were too high to navigate under the proposed bridge.[5]

An attempt to reach a compromise on the height issue was made at a meeting where Jonathan Jones, chief engineer of McClintic-Marshall Company in charge of the Detroit-Windsor bridge, answered the charges of anti-bridge groups and justified the proposed design. In a lengthy analysis of other bridges in the United States and Canada, such as the Brooklyn, Williamsburg, Manhattan, Queensborough, and Hell Gate bridges, all of which accommodated trans-Atlantic shipping, Jones explained that the center height of each of these structures was 135 feet. Moreover, Jones and Joseph Bower also presented testimony from T. M. Stephens, superintendent of the Marine Division of the Radio Corporation of America, which equipped the fleet of the Detroit and Cleveland Navigation Company. According to Stephens, the masts and antennae on these and other Great Lakes ships could be lowered without violating government radio regulations or the ships' efficiency.[6] Jones also insisted that increasing the height of the center of

the bridge would significantly increase construction costs and the amount of land required for the approaches. On March 25 the hearings were adjourned until Colonel Dent and his engineering staff of the United States War Department could review the bridge plans and the testimony.[7]

After several weeks of deliberation, Colonel Dent announced his decision. He recommended that the height of the bridge be raised to 152 feet at the center and 135 feet at the harbor line. His decision necessitated a redesign of the bridge, of course, and the staff of McClintic-Marshall rushed to their drawing boards to undertake the task.[8] The new plans were quickly completed and approved by the War Department on May 4, 1927.[9]

In the meantime, Bower had moved ahead on the local level to secure permission from the city councils of Detroit and Sandwich, Ontario, to construct the bridge over certain streets. On March 9 Bower, his Detroit attorney, Leo Butzel, and Jonathan Jones, the bridge's chief engineer, appeared before the Detroit Common Council to request such approval to cross Fort and Jefferson streets. According to local newspapers, they were courteously received by the council and assured by John C. Lodge, the council president, that permission would be granted once Bower had submitted a written request.[10]

On April 11 the council officially approved the written request, stipulating that the American Transit Company acquire another half block of property up to Porter Street, and that bridge construction would not interfere with the widening of Fort Street. The only negative remarks made at the council meeting were from Frank X. Martel, the colorful and powerful president of the Detroit Federation of Labor. Martel demanded that only American workers be employed on the American side of the bridge. But council members had expected

Martel's criticism on the international labor issue. A few months previously, he had urged that Canadians be prohibited from crossing the Detroit River to work in Detroit.[11]

On the Canadian side, progress was being made to begin construction of the bridge. On March 11 Charles McTague, counsel for the Canadian Transit Company, appeared before the Sandwich Town Council to request permission to build the bridge over Sandwich, London, and Peter streets, and also to close Victoria Street between Huron Line and Indian roads. McTague also requested an exemption from taxes for ten years.[12] On April 2, the Sandwich Town Council gave its tentative approval to McTague's request and forwarded the bridge plans to C. A. Dunning, minister of railways and canals, for approval of the Dominion Railway Board of Canada. At the same meeting, however, the town council rejected McTague's request for a tax exemption.[13]

Bower and his colleagues were pleased with the responses of the Detroit and Sandwich governing councils and proceeded to expedite the beginning of the actual construction of the bridge to meet their May 13 deadline. But their optimism was not to last long, for on April 19 Mayor John Smith of Detroit vetoed the action of the Detroit Common Council. First, he challenged the constitutionality of the council's action, contending that it violated article VIII, section 25, of the Michigan constitution, providing for the granting of franchises to private companies. "The right to build the American approaches to the bridge constitutes a violation because of its virtual permanence," Smith asserted. "A franchise . . . under Michigan law can only be granted by a favorable vote of three-fifths of the electors," he continued.[14] Furthermore, Mayor John Smith also criticized the council for failing to address the issue of the rates of

toll to be charged by the bridge company and for neglecting to establish procedures to govern future relations between the city of Detroit and the American Transit Company. Smith also challenged the council on the propriety of its practice of approving a "day-to-day" agreement for the bridge company. Moreover, he charged the council with overlooking the obvious fact that the bridge was to be a permanent structure whose franchise could not be removed by the council once it had been built.[15]

Smith's veto created open warfare between the mayor's office and the common council, of course. President Lodge and other council members were furious with the mayor for his stand on the bridge issue. They noted that the city corporation counsel, Charles P. O'Neil, an appointee of Mayor Smith, had approved the legality of council action and had clearly stipulated that the council resolution did not grant a franchise. Moreover, O'Neil had advised the council that their agreement with the bridge company gave full and appropriate protection to the city of Detroit.[16]

Lodge's indignation over the mayor's position continued as he made his views public. A few days after the council's heated meeting with the mayor, Lodge spoke out at a news conference, reminding everyone that the council had authorized the construction of numerous bridges over city streets, such as those built by the Cadillac Motor Company over Clark Avenue, by the Fisher Body Company over Beaubien Street, and by the Crowley-Milner Company over Library Avenue.[17] Councilman John Nagel, at the same news conference, attacked the mayor's disapproval of "day-to-day" agreements, charging that the Mayor had recently approved similar agreements with public utility companies, specifically Bell Telephone Company, City Gas Company, and Detroit Edison Company— measures which, Nagel noted, "involve ten to fifteen times the amount" of the bridge budget.[18] Finally, Lodge restated his frustration at the Mayor's break with the council in his concluding remarks: "I am mystified at this situation. . . . Why at the last minute should there be such a great difference between the governing bodies of the City?"[19] Later, after learning that the mayor "was disgruntled because he was not fully consulted about the bridge," Lodge criticized Bower and the bridge company for failing "[to take] it up with the Mayor in advance."[20] In response to this charge, J. W. Austin, treasurer of the transit companies, explained that he and Bower had met with Mayor Smith once earlier and "three times recently we have tried to call on the Mayor, but he was always engaged or out of the city." Indeed, Austin reported that he and Bower had finally seen the mayor one week previously and "tried to assure him then that there was not the slightest intention to ignore him."[21]

Bower also responded to Smith's demand to control the toll rates charged by the bridge company. "The rates of toll," explained Bower, "were within the jurisdiction of the United States War Department and the Railway Commission of Canada . . . , and not the Detroit City Council."[22] Furthermore, Austin expanded on Bower's statement in a briefing before the city council when he stressed the critical importance of meeting the May 13 construction deadline. "We cannot obtain an extension because Congress is not in session and I do not believe we could get a new franchise from Congress, judging from its attitude when the present one was extended for a year in May, 1926. We must start immediately," he continued, "or the project will be lost."[23]

Although John Lodge and other council members were impressed with the endeavors of Austin and Bower on behalf of the Detroit-Windsor bridge, they also rec-

ognized that construction of the structure must commence by May 13 or not at all. On April 26, despite the threats of Mayor Smith, the common council unanimously overrode his veto.[24] As he had promised, within ten days Mayor Smith countered council action with a lawsuit against Bower and the American Transit Company in Wayne County Circuit Court. Insisting that he was "only interested in the rights of the people," Smith asked the court to enjoin the American Transit Company from building the bridge.[25]

Judge Vincent M. Brennan was assigned to the case by the court and immediately scheduled a show-cause hearing for May 23. In the interim, he refused to stop construction on the bridge. The judge's ruling, heralded as a victory for the Detroit Common Council, Joseph Bower, and the American and Canadian Transit companies, removed the mayor's roadblock to starting construction on the bridge.[26]

Bower and his colleagues were obviously pleased with the judge's ruling because it allowed them to start work on the project before the May 13 deadline. But they were shrewd enough to realize that the court ruling was a hollow victory. Protracted litigation after the hearing later in May could seriously jeapordize the financing of the bridge and thereby cause lengthy construction delays.

In an attempt to break the deadlock, Bower decided to meet with Mayor Smith and to determine whether he could win the mayor's support or, at the very least, persuade him to withdraw his lawsuit. Finally, after a series of meetings between Bower and Mayor Smith, a deal was made. Bower agreed to pay for the cost of a citywide special election to allow the voters of Detroit to decide whether they wanted a privately owned toll bridge, as proposed by the American Transit Company. In turn, the mayor withdrew his lawsuit, allowing the company to proceed with the construction of the bridge on private property. Bower presented the city of Detroit with a check for fifty thousand dollars to cover projected costs for the special election to gain electoral approval for the bridge.[27]

Following Bower's lead, on May 24 the Detroit Common Council passed an ordinance authorizing the American Transit Company to cross certain westside streets, and to establish reasonable tolls under the regulation of the United States War Department. It also provided that the city had "first privilege" to operate streetcars or buses over the bridge. The council also set the date for the public referendum for June 28, 1927.[28]

In the meantime, acting under Judge Brennan's ruling, the American Transit Company started drilling on a site at the northwest corner of Jefferson Avenue and 21st Street. The date selected for this work was May 7, six days before the congressional authorization was to expire.

Recognizing the public relations value of the event, Bower planned a special ceremony for the occasion of starting bridge construction. When Bower was called away to New York on business, James Austin took charge of the ceremony. In attendance on May 7 were William B. Gregory of the Detroit firm of Gregory, Mayer and Thom and also president of the American Transit Company, who presided at the affair, and other bridge directors and officials, including William J. Pulling, Charles S. King, J. O. Reaume, A. F. Healy, and Hiram Walker. James Fozard and Sherman Callender also represented Bower at the function.

After a few speeches were given extolling the historic significance of the event, Helen Austin, the sixteen-year-old daughter of James Austin, treasurer of the bridge company, drove the ceremonial stake into the ground to mark the site of the initial drilling operation. A crew from Pathé News

Films were on hand to cover the ceremony, and newspapers gave coverage to it in Michigan and Ontario.[29]

Immediately after the ceremonies were concluded, drilling commenced by employees of the Pennsylvania Drilling Company, who had set up a temporary rig. Additional drilling equipment arrived from Pittsburgh on May 10, and the engineers located the remaining three corners of the anchorage pier on the American side of the river. By the end of the day on May 13, the drilling crew had reached a depth of 113 feet, having pierced successive layers of blue clay, quicksand, small boulders, and very coarse soil. At about 115 feet below the surface, the drills encountered sulphur dioxide, which poured out of the casing at the rate of one-half gallon per minute. When the crew completed drilling of the sixth hole on June 20, they loaded their equipment on a ferry and headed for the Canadian side of the river.[30]

Now there was an occasion for an opening ceremony in Canada. June 23, 1927, was the date for Canadian bridge proponents, politicians, and businessmen to win publicity for themselves. More than five hundred people gathered in the pouring rain to see Mayor Alexander McKee of Sandwich drive the stake into the ground to mark the site of borings at Sandwich Street and Huron Line Road. Joseph Bower was the keynote speaker and was applauded loudly for "translating the dreams of years into terms of steel and concrete."[31] Other speakers included Mayor McKee, who praised Bower for fighting the "selfish Detroit interests which were seeking to kill the project"; W. B. Clifford, warden of Essex County; George Hanrahan of the Border Chamber of Commerce; the Reverend H. P. Westgate, pastor of St. John's Anglican Church; and the Reverend Daniel L. Dillon, president of Assumption College. Also present were William Gregory, J. W. Aus-

Helen Austin, daughter of bridge vice-president J. W. Austin, leads the groundbreaking ceremony in Detroit, May 7, 1927. W. B. Gregory, the bridge director, holds the stake. (Courtesy of the D.I.B. Archives.)

tin, Hiram Walker, and other bridge officials. Again, as in Detroit several weeks previously, the media covered the event, and a film of the Canadian ceremony was shown in theaters frequently during the month of July.[32]

As June 28, 1927, approached, Joseph Bower and his associates were well aware of the chance they were taking. There was little time to organize a campaign, it would cost fifty thousand dollars to underwrite election costs, and Mayor Smith was openly opposed to the project, even though he had

dropped his lawsuit against the bridge project. Bower decided that it was worth the risk to wage a campaign and to continue construction on the bridge. If they waited until December, the cost of materials and labor would be higher, probably more than the cost of the special election. Also, since Mayor Smith planned to run for reelection in November, the bridge would be an election issue. Either way, the mayor's opposition had to be neutralized.[33]

Mayor John Smith was a controversial, yet popular, figure with the political power

Drilling to locate the site of one corner of the anchorage pier, May 7, 1927. (Courtesy of the D.I.B. Archives).

base in eastside Detroit districts. Born in Detroit on April 12, 1882, he was a self-made man. Like Joseph Bower, he had had to quit school before he finished fifth grade to help with family expenses. Later, he served in the army during the Spanish-American War. After the war, when he returned to Detroit, Smith accepted employment with the Detroit Shipbuilding Company as a steam fitter.

Smith's involvement in politics came soon after the war. He was seen at Republican Party meetings and soon attracted the attention of party leaders. In 1911 Governor Chase S. Osborn appointed Smith to the position of deputy state labor commissioner, and two years later he became a chief deputy of the Wayne County Sheriff's Department. Following his election to the Michigan state senate in 1920, John Smith was appointed postmaster of Detroit by President Warren G. Harding in 1922. And finally, when Mayor Frank Doremus resigned, Smith won the three-way race for the mayor of Detroit.[34]

With less than one month before the election, Bower organized a citywide campaign on behalf of the bridge. Public rallies and meetings were held and Bower and his associates accepted invitations to speak at dozens of community meetings. Bower also contacted business, trade, community, and other leaders and sought their endorsements. News stories and other full-page advertisements explained the advantages of the bridge and the need for a large voter turnout on June 28.[35]

Despite Bower's efforts, a counter-campaign against the bridge developed and gained ground. Robert Oakman, a prominent and wealthy Detroit real estate developer, led a well-organized movement against the bridge. As a close personal ally of Mayor Smith, Oakman also had been active in Detroit politics. He had served as administrative assistant to Governor Hazen Pingree and later as state tax commissioner. He was a strong supporter of Smith in the Mayor's recent election campaign. Furthermore, Oakman's influence held the respect of many wealthy voters; a successful real estate dealer, he sold and owned large tracts of land, including a strip stretching from the Highland Park Ford Plant on Woodward Avenue to the Ford River Rouge Plant. Moreover, he had extensive additional holdings in northwest Detroit.[36]

Under the auspices of a Detroit citizens' committee, Oakman attacked the Bower bridge plan on several grounds. He claimed that the proposed construction

Mayor John W. Smith (*left*) and Robert Oakman, vocal opponents of a privately owned bridge. (Courtesy of the Burton Historical Collection of the Detroit Public Library.)

costs were excessive, charging that "two-thirds of the cost would go to the promoters for profit and waste."[37] He insisted also that the tolls would be excessive, costing the citizens of Detroit "millions of dollars."[38] The design of the bridge was also the object of Oakman's criticism. He described it as "a commercial affair without sufficient regard to the fact that it will be the most prominent feature of our beautiful river." On a similar note, he later claimed that "our noble river will be forever disfigured by an ungainly structure that will be a torment to the people of all time."[39] Later in the campaign,

Oakman demanded that the common council enact legislation to provide that the control of the bridge revert to the City of Detroit after construction costs had been met.[40] Joseph Bower was a special target of Robert Oakman. Time and time again, Oakman charged that Bower had "lulled the Council to sleep with his siren voice."[41]

As Oakman's campaign became stronger, he found allies who supported him in his fight against the bridge. Frank X. Martel, the president of the Detroit Federation of Labor and a powerful politician in Detroit, expressed deep concern about the bridge because it would provide "a possible means of wider entry of Canadian workmen into the Detroit labor market."[42] Governor Fred M. Green also expressed doubts about the proposed bridge. He believed the bridge would be a major liability to Detroit and Michigan by "spilling 200,000 to 300,000 of Detroit's growing population into Canada." Green warned on May 29, 1927: "The man who works in Detroit, but lives and spends his money in Canada, is no help to Michigan."[43]

Oakman found another welcome ally to his cause when Harvey J. Campbell, the secretary and general manager of the Detroit Board of Commerce, made an official request on June 17 to the Detroit Common Council that it postpone the referendum on the bridge until November 3. According to Campbell, the board needed additional time to study the bridge proposal, especially its design and proposed location. Campbell expressed specific concerns about the grade on the American side of the bridge which he wanted limited to 4 percent. Campbell also called for a provision whereby the bridge would revert to the ownership and control of Canada and the United States after a certain time period. The design of the bridge needed careful review, he said, to "make it more attractive."[44]

The news of Campbell's recommendations shocked Joseph Bower and his supporters. They had been counting on the strong endorsement of the powerful Detroit Board of Commerce and its backing in the bridge campaign. After all, the board had been publicly in favor of a Detroit-Windsor bridge since 1903 and had been Charles Evan Fowler's strongest supporter just a few years earlier.

The controversy heated up further when Mayor Smith returned from Europe a week before the election. Although at first he told reporters that he had not had time to review the matter and did not intend to get involved, his neutral position did not last long. On June 24 he held a news conference to denounce the Bower plan and to

demand that the council postpone the vote until the regular November elections.[45]

Smith spelled out in more detail his opposition to the Bower proposal a short time later. He was opposed to the "great and vague rights granted by the City Council ordinance which practically gave the American Transit Company the opportunity to charge tolls forever."[46] The mayor also expressed his bitter opposition to toll roads in general, which he characterized as "an outworn expedient." Finally, he charged that the stock of the American Transit Company "appears watered."[47] On the day before the election, Smith chided Bower and bridge supporters thus: "That ordinance, the meaning of which nobody clearly understands, is what the people of Detroit will vote on, not Mr. Bower's newspaper promises."[48]

The motives of John Smith, Robert Oakman, and other opponents of the international bridge were scrutinized in the news media throughout the bridge campaign. Many charged that Oakman's opposition, in addition to his friendship with the mayor, arose from what he perceived to be a threat to his business ventures. According to an editorial in the *Border Cities Star,* Oakman was afraid that the bridge "might interfere with his land developments on the outskirts of Detroit, and of course, by bringing a certain number of lot buyers to the Canadian side."[49] Oakman, however, denied that this was a factor in his opposition.

Mayor Smith's motives in the matter were more complicated. Some political observers believed that he wanted to use the issue of a privately owned bridge as a campaign issue. John C. Lodge, the popular president of the Detroit Common Council, had announced his intention to run against Smith, and the mayor needed a newsworthy, controversial campaign issue to attract voters away from Lodge. According to the

Border Cities Star, Smith planned "to pose as a vigilant watchdog of the public welfare, who preserved City rights from the clutches of Wall Street and the British government."[50]

Other city leaders, including several members of the Detroit Common Council, suggested more ulterior motives, charging that the Mayor and Robert Oakman were influenced by "persons interested in a vehicular tunnel, or possibly another bridge."[51] Smith's political opponents delighted in spreading this story.

It is obvious that politics was a key factor in Mayor Smith's opposition to the bridge and that he wanted the referendum on the bridge postponed until the fall when he would run again for reelection. "Johnny" Smith was, after all, a shrewd politician. But his opposition was based upon other factors as well. Since 1925 he had been on record as in favor of a municipally owned Detroit-Windsor bridge. In that year, he had met several times with Mayor Frank Mitchell of Windsor and other Essex County leaders on behalf of such a municipal venture. Furthermore, Smith had earlier in his political career waged a strong campaign against a privately owned Detroit street railway company.[52]

What is not clear is why John Smith agreed to the election compromise. He could have seriously damaged the Bower project by protracted litigation. Joseph Bower could not understand Smith's position. Many years later, Bower explained that he had "no knowledge of why Mayor Smith was so opposed." "Maybe," Bower conjectured, "he was opposed to the bridge because the ferry companies didn't want it."[53]

During the heated campaign of 1927, attention was also given to Joseph Bower's motives. In a press conference held a few days before the election, Bower was quoted as saying, "I spent my boyhood in Detroit,

and back in those days they were talking about a bridge over that magnificent stream. I dreamed of such a bridge when I was an office boy in the financial district here, and as the years rolled on and I finally realized I could build such a structure the thought remained uppermost in my mind."[54]

Bower also used the interview to respond to the criticisms of the aesthetic appearance of the proposed bridge. "I would be the last man in the world to erect anything but a beautiful span across the river in which I swam as a boy," he exclaimed.[55] Again he recalled his early life in Detroit: "The Detroit River recalls pleasant memories to me and I would never think of changing those memories."[56]

As the election approached, Bower recognized that he needed additional strong business and community endorsements on behalf of the bridge. The action of the Detroit Board of Commerce was a major setback and Bower feared that it might lead to the desertion of other key business groups. After days of intensive campaigning, endorsements of the bridge were received from the Detroit Real Estate Dealers Association, the Detroit Automobile Club, and the Detroit Citizens League. Prominent citizens also lent their support to the bridge proposal, including John C. Lodge; Charles Van Dusen, vice-president of the S. S. Kresge Company; Leo Franklin, rabbi of Temple Beth El; and Sidney Waldron, president of the Detroit Rapid Transit Commission. Full page advertisements containing the endorsements of hundreds of Detroiters appeared in all of the Detroit newspapers during the closing days of the campaign.[57]

Bower made a special effort to get the personal endorsement of Henry Ford. With the helpful assistance of Wallace Campbell, vice-president of the Ford Motor Company of Canada, Bower met with Ford a few days

VOTE "YES" FOR THE BRIDGE

Specimen Ballot, Special Election, June 28, 1927

INTERNATIONAL BRIDGE ORDINANCE

Do you favor adopting ordinance enacted by the Common Council **May 24th, 1927,** the substance of which ordinance grants permission to American Transit **Company, a** corporation, its successors and assigns, to construct and maintain over and across **certain** streets and alleys in the City of Detroit, the approaches to an international bridge **to be** constructed across the Detroit River from a point in the vicinity of Twenty-first **Street,** Detroit, Michigan, for travel between United States and Canada; and provides for **super-** vision and regulation thereof, the title of which ordinance is as follows:

AN ORDINANCE TO PERMIT THE AMERICAN TRANSIT COMPANY TO CONSTRUCT AND MAINTAIN OVER AND ACROSS CERTAIN STREETS AND ALLEYS IN THE CITY OF DETROIT THE APPROACHES TO AN INTERNATIONAL BRIDGE FOR TRAVEL BETWEEN DETROIT AND CANADA; AND TO PROVIDE FOR SUPERVISION AND REGULATION AS IN THIS ORDINANCE PRESCRIBED.

FOR THE ORDINANCE - - - - - ☒

AGAINST THE ORDINANCE - - - ☐

Campaign literature in the special election, June 28, 1927. (Courtesy of the D.I.B. Archives.)

before the election. Ford was impressed with Joseph Bower and his plans for a bridge. On June 25 Ford publicly endorsed the plan and issued the following statement: "The only way things can be done today is by private business. The Detroit International Bridge is an international matter and I believe that if it is constructed by private enterprise and capital it will be built quickly and well."[58] Ford's endorsement received widespread publicity.

Another coup for Bower occurred on June 24 when the directors of the Detroit Board of Commerce reversed their earlier position and voted unanimously to endorse the Bower plan.[59] On the same day, newspapers announced that Andrew Mellon, U.S. secretary of the treasury, also supported the bridge proposition. The papers noted that Mellon had strong financial ties with the McClintic-Marshall engineering firm, already identified with the bridge

project.[60] The *Detroit Free Press*, the *Detroit News*, and the *Border Cities Star* each gave strong editorial endorsements on behalf of the bridge.[61]

Joseph Bower and his supporters had waged an effective campaign, and it was evident that as the election neared, they were gaining support. Mayor Smith was aware of this trend and admitted that his position was increasingly unpopular with the voters. He and Oakman became vitriolic in their statements and actions. Smith's greatest faux pas occurred a few days before the election. While he was entering the radio studio of station WGHP to give a speech denouncing Bower and the common council bridge ordinance, he met H. H. Esselstyn, a reputable engineer who was president of the Detroit Engineering Society and also a Smith appointee to the Detroit Railway Commission. The Mayor confronted Esselstyn and demanded to know what he was doing at the radio station. When Esselstyn explained that he was there waiting to appear on a later program to discuss the engineering aspects of the bridge plan, Smith fired him on the spot. "I'm through with you," the Mayor shouted, "You report to my office tomorrow morning with your resignation as Commissioner of Street Railways."[62]

In the station interview which followed, Esselstyn announced that he would refuse to offer his resignation, as demanded by Mayor Smith. "I want all Detroiters to know," he stated, "that because I have made this short speech, I have been discharged as Commissioner of Street Railways."[63] The episode received front-page coverage in all the local newspapers the day before the election. Esselstyn became a hero and Johnny Smith the goat.[64]

On June 28, a record number of 74,557 voters, twice the number expected, turned out to cast their ballots on the bridge referendum. The proposed bridge ordinance won by an eight-to-one margin, 66,353 to 8,204. Each of the city's 604 voting districts endorsed the bridge proposal. Robert Oakman's home district voted in favor of the bridge by a five-to-one margin. Joseph Bower had won a major victory.[65]

In the aftermath of the election, Robert Oakman vowed to go to court to stop construction on the bridge. Bower graciously thanked the citizens of Detroit for their support and promised to construct a bridge which will "beautify the Detroit River" and to charge a reasonable toll for crossing the structure.[66]

Mayor Smith accepted the results with more poise than did Robert Oakman. "I bow to the will of the people," he stated; "They want a bridge and they must have a bridge." "But," he added, "if the election were held again tomorrow, and if I were the only person voting against it, I would still feel it my duty to oppose it."[67]

Joseph Bower was elated with the results and tired of waiting. He captured the spirit of the citizenry after the election, saying, "We're through arguing. Let's build!"[68]

CHAPTER 5

The Necessary Resources:
Experts and Dollars

The days following the Detroit election found Joseph Bower and the directors of the American and Canadian transit companies busy with a myriad of legal and administrative details. Most of the work fell upon Bower's New York attorney, Alfred Cook. The sale of bridge securities required approval from a number of federal, state, and local agencies, and the purchase of land for the United States and Canadian approaches and terminals likewise required the services of attorneys and real estate developers. Bower relied as well upon Alfred Cook in his plans to organize the bridge companies.[1]

Despite these major tasks, Bower found time to credit the people who had worked on behalf of the bridge proposal in the recent election. On June 29, 1927, he held a "victory dinner" at the Barlum Hotel in Detroit, which was attended by more than four hundred persons who had helped Bower in the referendum election on June 28. It was a festive occasion and Bower charmed the group with descriptions of his plans for building the Detroit-Windsor bridge.[2]

Under the terms of an agreement of May 27, 1927, between Bower and the transit companies, Bower had been "given the exclusive option until September 1, 1927, to purchase all of the property and assets of the American and Canadian Transit Companies."[3] Once this transaction was completed, Bower reorganized the company. In June 1927 he formed the Detroit International Bridge Company under the laws of the State of Michigan, and received authorization from the state "to construct, own and operate the bridge."[4] After a series of complicated legal maneuverings, the Detroit International Bridge Corporation, incorporated in the state of Delaware in July 1927, took over control of the American Transit Company, a Nevada-based corporation, and it, in turn, was acquired by Bower's Detroit International Bridge Company on August 12, 1927. The charter of the Canadian Transit Company remained intact, although it was controlled by Bower's new company.[5]

Under the terms of the option agreement, Bower assumed "the indebtedness of the American and Canadian Transit Com-

[handwritten margin notes:]
Skating Jan. 1, 1893
opened

Dept. of Parks + Blvds
7 Annual Report 1892
912 p. 23, 34   ∨ 24

~~xx 11-1860s~~
LIGHT
✗P 4-3-38

∨ 1970-7-2 4B 1:3

WIRSS Lease
  N 1970-7-28 3A
F 1970-9-14 3A
  1970-9-9 3A
F 1971-3-17-9A

F 1976-6-25 3A

all sub-
ls of the
t on said
imburse
k of the
cash ac-
rvice to
ents to
ash and
stock;
t, and
n cash;
verdale
w York
Cook,
alue of
5,000 in
eferred
Chase,
,000 in
eferred
ipated
ct.[7]
of the
eciation

to a number of persons who had been of special assistance to him. Preferred stock certificates were sent to the following: J. W. Austin, $30,000; Jonathan Jones, $10,000; and $5,000 to J. L. Fozard, H. DeWitt Smith, F. M. Radford, William B. Gregory, Hiram Walker, W. J. Pulling, C. S. King, A. F. Healy, J. O. Reaume, Henry Becker, and Sherman D. Callender.[8]

Bower proceeded to reorganize the boards of directors of the Detroit International Bridge Company and its subsidiary, the Canadian Transit Company. Bower, of course, was elected president of both companies, and with him on the former served J. L. Fozard as vice-president and general manager, J. W. Austin as vice-president, Sherman D. Callender, secretary-treasurer, Frederick D. Brown, assistant secretary, and David Graham, assistant treasurer. Bower, Callender, Austin, and Graham

were joined on the board of directors by Jansen Noyes, Alfred C. Dent, and Alfred A. Cook. The Canadian Transit Company elected Bower as president, J. W. Austin as vice-president, J. L. Fozard as secretary-treasurer, Frederick C. Brown as assistant secretary, and David Graham as assistant treasurer. Bower, Austin, Fozard, Dent, Noyes, Cook, and Graham made up the board of directors.[9]

To assist with the complicated legal transactions, Bower retained five distinguished law firms: Stevenson, Butzel, Eamon and Long of Detroit; Cook, Nathan and Lehman of New York City; McTague, Clark and Racine of Windsor; McGiverin, Hayden and Ebbs of Ottawa; and Tilley, Johnson, Thompson and Parmenter of Toronto. Alfred Cook of New York was given major responsibility for the preparation of the incorporation papers, the transfer of ownership from the American Transit Company to the Detroit International Bridge Company, and the contracts with the banks and underwriters, with McClintic-Marshall Company, and with the Mellon banking interests.[10]

As a result of the design changes required by the U.S. War Department, new plans and budget estimates were prepared for submission and review by the city councils of Sandwich and Detroit, as well as by state and provincial agencies. The attorneys also negotiated agreements with the Pere Marquette and Wabash railroad companies for permission to construct a bridge approach over their property and tracks.[11]

The acquisition of private property for the bridge approaches also proceeded rapidly in the summer of 1927. Although Bower's real estate agents obtained options on most of the land needed, there were holdouts which required condemnation proceedings. In Sandwich, one woman homeowner who refused to accept $30,000 approved by the Canadian Transport Commission found her furniture and belongings out on the street. The local newspaper, which published a photograph of her surrounded by her possessions under the caption "Among My Souvenirs," quoted her as saying, "I hope the bridge falls in the River."[12]

Financing of the bridge was handled directly by Joseph Bower in New York. On July 19, 1927, the bridge companies signed an agreement with the prestigious New York firms of Hemphill, Noyes and Company and Peabody, Haughteling and Company to sell $12 million in "First Mortgage Sinking Gold Fund Bonds" and $8 million of "25-year Participating Sinking Fund 7% Gold Debentures." In addition to the bonds, $1.4 million of preferred stock and $100,000 in shares of common stock were issued to Joseph Bower. As collateral security, Richard B. Mellon, H. W. McClintic, and C. D. Marshall deposited in the Mellon Bank of Pittsburgh on August 1, 1927, 60,000 shares of preferred common stock of the Aluminum Corporation of America and 70,000 shares of common stock of the Gulf Oil Company of Pennsylvania for a total fair market value of at least $12 million. On August 16, 1927, the bond underwriters transferred $20 million to the New York Trust Company as trustee of the bridge project. The complete funding of the Detroit-Windsor bridge was accomplished within a single month.[13]

The changes in the height of the bridge as required by the U.S. War Department not only necessitated changes in the bridge's design and the Canadian and American approaches, but also required changes in the construction budget. On June 11, 1927, after his staff had prepared new designs and specifications, C. D. Marshall notified Joseph Bower that the total cost of the bridge alone would be $11,387,200, an increase over the earlier budget. This total was allocated as follows:[14]

Construction of bridge, approaches, lighting, and terminal structures	$9,852,200
Customs, duties, and sales tax, Canadian	570,000
Construction bond (3 years)	250,000
Engineering and consultants' fees	480,000
Legal and office expenses	100,000
Taxes during construction	135,000
Total	$11,387,200

Marshall was careful to point out to Bower that the budget estimate did not include the purchase of real estate, easements over railroads or other property, or payment for any past services of engineers, attorneys, or others associated with the company.[15]

After the bridge designs, specifications, and budget were reviewed and approved by Ralph Modjeski and Clement Chase, engineers whom Bower had hired as consultants to represent him in his dealings with McClintic-Marshall, a detailed construction contract was prepared. It provided that McClintic-Marshall agreed to "do all the work and furnish all the labor, material, plant, tools, power and equipment necessary for constructing the bridge."[16] The general plans and the specifications approved by both parties were to be followed in general except that McClintic-Marshall, with the approval of Bower and appropriate government authorities, "may make such modifications in such plans and specifications . . . as will improve the bridge." Both parties also agreed to hire expert consultants to advise them in all aspects of the construction.[17]

McClintic-Marshall agreed to complete the bridge "in not more than three years from the date of the deposit" of the necessary funds. If construction should exceed three years, the contractor agreed to pay the Detroit International Bridge Company and the Canadian Transit Company a "sum equal to interest at the rate of 6½ percent

The bridge team. *From left:* Joseph A. Bower, C. D. Marshall, J. W. Austin, Ralph Modjeski, and C. E. Chase.

per annum on the outstanding bonds of the Company and 7 percent on the outstanding debentures."[18] If, however, the bridge was completed in less than three years, the contract provided that the contractor would receive "one half of all receipts from tolls, less ½ of the actual operating expenses, including taxes and allowances for depreciation." The total payment to McClintic-Marshall was set at $11.5 million. The contract was signed on July 20, 1927, by J. W. Austin and Sherman Callender of the Detroit International Bridge Company, Charles King and J. L. Fozard of the Canadian Transit Company, and C. D. Marshall of the McClintic-Marshall Company. The effective date of the agreement was August 16, 1927.[19]

The contract was an important factor in the sale of the bonds for the bridge. The guaranty of completion within a given period, backed by a surety bond, "eliminated any uncertainty from the financing and permitted a quick determination of the total amount of securities required to be sold."[20] According to C. D. Marshall, without such a guaranty, "private financing for the bridge would have been impracticable and the project would have had to await the distant and unlikely contingency of joint action toward building and ownership by the two governments concerned."[21]

The three-year completion guaranty was not the only unique feature of the contract. In most bridge contracts, a steel fabricator, like McClintic-Marshall, would be responsible for only one part of a bridge project. Under this agreement, however, most of the construction of the piers, anchorages, roadway, approaches, and customs facilities were sublet to other companies under supervision of the staff of the main contractor. The flexibility given to the contractor to make changes "in the structural details and in the arrangements for traffic circulation and control" was another unusual provision of the contract.[22]

To a large degree, the construction contract, with its innovative provisions, represented the trust which Joseph Bower and his partners had in C. D. Marshall and H. H. McClintic and the expertise of their staff. By 1927 McClintic-Marshall was prominent and reputable in the steel fabrication business of the United States. This Pittsburgh-based company, incorporated in 1900, was later purchased by Andrew W. Mellon, the financier. Mellon then hired H. H. McClintic and C. D. Marshall to operate the original bridge construction business, and after a time sold the firm to McClintic and Marshall.[23]

By 1913 McClintic-Marshall had become the largest independent steel fabricator in the United States and had built such bridges as the one over the Ohio River at Beaver, Pennsylvania, and the lock gates of the Panama Canal. Marshall was in charge of the engineering facets of the company's operation, including the administration of the main and regional offices. McClintic was responsible for the mechanical operations and shops. The company prospered as it expanded its services to include office, mill, and factory buildings, machine shops, furnace and power plants, ore trestles and bins, as well as all types of railroad and vehicular bridges.

McClintic-Marshall owned and operated fabricating steel works in Pittsburgh, Chicago, Los Angeles, San Francisco, and Potsdam and Carnegie, New York, with a total annual steel capacity of 450,000 tons. In addition, offices were located at the above cities and in New York, Philadelphia, Boston, Detroit, Cleveland, Baltimore, Cincinnati, St. Louis, and Charlotte, North Carolina.

By 1927, McClintic-Marshall had completed hundreds of railroad and vehicular bridges and had numerous others under construction, including the Hudson River Bridge, between 178th Street in New York City and Fort Lee, New Jersey; Bear Mountain Bridge, across the Hudson River; Outerbridge Crossing over the Arthur Kill; Mount Hope Bridge, connecting Bristol and Portsmouth, Rhode Island, over Narragansett Bay; and Carlton Bridge over the Kennebec River at Bath, Maine. The company (since 1931 a part of Bethlehem Steel Company) would, of course, gain even more fame for its construction of the Golden Gate Bridge, linking San Francisco and Marin County, California.[24]

It is not surprising that Joseph Bower selected this company to plan and complete the Detroit River bridge. This is an example of Bower's sound business experience and good judgment.[25] The contract also represented the high esteem in which Marshall and McClintic held Joseph Bower. Neither Bower nor the McClintic-Marshall company ever regretted their partnership in the building of the Ambassador Bridge.

CHAPTER 6

A Bridge Takes Shape

During the summer of 1927, while the election battle was waged and the financing of the bridge was secured, the engineers of McClintic-Marshall were busy preparing final plans for the bridge and contracts for the services of the various firms which would contribute to the difficult aspects of construction. Subcontractors were engaged to perform specific tasks of the long construction scheme.

The general design of the bridge was typical of other suspension bridges.[1] At the harbor lines on each side of the Detroit River, massive piers were built deep into the ground. On these were erected towers stretching 380 feet above the river. Inland, away from the riverbank, anchorages resting upon the bedrock 120 feet below the surface were constructed. Two cables, each made up of thousands of small wires, were strung over the towers, on saddles, and attached to the anchorages. Wire suspenders were dropped from the main cables to hold up the central span or roadway across the river. The total length of the structure from entrance to exit was 9,200 feet; the distance between the two main towers, the suspended section of the bridge, was 1,850 feet. At the time of its construction, it was the longest suspension bridge in the world, exceeding by 100 feet the Philadelphia-Camden Bridge completed in 1926.

Following the requirements of the U.S. War Department, the span was 152 feet above the river at the center and 135 and 133.5 feet above the river at the United States and Canadian harbor lines, respectively. The center height allowed the passage by 20 feet of any vessel operating on the Great Lakes at that time. The maximum grade of the roadway on the American side was 5 percent for a distance of over nineteen hundred feet. On the Canadian side, the greater availability of land allowed a maximum grade of 4 percent. The roadway of the bridge was 47 feet wide, accommodating, at the time of its completion, five lanes of traffic. An 8-foot sidewalk was provided for pedestrians. Heavy railings were constructed to resist the impact of skidding vehicles.

According to plans, the bridge was to

be lighted by two independent currents, one American and the other Canadian, installed on either side of the roadway. In the event that one source of electricity failed, there would be at least partial illumination on the bridge. The bridge plans also called for pneumatic tube systems to facilitate the central sorting and retrieval of automobile licenses, which in 1929 were collected by United States and Canadian customs officials from foreign autos and returned upon reentry. Customs terminals were built on both sides of the bridge to accommodate the examination of vehicles and their contents. Buildings to house customs staff and bridge employees were also planned.

Although the McClintic-Marshall Company was awarded the contract for the entire bridge, it was interested primarily in that part of the construction which involved the steel fabrication of the bridge structure, including the fabricated steel units of the United States approach trusses and viaduct, the main towers, the floor beams, and the stiffening trusses of the main suspended span. These parts were carefully designed and assembled at the company's main plant in Rankin, Pennsylvania, and shipped to Detroit for assembly on the bridge location.[2]

Subcontracts were let out for bid on other parts of the bridge, including main and auxiliary piers and superstructure, anchorages, pavements, curbs and sidewalks, bridge cables, building and mechanical work, exterior lighting, Canadian approach trusses and viaduct approaches, terminals, masonry, and granite block pavement. By the end of September 1927, the contracts for the main piers and anchorages were let and construction commenced simultaneously on key sections of the bridge.[3]

Even before the selection of subcontractors, the engineering staff of McClintic-Marshall had been busy with its preliminary work. The drill borings which had be-

gun in May 1927 gave a profile of the soils and revealed progressive layers of yellow clay, blue clay, quicksand, and hardpan of varying thicknesses. The hardpan, located 110 feet below the surface, contained huge boulders, some of which were 15 feet in diameter. At first, the engineers studying the boring samples planned to anchor the cables in this formation, but because of the tremendous loads on the main towers and the tendency of the anchorages to slip under pressure, they decided to go deeper to the bedrock, geologically termed "Dundee Limestone." It is significant that although the borings were made 3,600 feet apart on the American and Canadian shores, the limestone foundation was uniformly flat, varying only 6 feet in elevation. It was into this solid rock formation that the main piers and anchorages were attached.[4]

After the borings were analyzed, survey parties laid out the positions of the piers, anchorages, and approaches. The cross-river triangulation system was rechecked and "minor corrections" were made. The demolition and removal of buildings on the site of the American approach and terminal had been completed by August 31, 1927. Headquarters for McClintic-Marshall were established in a building acquired by the bridge company at 1245 21st Street. Six staff engineers were assigned to work exclusively on the Detroit-Windsor river project.[5]

McClintic-Marshall selected Jonathan Jones, the assistant chief engineer of the company, to assume major responsibility for the final design and construction of the bridge. He was ideally suited for the assignment by experience, temperament, and administrative ability. Jones was a nationally recognized expert on structural bridge design and had experience in all phases of construction. A graduate of the Engineering College of the University of Pennsylvania in 1906, he served as engineer of bridges for the city of Philadelphia from 1913 to 1920. In that year he joined the engineering staff of McClintic-Marshall and by 1929 had risen to the position of chief engineer. He was initially involved with the planning of the Detroit-Windsor bridge in 1922 when his company served in a consulting capacity to Charles Evan Fowler.[6]

During the construction of the Detroit-Windsor bridge, Jones commuted between Detroit and the company's headquarters in Pittsburgh. In addition to the six engineers assigned to the project, Jones initially selected E. J. Paulus as engineer of construction, and E. H. Proctor as his assistant. Jones assigned Paulus and Proctor full time to Detroit. Robert MacMinn replaced Paulus in November 1927 and continued in that position until the bridge was completed. Jones and his special team of engineers did the preliminary surveys, prepared the design of the bridge, and supervised the companies which had won the subcontracts for different sections of the bridge. Jones also coordinated the fabrication of the steel sections of the bridge produced at his company's Rankin Mills subsidiary near Pittsburgh.[7]

Following common bridge construction practices, additional experts were hired as consultants on different phases of the project. E. A. Proctor, of the New York firm of Moran, Maurice and Proctor, was hired as consultant on the design and construction of the main piers, anchorage substructures, and approach piers. An expert on foundations, Proctor was already familiar with Detroit, having been involved with the design and construction of several of Detroit's tallest buildings. He also served as consultant on the design of the Philadelphia-Camden Bridge, the proposed Hudson River bridge and the "Great Dam being constructed across the Susquehanna River at Conwingo, Maryland."[8]

The Detroit firm of Smith, Hinchman and Grylls was hired to advise on the design of the anchorages, towers, and terminal buildings, and on the aesthetic appearance of the bridge. Other consultants included Clayton Pike for the bridge's lighting system, Clarence Proctor for asphalt paving, and the Perry Testing Laboratory of Detroit for tests of concrete used in the bridge.

For the suspended structure of the main span, Jones hired Leon S. Moisseiff of New York City. An engineer and mathematician of great distinction, Moisseiff had the intricate mathematical gift "for the accurate and economical determination of stresses for bridges."[9] By using his "deflection theories" developed at the turn of the century, bridge builders were able to determine the interaction between the wind and other weather elements and the traffic load on suspension bridge structures.[10]

Moisseiff introduced many of his ideas on the design of the Detroit-Windsor bridge, including the elimination of the unsightly overhead bracing so typical in many earlier suspension bridges, which gave the motorist "the feeling of passing through a tunnel."[11] Moisseiff also recommended the use of silicon steel on the bridge which provided a 50 percent increase in strength and carrying capacity at little additional cost per pound. The slender appearance of the Detroit-Windsor bridge structure, which was markedly different from the massive bulky structure proposed earlier by Charles Evan Fowler, reflected the influence of Leon Moisseiff.[12]

The major engineering consultants hired by McClintic-Marshall to oversee all phases of the entire project including traffic projections were Colonel C. N. Monsarrat and Philip L. Pratley, partners in a Montreal engineering firm. Colonel Monsarrat had been associated with the Detroit-Windsor bridge project since 1922 when he served on the board of examiners for the American and Canadian Transit companies. Later, in the fall of 1925, Colonel Monsarrat was hired by the Essex County Transportation Committee to review the Bower plans for a suspension bridge.

Philip Louis Pratley, the co-founder of the Montreal firm in 1921, also had a distinguished record as a bridge engineer. Born and educated in England, he came to Canada in 1906 to join the staff of the Dominion Bridge Company of Montreal as designing engineer. In this capacity, he designed several major bridges, including the large highway arch bridge over the Saint John River, near Saint John, New Brunswick. In 1908 he became chief designer for the Quebec Board of Bridge Engineers, and later, the designing engineer for the Quebec Bridge. In 1920 Pratley returned from the Dominion Bridge Company to enter private practice with Colonel C. N. Monsarrat.

Later in his career, Pratley served as consulting engineer on a series of major bridges, including the Jacques Cartier Bridge, Angus L. MacDonald Bridge, Burlington Skyway High Level Bridge, Thousand Islands Bridge, and the Lions' Gate Bridge in Vancouver. Pratley was associated with the Detroit-Windsor bridge, not only during its construction, but later, after its completion, as consulting engineer in charge of inspection and maintenance.[13]

Jonathan Jones summed up the importance of Monsarrat and Pratley to the bridge project when he wrote to Joseph Bower on August 31, 1927: "We have a high regard for Mr. Pratley's technical ability, experience and thoroughness, beside which we regard Colonel Monsarrat's influence in Canada as a value to ourselves and the Bridge Company."[14]

The Detroit International Bridge Company also hired engineering consultants to represent its interests on the project. The firm of Coverdale and Colpitts of New York City and Montreal continued to conduct traffic and revenue surveys for Joseph Bower. The data gathered became increasingly valuable in light of the proposed construction of the Detroit-Windsor tunnel.[15]

Meanwhile, the New York engineering firm of Modjeski and Chase was hired by Bower to advise him on all aspects of the bridge design and construction and to certify that the work conformed to the contract. They were one of the premier bridge engineering firms in the United States and had been involved in other major suspension bridges. Indeed, Ralph Modjeski was acknowledged as the leading bridge designer in the country and had built more great bridges than any other living American engineer.[16]

Modjeski had served as consulting engineer on bridge projects for the United States government, the Dominion of Canada, the Northern Pacific and other railroad companies, and numerous state and local governments. He was chief engineer on such bridges as those over the Mississippi River at Rock Island and Thebes, Illinois, the Columbia River at Celilo, Oregon, and the Philadelphia-Camden Bridge. From 1908 to 1918 he was a member of the board of engineers for the Quebec Bridge over the St. Lawrence River. Two of his later achievements were the Delaware River Bridge which opened in 1926 and the San Francisco–Oakland bridge, completed in November 1936.[17]

Under the contract with Joseph Bower and the Detroit International Bridge Company, Modjeski and Chase agreed "to supervise all work of construction in mills, shop and field," to inspect all materials used on the bridge, and to inspect and certify the bridge when completed. They also agreed to assign a resident engineer to the project and for this position they selected Russell G. Cone.[18]

In addition to consulting engineers hired by the Detroit International Bridge

Company, McClintic-Marshall, and Modjeski and Chase, the American Cable Company, which won the subcontract to supply the cable wire, employed David Steinman and Holton Robinson as consultants. Both had national reputations for their work on suspension bridges and were also currently engaged in building the cables on the Mt. Hope Bridge across Narragansett Bay in Rhode Island.[19] Steinman, of course, was already familiar with the Detroit-Windsor bridge project, having served earlier as a consultant to Charles Evan Fowler.

Despite the number of consulting engineers and firms involved in the Detroit-Windsor bridge, there were few problems or delays. The consultants differed occasionally on details of the design, testing procedures, and construction techniques, but the matters were always resolved amicably and professionally due to the efforts of Jonathan Jones.

The McClintic-Marshall Company, under the direction of Jones and Robert MacMinn, the resident engineer, controlled the construction of the entire project and fabricated and erected the structural steel except for the Canadian viaduct. The remainder of the work was subcontracted "to experienced firms in the several special fields involved."[20] Special consideration was given to Michigan and Ontario firms, if available, to work on their respective sides of the bridge.

McClintic-Marshall subcontracted certain materials and services for the Canadian side of the bridge as follows: demolition, Canadian approach, to General Wrecking Company, Detroit; Canadian approach piers, abutment, and terminal fill, to Merlo, Merlo and Ray Company, Ford City, Ontario; and Canadian approach steelwork, Canadian Bridge Company, Walkerville, Ontario.

Subcontracts for the American side were awarded thus: demolition, American approach, to Fulton Lumber and Wrecking Company, Detroit; American approach piers, to Walbridge Aldinger Company, Detroit; and American auxiliary piers, abutment, and terminal fill, H. H. Esselstyn, Detroit. American companies were also given subcontracts for the remaining work on the bridge. Pennsylvania Drilling Company of Pittsburgh, for example, was to conduct core borings; the Foundation Company of New York would complete the main piers and anchorage substructures; and the Keystone State Corporation of Philadelphia agreed to erect main span cables, suspenders, and hand rope.[21]

The number of workers employed on the bridge varied according to the stage of construction and the type of work involved. At times, there were more than six hundred workers on both sides of the bridge, and under constant pressure from labor unions in Detroit and Windsor a concerted effort was made to hire local workers—more specifically, Canadian citizens to work on the Canadian sections of the bridge and American workers to work on the American sections.[22]

For the specialized bridge work such as anchorage, tower, and cable erection, experienced work teams were recruited from other parts of the country. As one bridge project was completed, these "migratory" workers moved on to other sites, usually recruited by the contractors. Thus many of the workers who came to Detroit had recently been employed on the Bear Mountain Bridge over the Hudson River in New York, which was completed in 1927.[23]

The first step in the construction plan was to take borings of the subsoil under the piers and anchorages. The Pennsylvania Drilling Company of Pittsburgh was hired to perform this task. Under the supervision of Lee Young, a team of drillers commenced work in May 1927 and took borings at

Canadian anchorage site, October 27, 1927. (Courtesy of the D.I.B. Archives.)

Canadian main pier under construction, March 13, 1928. (Courtesy of the D.I.B. Archives.)

eleven sites up to 130 feet below the surface. The cores obtained during the drilling were analyzed by the bridge designers and made available to potential bidders on the substructure of the bridge.[24] After field surveyors laid out the positions of the piers and charted the locations of the approaches, viaducts and terminals, demolition crews cleared or removed the necessary buildings. This allowed the work on the bridge's substructure to begin.[25]

The foundations for the two main piers and the anchorages were built by the Foundation Company of New York. The work on the piers, which commenced on September 20, 1927, involved the excavation of soil and the construction of pairs of cylindrical concrete caissons deep below the surface of the river until hardpan was reached. The actual process, developed after years of experience and experimentation, provided that cylindrical caissons, each 38 feet in diameter and with steel cutting edges on the bottom, were placed in the excavated area. The caisson walls were then extended upward, building upon the base extending out of the ground. The weight forced the entire structure farther down toward the bedrock below. After the soil inside the caisson was excavated, another was placed on top. When the caissons reached bedrock they were sealed by pouring more than 8,000 cubic feet of concrete in the shaft until it reached the top of the working chamber roof. Eventually the working chamber, too, was filled with concrete.[26]

The construction of the Canadian main piers was more complicated because of their location, about 250 feet from the shoreline in 15 feet of water. An artificial island was built at the site of the pier and a ramp constructed to connect it to the shoreline. The unstable underwater clay on the Canadian side created additional construction problems.[27]

The work on the foundation was strenuous, difficult, and dangerous. The workers, called "sand hogs," had to work under pressure of thirty pounds per square inch to keep out the water. Each gang worked two shifts a day, two hours below the surface, with four hours of rest following. When the air pressure was maximum they worked only one hour a day in two half-hour shifts.[28]

Because of the potential danger of the bends, a temporary "hospital" was constructed, consisting of a huge boiler divided into two compartments where the pressure could be regulated and reduced gradually. Although a number of workers were treated at the hospital, there were no fatalities. One worker was killed, however, when he fell nearly 100 feet into the anchorage excavation. Another died from injuries sustained when he was struck by a "concrete mixer skip on the Canadian side."[29]

When the foundation excavation work was completed in April 1928, the sand hogs, described as "having a roving tendency that sends them around the country in a migratory shift from one job to another," left Detroit and moved on to other bridge construction projects.[30]

After the main piers were completed, the construction of the towers began. These slender steel structures, each rising 363 feet above the base of the piers, were constructed of silicon steel. Each tower was composed of two columns, 67 feet apart and crossbraced to withstand wind pressures. Each carried a load of twenty thousand tons to the piers below.

Because of the weight of the tower columns and their slender design, somewhat greater construction problems were encountered than on other recently completed bridges. For example, the top center section of the tower weighed sixty tons and the other sections weighed between fifty-five and sixty tons. Each section had to be

Caisson at the Canadian main pier, December 15, 1927. (Courtesy of the D.I.B. Archives.)

Surfacing machine, east Canadian main pier, April 20, 1928. (Courtesy of the D.I.B. Archives.)

raised into place by the use of a steel stiff leg derrick or "tower creeper" as it was called, carried on a special underframe and then raised progressively up the river face of each tower. After the lifting process had been completed to the desired height, saddles and rollers were hoisted up and attached to the top of the tower to receive the main cable.[31]

Under the supervision of G. A. Coffall, Morton McClain, and A. Toohey, the erection of the main United States tower was commenced on March 31, 1928, and completed on July 14, 1928. The Canadian tower was started on April 20 and completed on July 27, 1928.[32] The two anchorages, located respectively just north of West Jefferson Avenue in Detroit and north of London Street in Sandwich, rivaled the main towers as the most impressive parts of the bridge. Each anchorage consisted of two sections, one sunk below ground until it reached bedrock at more than one hundred feet below the river level and the other rising one hundred feet above ground. The structure was as high as a sixteen-story commercial building, half of which extended below ground.

The construction of the anchorage substructure also involved the sinking of a pair of vertical caissons to the bedrock, twenty-two feet wide and one hundred feet long, running parallel to the bridge cables. A huge cross block of concrete, fifty feet by thirty-six feet by ninety-seven feet, was constructed between the caissons to hold the eye bars to which the bridge cables were attached. Each anchorage superstructure rose to the roadway and supplied it with additional stability and resistance to the pull of the cables, each about eight thousand tons. The work on the anchorages was completed on June 22, 1928.[33]

In April 1928, as the main towers and anchorage superstructures rose skyward, Joseph Bower decided that it was time to

Announcement of the opening of the Ambassador Bridge, April 26, 1928. (Courtesy of the D.I.B. Archives.)

First truss, U.S. approach, May 18, 1928. (Courtesy of the D.I.B. Archives.)

Canadian main tower, May 26, 1928. (Courtesy of the D.I.B. Archives.)

Looking southwest from the U.S. side, June 6, 1928. (Courtesy of the
D.I.B. Archives.)

Tower creeper and derrick on the first section of the U.S. tower, June 15, 1928. (Courtesy of the D.I.B. Archives.)

name the bridge. He thought the name "Detroit-Windsor International Bridge" was too long and lacked emotional appeal. Some of the bridge's board of directors urged him to name it the "Bower Bridge," but Bower objected. "I didn't think that would be proper," he explained. "I thought of the bridge as an ambassador between two countries, so that's what I called it. I want it to symbolize the visible expression of friendship of two peoples with like ideas and ideals." Thus, on April 26, 1928, the bridge received its name.[34]

After the completion, in the summer of 1928, of three of the main components of the Ambassador Bridge—the main piers, the two main towers, and the anchorages—the erection and hanging of the cables began. As a preliminary step, it was necessary to construct two footbridges running between the main towers and thence to the respective anchorages. These platforms,

Canadian main tower erection and derrick laying roadway, July 12, 1928. (Courtesy of the D.I.B. Archives.)

The Canadian viaduct north of Wyandotte Street, July 26, 1928. (Courtesy of the D.I.B. Archives.)

Erection of the U.S. tower, August 5, 1928. (Courtesy of the D.I.B. Archives.)

drawn to the precise deflection desired, were essential to all phases of bridge construction, allowing the engineers to observe and monitor the spinning of the cables and to assist the workers in compacting the cables and attaching wire rope suspenders. Since the Ambassador Bridge was to be built with two cables, two footbridges were needed.

The method of raising the wires for the footbridges had been invented by John A. Roebling in the 1880s for the construction of the Brooklyn Bridge and refined in the building of each succeeding long-span suspension bridge. As a first step it was necessary to extend a rope or cable across the river to hold the footbridge. This procedure had been handled in different ways in the past. In prehistoric times a small thread was attached to an arrow and shot across the river or stream. At the Niagara River, this feat was accomplished by tying a string to a kite and flying it over the Niagara Gorge on the wind. Once across the river, heav-

The Pere Marquette Railroad engine roundhouse, June 30, 1928. (Courtesy of the D.I.B. Archives.)

The Canadian viaduct, London Street, October 5, 1928. (Courtesy of the D.I.B. Archives.)

Lafayette Street crossing on the U.S. side looking east, January 2, 1928. (Courtesy of the D.I.B. Archives.)

The U.S. anchorage ready for cables, June 19, 1928. (Courtesy of the D.I.B. Archives.)

Eyebars for the cables, U.S. anchorage, June 2, 1928. (Courtesy of the D.I.B. Archives.)

ier carrier ropes were successively pulled across.[35] Because of the distance across the Detroit River, a more proven technique was employed—having a tugboat carry four galvanized wire ropes, each one and seven-eighths inches in diameter, across the river, and when secured on both sides, releasing them to settle to the bottom of the river, out of the way of passing vessels. At a pre-arranged time, when the river was clear of vessels, they could be raised to the proper height above the main towers.

Joseph Bower recognized the symbolic importance of the event; he also recognized the public relations value of a public ceremony to witness the raising of the cables. With the support of business, government, and community leaders, he arranged for a special ceremony to take place at two o'clock on August 8, 1928. Newspaper advertisements and feature stories announced the plans, and invitations were sent to hundreds of the bridge's supporters.[36]

Early on the afternoon of the 8th,

U.S. anchorage construction. (Courtesy of the D.I.B. Archives.)

U.S. anchorage under construction, September 9, 1929. Cable strands had been attached to the eyebars on September 7, 1929. (Courtesy of the D.I.B. Archives.)

thousands of spectators lined the shores of Detroit and Sandwich at the site of the bridge. An estimated four thousand arrived at the Boulevard Dock, about three blocks west of the Detroit main tower. On the Sandwich side, the riverfront was also lined with spectators, many of whom had arrived by trolleys and automobiles. Hundreds of boats and yachts laden with interested viewers arrived to watch the event from the river below. All of the boating clubs in the area participated in celebrating the event. For added entertainment and local color the Essex Scottish Regiment, clad in striking highland uniforms, performed for the waiting spectators, as did the Detroit Police Band on the opposite bank.[37] Among the guests were the leading citizens from communities on both sides of the river, many of whom had actively supported the bridge for many years. The officials of the bridge

Spectators gathered to witness the raising of the footbridge cables, August 8, 1928. (Courtesy of the D.I.B. Archives.)

companies and the engineering firms were also on hand for the occasion.

At two o'clock the ceremonies were to start with the firing of aerial bombs simultaneously on both sides of the river. Mayor Ernest Thrasher of Sandwich lit the fuse on time, but acting mayor of Detroit, John C. Nagel, was delayed by heavy traffic, arrived several minutes late, and was tardy in setting off Detroit's aerial bomb.[38]

The sounds of the huge cranes and winches on both sides of the river were heard first. Then slowly the first wire cable emerged from the Detroit River. Pieces of seaweed, gathered during the few days the cables had lain at the bottom of the river, gave the appearance of pennants. As the cable reached the proper positions, Canadian and American flags were unfurled from the tops of the main towers and the respective bands played "The Star Spangled Banner" and "God Save the King."[39]

The roar of airplanes added to the festivities and a "silver one flew over the top of the towers scattering toy balloons."[40] As soon as the cable reached its prearranged height, the sea plane *Kin Jockety*, owned by Detroit sportsman Gar Wood and piloted by George Cobb, flew between the cable and the river surface, a stunt that was repeated several times for the cheering crowds.

Once the cable was raised from the river bottom, there was a flurry to see which vessel would be the first under the bridge. The Bob Lo steamer *Columbia*, bound upstream from Bob Lo Island, captured this distinction much to the enjoyment of hundreds of passengers. Shortly thereafter, the *Wacondah*, heading downstream from Little Current, Ontario, with a cargo of newsprint for the *Detroit Free Press*, passed under the cable.[41]

The first speedboat to pass under the bridge cable from a fleet of them lying at anchor in the river channel was the *Baby Gar*, also owned by Gar Wood and piloted by Orland Johnson. A few seconds later, *Gar Senior*, piloted by Wood himself, crossed beneath the steel rope. Wood and Johnson were the crew of *Miss America*, then the world's fastest speedboat. George Harrison Phelps' *Skylark III* followed—and then Robert Oakman in his yacht, *Mamie O.* The news accounts of the ceremony did not indicate whether Oakman, one of the outspoken opponents of the bridge a year earlier, now favored the bridge project.[42]

Forty-five minutes later the second cable was hauled into place, followed by two more in sequence, and the formal ceremonies were over. Newspaper interviews with spectators give an interesting account of the occasion. It was not the raising of the cables out of the river that had the greatest impact. As one reporter wrote, "It all seemed so ordinary." Rather, it was the sheer size of the towers and the bridge that was most impressive. So, too, were the activities of the bridge workers who "swarmed up and down the steel work, tying a rope here and there to facilitate the hoisting of the cables." Other workers assigned to tasks on top of the main towers "looked like tin soldiers" to the spectators.[43]

Although there was no formal ceremony at the gathering, about a hundred special guests were invited by Joseph Bower to a reception aboard the Canadian pleasure craft, the *Semiramis* of Toronto. Among the guests were the mayors of most of the Windsor-area cities, members of the Detroit City Council, prominent and border cities business leaders, federal government officials, and engineers. C. D. Marshall, Jonathan Jones, and Robert MacMinn of McClintic-Marshall Company, Colonel C. N. Monsarrat and Ralph Modjeski, Clement Chase, and other consulting engineers were joined by J. W. Austin, James Fozard, and other bridge company directors. They traveled to Lake St. Clair and then returned to the Queens Dock in Sand-

Mayor John C. Nagel of Detroit lights an aerial bomb, August 8, 1928.
(Courtesy of the D.I.B. Archives.)

The BobLo steamer *Columbia* was the first vessel to pass under the footbridge cables on August 8, 1928. (Courtesy of the D.I.B. Archives.)

From left: Ralph Modjeski, Robert MacMinn, Lt. Col. C. N. Monsarrat, C. E. Chase, Jonathan Jones. Detroit, August 8, 1928. (Courtesy of the D.I.B. Archives.)

From left: Ralph Modjeski, G. C. Moon, C. D. Marshall, Lt. Col. C. N. Monsarrat. Detroit, August 8, 1928. (Courtesy of the D.I.B. Archives.)

Joseph A. Bower, August 8, 1928. (Courtesy of the D.I.B. Archives.)

wich, passing under the cables twice.[44] The only mishap during the ceremony was the dunking of a Detroit newspaper photographer who fell off a bucking speedboat while photographing the rising cable. Fortunately, he swam safely one hundred yards to shore.[45]

Once the four wire ropes were raised over the towers and secured at each anchorage, they were placed in a predetermined position, exactly parallel to the final position of the two main cables. A platform or catwalk was then built by placing precut timber floor beams, spaced about twenty feet apart, at the bottom sides of the cables and carefully secured by U-bolts. Five-foot-long sections of the wooden walk were slid down the cables from the top of the towers and two men climbed down the walk and bolted these sections to the swaying cables. Handrails were also installed to provide some protection for the cable workers. At

C. D. Marshall, Detroit mayor John C. Nagel, and Joseph A. Bower. (Courtesy of the D.I.B. Archives.)

Footbridges between the main towers, August 29, 1928. (Courtesy of the D.I.B. Archives.)

Helen Austin, shown here with her father, J. W. Austin, after she had completed her walk across the Detroit River, September 15, 1928. (Courtesy of the D.I.B. Archives.)

periodic intervals, crossover catwalks were built between the two footbridges.

The construction of the footbridges and the main cables was under the supervision of George Bowers, longtime employee of the Keystone State Corporation of Philadelphia, which was awarded the subcontract for this work. At age sixty-three, with more than forty years' experience on bridge building in the United States, South America, Mexico, and South Africa, he was one of the veteran builders in the country and had recently supervised the cable work on the Bear Mountain Bridge and the Philadelphia-Camden Bridge.[46]

The construction of the footbridges and the main cables is the most dangerous work on a suspension bridge. Accidents on other such bridges were commonplace and the lives of many workers were lost on the swaying, windswept, and undulating footbridges. Bowers took special care to avoid accidents on the Detroit-Windsor bridge. During the winter of 1928 to 1929, when the wind was excessive and the ice and snow made walking on the footbridges treacherous, he canceled work on those days. Joining Bowers on the Detroit project were his two sons and other veteran cable builders.[47]

Ironically, George Bowers was the only casualty among his crew. Early in October 1928, while he was high on the footbridge supervising the adjustment of the main cable, a block and tackle broke, hitting him in the chest, breaking three of his ribs and his collarbone. He saved himself from a fatal fall by grabbing hold of the handrail until his crew could come to his aid. After spending several weeks in a Detroit hospital, he returned to complete work on the main cables.[48]

The first "public" crossing of the Detroit River over the footbridge was scheduled on September 15, 1928.[49] Joseph Bower and his colleagues recognized the public relations value of such an event and announced to the news media their plans to "walk over the River." At ten o'clock on the morning of September 15, Bower, J. W. Austin, Walter Henderson, Sherman Callender, James Fozard, and Charles McTague, accompanied by newspaper photographers and a Pathé News cameraman, rode the construction elevator to the top of the main tower.[50]

Helen Austin, the sixteen-year-old daughter of the vice-president of the Detroit International Bridge Company who had driven the ceremonial stake to commence the drilling operations in Detroit in May 1927, accompanied her father to observe the historic occasion. When the party reached the top of the main tower, 363 feet above the Detroit River, there was an abrupt change in plans. To the surprise of the assembled group, Joseph Bower became terrified of the height and, according to one witness, "was so scared he could hardly stand."[51]

As the bridge officials sought a way out of the embarrassing situation, young Helen Austin accepted the invitation of Frank Zundt, the paymaster of McClintic-Marshall, to walk across the footbridge with him and his small dog. "When we were twenty feet out," she recalled many years later, "My father frantically waved, 'Come back! Come back.'" She disregarded his entreaties and continued on her way. When she reached the Canadian tower she and Zundt discovered that the construction elevator was not working, so they turned around and retraced their steps back to the American side. She was greeted by an anxious father and the officers of the bridge company. Her historic trip as the first woman across the Ambassador Bridge was captured by the Pathé News photographer. For days after her walk, Helen invited her high school classmates to a local theater to see the Pathé News coverage of her exploit.[52]

The purpose of the footbridges, however, was more than to attract celebrities and gain publicity for the bridge work. They were essential to the erection of the main cables. To facilitate this engineering procedure, sturdy "gallows frames," or "timber bents," were constructed five feet above the footbridge at 150-foot intervals. These frames supported a device called a "hauling rope" which, driven by electric machinery, carried a sheave or spinning wheel four feet in diameter back and forth between the anchorages. Huge reels of galvanized wire, mounted on special racks at the anchorage sites, provided an endless supply of wire for the operation.[53]

When the spinning wheel carrying the wire reached the opposite anchorage, the wire was looped around a horseshoe-shaped device called a strand shoe, which was anchored solid to the bedrock by eye-bolts. The wire was then returned to the original starting point and there passed around a similar strand shoe. This operation continued until the wire had passed over the river 206 times, and the free end was then spliced to the original end. After 37 of these strands were formed—a total of 7,622 individual wires each with a lifting capacity of four tons—they were laid together in a carefully designed hexagon pattern. The bottom row of the cable consisted of 4 strands, then 5, then 6, and a middle row of 7. Above, it dropped in the reverse order to 4 strands. The hexagon cable measured 21 inches from corner to corner and was 19¼ inches in diameter when compacted.[54]

The strands of each of the two hexago-

Bridge officials pose on top of the U.S. tower, September 15, 1928. *From left:* Joseph A. Bower, Sherman D. Callender, Walter L. Henderson, James L. Fozard, and J. W. Austin. (Courtesy of the D.I.B. Archives.)

Temporary footbridges with cable spinning equipment in place by October 1928. (Courtesy of the D.I.B. Archives.)

Cable saddle at the U.S. tower, October 7, 1929. (Courtesy of the D.I.B. Archives.)

Seizing strands at the U.S. anchorage, December 6, 1928. (Courtesy of the D.I.B. Archives.)

Squeezing cables at two-hundred-foot intervals prior to compacting, December 18, 1928. (Courtesy of the D.I.B. Archives.)

nal cables were then pressed together into a circular shape with the aid of six hydraulic jacks operating at pressures as high as six thousand pounds per square inch. The cables were covered with a light film of protective material and coats of zinc. Much later, when the bridge was nearly completed and after the cables were carrying the full weight of the bridge (the full "dead load stress"), they were wrapped with a continuous length of annealed, galvinized steel wire. This process was performed with an electrically driven wrapping machine which enveloped the cable as it was rotated. The purpose of this elaborate wrapping procedure, which had been invented by John Roebling in the construction

Cable wrapping machine, October 7, 1929. (Courtesy of the D.I.B. Archives.)

Compacting machine, December 12, 1928. (Courtesy of the D.I.B. Archives.)

of the Brooklyn Bridge, was to protect the cables against rain, snow, and harmful atmospheric pollutants.[55]

The construction of the cables followed procedures which had been developed slowly over a half century since the building of the Brooklyn Bridge and other suspension spans. There was one key difference, however. A new type of cable wire was used on the Ambassador Bridge. Up to that time, a cold-drawn, acid steel wire was used in the cables of suspension bridges, and indeed, the original specifications for the main cables of the Ambassador Bridge provided for the use of such wire. In the fall of 1927, the American Cable Company introduced a new cable wire—a heat-treated,

high-carbon steel wire. According to its tests, the new wire was stronger than the old cold-drawn wire and cost considerably less. Furthermore, the American Cable Company announced that the new heat-treated wire was ready for commercial production immediately.[56]

Jonathan Jones promptly recognized the potential value of the wire and ordered his own tests to be performed to determine its strength. When they produced favorable results, Jones requested that Leon Moisseiff, Ralph Modjeski, Clement E. Chase, Colonel Monsarrat, and Philip Pratley give their opinions on the new wire.[57] After visiting the Monessen, Pennsylvania, plant of the American Cable Company and examin-

Erecting the suspended span. (Courtesy of the D.I.B. Archives.)

ing first hand the production of the wire, all of the consultants approved of the substitution.

Ralph Modjeski summed up their conclusions on November 15, 1927: "Inasmuch as the other requirements of the specifications as to the chemical and physical tests on the acid steel wire will not be changed if basic steel is used, we feel that the quality of the work on the Bridge and the ultimate results will not be in any way inferior to that which would have been obtained with acid steel." He concluded his letter to Jones: "We therefore authorize you to substitute basic steel on the cables of the Detroit Bridge."[58] Monsarrat and Pratley also gave their approval for the change.[59] Holton Robinson and David Steinman had earlier agreed to use the heat-treated wire on the Mount Hope Bridge which they were constructing across Narragansett Bay in Rhode Island.[60]

The use of the new type of cable wire was a major innovation on the Ambassador Bridge and news of its use was reported widely in engineering journals. On September 24, 1928, the erection of the cables commenced; three months later, on December 27, the work was completed.

The suspended structure of the main span of the bridge, stretching 1,850 feet between the main towers, was made up of two sections—the floor and the stiffening trusses. These elements provided the stability of the bridge and were designed to prevent the undulations which occurred in cables during the passage of heavy separated loads across the bridge.

In designing the bridge and in calculating the impact of heavy loads and wind, McClintic-Marshall turned to Leon Moisseiff, one of the world's leading authorities on the impact of stress upon suspension bridges. His detailed study of the design first prepared by the staff of McClintic-Marshall led to significant changes.[61] Using

newer techniques of computing bridge stress that he had developed, Moisseiff recommended reducing the depths of the stiffening trusses by nearly one-half and thus eliminating the bulky and oppressive system of overhead bracing, which in earlier bridges gave the "feeling of passing to and through a tunnel." Moisseiff took advantage also of the recent introduction of structural silicon steel on long span bridges which had allowed a sharp increase in carrying capacity without additional cost. It also contributed to the light and graceful lines of the bridge and the "feeling of opening the Bridge to the sky."[62]

The main span—comprising the floor and stiffening trusses—was held in place by wire rope suspenders which were passed over the steel bands clamped to the cables at predetermined panel points. The two pairs of wire ropes, or suspenders, each one and seven-eighths inches in diameter, had cast steel sockets on the loose ends. These sockets fit attachments on each of the fabricated steel parts which made up the suspended span of the bridge.

On January 23, 1929, the construction of the main suspended span began, starting at the main piers and working toward the center of the bridge. The five deck panels were erected by stationary derricks at the tower, then a special "traveler" derrick was used to hoist the fabricated steel parts from barges anchored below on the river. All of the steel parts, including the cross beams, stringers, and trusses, had been manufactured at the Rankin plant of McClintic-Marshall and transported intact to Detroit. They were there loaded on barges in the order of erection and hoisted and placed from derricks above.[63]

Cross beams were lifted into place and attached to the socketed wire suspenders dropping from the cables above. Stringers were laid over the cross beams, parallel to the span, to guide and roll the erection traveler as it moved toward the center of the bridge. On the first pass of the traveler, the floor beams, bottom chords, and stringers were laid. Then the top chords were hoisted in place and attached along with the sidewalk framing and the railings. On its final pass, before it was dismantled, the traveler installed the roadway railings and the remaining floor steel. In addition to the suspended span between the two main towers, each side of the bridge had two main sections of roadway, one extending from the main tower to the anchorage and the second connecting the latter and the terminals.[64]

The approach deck truss spans were made of prefabricated steel deck trusses. They were lifted into place by huge cranes onto piers, steel columns or "bents" and braced towers which had been erected in advance. Transverse floor joists, spaced at six-foot intervals on the top of the trusses, were used on the bridge approaches. They were hoisted from the ground and put into place by a traveler derrick operating along the roadway.[65]

The construction of the approaches proceeded simultaneously, although there were minor differences. On the American side, because of the location of the bridge approach over major city thoroughfares, attractive concrete piers were constructed at such crossings. The location of the main enginehouse and yards of the Pere Marquette Railroad under the main Detroit approach also required special attention. Jonathan Jones and his engineering staff solved this problem by constructing two columns through the roof of the enginehouse between two locomotive stalls.[66]

The approach viaducts also differed in length and other features. The United States viaduct was 1,431 feet long and had a maximum 5 percent grade, whereas the Canadian approach was 2,409 feet long with a maximum grade of 3.25 percent. On the United States side, the erection of columns, bracing, and girders was achieved by using huge cranes operating from the ground and by tractor cranes moved to the completed roadway. The construction of the roadway viaduct in Canada involved an A-frame derrick on the deck, moved on skids.[67] The roadway was constructed by placing four longitudinal lines of steel girders with transverse floor joists. In order to avoid streets and buildings, steel girders, ranging in length from 36 to 96 feet, were used.[68]

After the completion of the suspended span, the pavement of the roadway began, starting from the center of the bridge. Concrete mixing plants were erected on either side of the bridge and, using a block and pulley, the mixed concrete was hoisted to the roadway to three-wheel gasoline tractors which transported the concrete along temporary planking constructed on the sidewalk of the bridge. The concrete pavement was covered with two and one-half inches of asphalt.[69]

On the American side where the grade was steeper, granite blocks, four inches deep, were used to provide greater traction, especially for trucks and horse-drawn wagons. The granite blocks were quarried in Newberry, South Carolina, tested, and shipped to Detroit for installation.[70]

The work on the deck truss spans proceeded simultaneously with the construction of the anchorages and the laying of the cables. In fact the approach deck spans, erected from the main towers inland, were essential to provide stability for the main towers as their construction proceeded upward, as well as to provide a counterweight to the derrick creepers located on the river side of the towers.

The railings along both sides of the roadway were installed as the bridge flooring was put in place. On the east side of the bridge, sturdy rails made of longitudinal

Setting roadway slab reinforcing steel on the Canadian side, November 15, 1928. (Courtesy of the D.I.B. Archives.)

Concreting the roadway, U.S. viaduct, March 23, 1929. (Courtesy of the D.I.B. Archives.)

The Canadian approach, April 26, 1929. (Courtesy of the D.I.B. Archives.)

Laying the granite blocks on the U.S. approach, July 1929. (Courtesy of the D.I.B. Archives.)

Laying the top course of pavement, July 20, 1929. (Courtesy of the D.I.B. Archives.)

channels, with smooth vertical surfaces exposed to the roadway, were used. The railings and posts were "designed of unusual strength" in order to resist the impact of skidding vehicles. On the west side, an ornamental pipe and picket railing was used because the sidewalk, separated from the roadway by a ten-inch curb, would reduce the impact of out-of-control vehicles.[71]

Motorists in recent years have wondered why the railings on the west side of the bridge give an excellent view of the river whereas on the side looking toward downtown Detroit and Windsor the views are obscured. The question was not raised at the time the bridge was opened because most of the automobiles were higher off the ground and the occupants could easily see over the railings.

The Ambassador Bridge required more extensive terminals than had earlier bridges constructed in Canada and the United States. The space requirements for the customs and immigration offices were great, especially for the inspection of automobiles and trucks. Warehouse facilities were also required for the storage of goods in hand. Office space was needed for the support staff of the customs and immigration agencies and, of course, for the staff of the bridge itself.

The terminal facilities in Canada required seven and one-half acres of land; in the United States, six acres. On each side, the collection and inspection islands were arranged in an arc. There were originally twelve such booths on either side, nine for customs inspection and three for toll collection. The raised canopy on either end of the arc adjacent to the administration building accommodated trucks, trailers, and other high vehicles. The use of the islands was determined by the volume of vehicular traffic. On each side, administration buildings were constructed adjacent to the inspection islands. The two-story structures were built

of a limestone veneer on a reinforced concrete frame, with steel sash, limestone parapets, and flat roofs. In addition, a smaller building was provided for toll collectors and for customs officers who coordinated the collection, sorting, and return of motorist registration cards. Pneumatic tubes connected the excise buildings, as they were called, with the inspection islands. On the United States side, a one-story detention building was constructed for the examination of heavily loaded vehicles.[72]

Because of the location of the terminals, twenty feet above street level, it was necessary to provide a substantial amount of landfill, in all more than 192,000 cubic yards. On the Detroit side, this fill was obtained from soil excavated from the construction of the main tower and anchorage, and from office building construction sites in downtown Detroit. On the Windsor side, landfill was obtained from dredging operations on Lake St. Clair and transported by barge to Sandwich and thence by truck to the terminal site.[73] Reinforced concrete walls, 4 to 20 feet high, were constructed to contain the earthen fill.

The lighting system for the Ambassador Bridge was divided between the United States and Canada. One current was provided by the Detroit Edison Company, the other by the Ontario Hydroelectric Power Commission. In the event of a failure of one of the systems, partial illumination would still be available. The bridge roadway was lighted with six hundred candle power lamps located about 150 feet apart and 20 feet above the roadway. The terminal areas were illuminated by floodlights. High above the span, on top of the main towers, an electric sign, "Ambassador Bridge" in letters 6 feet high, marked the location of the bridge to motorists and ships on the Detroit River. Navigation lights were installed on the bridge to aid vessels sailing on the river.[74]

CHAPTER 7

The Cable Setback

Work on the Ambassador Bridge proceeded well ahead of schedule. Despite harsh winter weather, there were no work stoppages, labor problems, or delays in receiving the fabricated steel and other bridge parts. By January 1929 the bridge cables were completed, and work on the suspended span commenced. Formation of the terminals, viaducts, and other sections of the bridge was also far ahead of schedule. Already, plans were being made to open the bridge on July 4, 1929, about fourteen months earlier than the date required by the contract with McClintic-Marshall.[1] Bower and his backers were delighted with the progress.

Their euphoria did not last long, however. Early in March, Jonathan Jones temporarily stopped all work on the bridge until a detailed examination could be made of the main cables of the structure. There was no evidence that the cable wires were defective, but the discovery of weak cables on another bridge in Rhode Island led to Jones's decision.[2] The Mount Hope Bridge connected Bristol and Portsmouth, Rhode

Island, across a section of Narragansett Bay, and was under construction at the same time, actually a few months ahead of the Ambassador Bridge. McClintic-Marshall was the main contractor for the steel work on both bridges and had access to the most up-to-date information on both projects.[3]

Late in January 1929, after the Mount Hope Bridge was nearly completed, inspectors discovered a number of broken wires in the Bristol anchorage, all of which were located where the wires left the strand shoes. David Steinman, who was chief engineer on the project, attempted to splice the broken wires, but he soon reported that "more wires are breaking, faster than they can be spliced."[4] By March 4, 260 wires out of a total of 360 in one strand shoe were discovered to be defective. Additional broken wires turned up later. Steinman was warned by the U.S. Corps of Engineers that he would be liable for the cost of removing the wreckage if it fell into Narragansett Bay. It was at this juncture that Steinman met with Marshall and McClintic and demanded that the cables be condemned.[5]

Removing the steel main span, April 2, 1929. (Courtesy of the D.I.B. Archives.)

Cutting cable into thirty-two-foot lengths, May 25, 1929. (Courtesy of the D.I.B. Archives.)

Stiffening trusses and floor beams, prefabricated at McClintic-Marshall's Rankin, Pennsylvania, plant, were hoisted into place from barges below. (Courtesy of the D.I.B. Archives.)

Removing cables from eyebars, May 4, 1929. (Courtesy of the D.I.B. Archives.)

The span rebuilt, September 1929. (Courtesy of the D.I.B. Archives.)

Completing construction of the U.S. anchorage. (Courtesy of the D.I.B. Archives.)

They agreed, and on March 25 gave orders to remove the cables, span, and suspenders.[6]

On March 1, as soon as the extent of the defective wires on the Mount Hope Bridge was recognized, Jonathan Jones stopped all work on the suspended span of the Ambassador Bridge and began an extensive examination of all of the strands in the cables. Although he discovered only two broken wires, also located at the strand shoes, he awaited a resolution of the Mount Hope crisis before proceeding with construction on the Ambassador Bridge. On March 25, he wired Colonel Monsarrat and Philip Pratley and informed them about the condemnation of the cables on the Mount Hope structure and advised them to visit the Rhode Island site immediately and meet with David Steinman. They had been advised earlier by Jones of the problem, so it did not come as a surprise.[7]

Their visit confirmed their worst fears. The cables of the Ambassador Bridge must

The Canadian anchorage, September 20, 1929. (Courtesy of the D.I.B. Archives.)

Suspended steel span erection completed, September 27, 1929. (Courtesy of the D.I.B. Archives.)

Constructing the floor of the suspended span. (Courtesy of the D.I.B. Archives.)

The U.S. approach from the main tower, October 7, 1929. (Courtesy of the D.I.B. Archives.)

Concreting the main span, November 4, 1929.
(Courtesy of the D.I.B. Archives.)

The Canadian approach from the main tower,
November 4, 1929. (Courtesy of the D.I.B.
Archives.)

also be condemned. McClintic and Marshall
did not hesitate to act on the Ambassador
Bridge. Although it cost them one million
dollars, they decided to remove the cables
and replace them with the traditional cold-
drawn wire.[8]

Joseph Bower received the bad news
while he was attending a dinner in his
honor in New York City. Many years later,
he looked back on that evening and recalled, "There were two men from the engineers. They told me that the suspension
cables were splitting; they wouldn't hold
the strain. The whole thing would have to
be torn down and replaced. . . . I didn't
want any more food that night nor wine
either."[9]

Although Bower was deeply disappointed at this turn of events, he had no
choice but to follow the decision of Mc-
Clintic and Marshall. Fortunately, the Detroit International Bridge Company was not
liable for the cost of replacing the cables;
furthermore, the project was still well
ahead of schedule. On March 27, Bower issued the following statement to the press:

> McClintic-Marshall & Company of Pitts-
> burgh, Pa., the general contractor for the
> building of the Ambassador Bridge, had
> decided to rebuild the cables because of
> the fact that due to certain physical char-
> acteristics recently developed in wire sim-
> ilar to the wire used in the cables of the
> Ambassador Bridge, the question has
> been raised as to the advisability of using
> these cables until further proof of the de-
> pendability of the wires has been ob-
> tained.
>
> In order to avoid delay and to elimi-
> nate all uncertainty the contractor had
> concluded to replace the cables with new
> cables.[10]

The procedures for dismantling the
cables and the suspended span had to be
devised by McClintic-Marshall and a team
of bridge engineers. Not only were there no

precedents to fall back upon or engineers with experience with such work, but the time pressure was intense. Even the work on the Mount Hope Bridge, which had already started, was not much help because of the different design and cable sizes.

The first step was to remove the structural steel of the suspended span, which, prior to cessation of construction, had reached 340 feet from each tower. In procedures reversing the order of construction, the floor beams, the bottom chords of the stiffening trusses, and the four lines of stringers were unfastened and lowered to the barges anchored in the river. The removal of the suspended span took eight days, from April 2 to April 10, 1929.[11]

Next to be removed were the clamps holding the wire suspender ropes and binding the cables. During this process, many additional broken wires were discovered under the clamps.[12] Dismantling the cables was more difficult. In order to release the cable strands and the anchorages so that the eye bars were exposed, 150 cubic yards of concrete had to be removed with pneumatic drills.[13]

New footbridge cables had to be constructed, since the original ones had been dismantled after the cable work was completed. When they were ready, a team of 175 workers, under the supervision of George Bowers and provided by the Keystone State Corporation of Philadelphia, started removing the cables. Eight crews were assigned the task and, with the aid of flame cutting equipment, twelve-foot sections on either side of the main tower saddles were cut; then each of the thirty-seven strands of each cable was cut into thirty-foot lengths. They were dropped off the catwalk to a "bone yard" below and hauled away by trucks and railroad cars to scrapyards.[14]

Joseph Bower and others involved in the construction of the Ambassador Bridge were deeply depressed by the delays caused by the defective cable wire. The planned Fourth of July bridge celebration was postponed until the New Year, or December or November 1929 at the earliest. Moreover, the steady progress in the construction of the competing Detroit-Windsor tunnel did nothing to boost the spirits of the bridge promoters.[15]

The frustration of Joseph Bower and his colleagues was summed up earlier by a statement of Alfred Cook, Bower's New York legal counsel: "If every little matter in connection with large concerns involves all of the difficulties that we have had here, I wonder how it is that anything moves, unless it be the earth around the sun."[16]

The long delay in removing the cables gave McClintic-Marshall engineers ample opportunity to run tests on the cold-drawn wire to be substituted on the bridge. Extensive tests were conducted on the steel wires at laboratories at Lehigh University and the Massachusetts Institute of Technology. Expert metallurgists were hired to examine the wire and observe its production. Philip Pratley, Leon Moisseiff, and Ralph Modjeski also reviewed the specifications for the new wire.[17]

On June 14, 1929, the spinning of the new cables on the Ambassador Bridge began. Extra workers were hired, overtime schedules established, and new deadlines set in order to complete the bridge before winter arrived. In less than ten weeks, by August 15, 1929, the erection of the cables had been completed and work on the suspended span began by the first of September.[18]

During this time, the construction of the Canadian and American viaduct approaches proceeded without interruption. Laying the concrete slabs was completed on June 11 and paving the terminal area was finished on October 10. The roadway was completed by placing a two-and-a-half-inch layer of asphalt on top of the concrete pavement, except for the steep American approach, where granite blocks had been placed to provide greater traction. All of the road work was done by November 6, 1929, and the Ambassador Bridge had survived the defective cable crisis. It would soon be finished.

CHAPTER 8

Completion and Dedication

As the progress on the bridge proceeded without delay in the fall of 1929, Joseph Bower started to make plans for the dedication and opening of the bridge. Armistice Day, Monday, November 11, was selected for the ceremonies. J. W. Austin and Charles McTague were assigned the task of arranging the formal festivities.

Actually, there had been two public ceremonies earlier in 1929 to dedicate the terminal buildings on each side of the bridge. On January 3, several hundred invited guests gathered for the official laying of the cornerstone on the Administration Building on the American side of the bridge. A copper box containing copies of the *Border Cities Star* and three Detroit newspapers, a collection of photographs of the bridge in various stages of construction, and other documents were placed in the cornerstone marked "1929." J. W. Austin, Sherman Callender, and C. D. Ferguson, U.S. collector of customs for Michigan, were the featured speakers. A special luncheon at the Detroit Club, hosted by J. W. Austin, followed.[1]

A similar ceremony was held for the dedication of the Canadian terminal on April 29, 1929. Following a luncheon at the Norton-Palmer Hotel, several hundred gathered at the bridge entrance to hear speeches by Charles McTague, A. H. Dalziel, customs collector for the Port of Windsor, and Orval G. Adams, chief inspector of the local immigration staff. R. Bryson McDougald, the newly appointed manager of the Canadian Transit Company, and James Fozard, the vice-president and general manager of the Detroit International Bridge Company, also participated in the program.[2]

Although these ceremonies were well attended and widely covered in the news media, they were minor affairs compared to the plans for dedication of the bridge. Bower wanted to use the occasion not only to cap the efforts of the McClintic-Marshall Company and all those who worked on the structure, but also to woo customers from the Detroit-Windsor and Walkerville-Detroit ferry companies. Furthermore, Bower was only too aware of the imminent

The Canadian cornerstone laying ceremony, April 26, 1929. *Second and third from the left:* R. Bryson McDougald and James L. Fozard. (Courtesy of the D.I.B. Archives.)

competition from the Detroit-Windsor tunnel, which was scheduled to open within a year after the completion of the Ambassador Bridge. The news that another international bridge was to be built connecting Amherstburg, Ontario, and Grosse Isle was also a deterrent to complacency. The ground-breaking ceremonies for this structure, a few miles south, took place on May 16, 1929, at Stony Island. Ralph Modjeski was the consulting engineer on this $5 million cantilever bridge, scheduled for completion in May 1931.[3]

For weeks before the opening, Bower planned and implemented media coverage of the upcoming event. Radio and newspaper stories featured Bower, J. W Austin, Charles McTague, and accounts of the bridge's construction. The story of the replacement of the cables to ensure safety of the bridge was also covered widely. Photographic coverage of the construction was provided by newspapers and engineering journals and magazines. Thousands of copies of a full-page advertisement which appeared originally in Detroit and Windsor newspapers were distributed throughout Essex County and southeastern Michigan.[4] During the summer of 1929, tens of thousands of tourists lined both sides of the Detroit River to witness the erection of the new cables and suspended span.

As the date of the formal opening approached, Bower sent personal invitations to thousands of Ontario and Michigan citizens who had supported the bridge over the past decade. Government officials, business and community leaders, and colleagues were invited to sit at the viewing platforms on either side of the bridge.[5]

For his New York business associates and friends, Bower offered a special inducement to witness the dedication of the Ambassador Bridge. He leased a train from the Pennsylvania Railroad for their exclusive use. It left New York City on the evening of Sunday, November 10, and returned on Tuesday morning. Judging from the compliments paid to Bower after the train excursion, it is clear that he was as successful at entertaining New York's business and financial leaders as he was in securing the financial support for the bridge.[6]

The opening ceremony was also testimony to the great care and planning of Joseph Bower, J. W. Austin, Charles McTague, and their colleagues. On both sides of the river, military parades marked the opening ceremonies. In Detroit, twenty thousand World War I veterans marched from Grand Circus Park, south on Woodward Avenue to Fort Street, then along Cass Avenue and Lafayette to 23rd and Porter. It took forty-five minutes to reach this destination at the Bridge terminal and the reviewing stands.[7]

On the Canadian side, veterans groups representing all of the Essex County legion posts took part in the parade from downtown Windsor to the bridge. Led by Colonel E. S. Wigle as parade marshall and the Essex County Scottish Band, they ar-

rived at the Canadian terminal at three o'clock. By this time, huge crowds of spectators had gathered on both sides of the bridge—an estimated fifty thousand at the Canadian entrance and double that number on the American side.[8]

Even before the formal ceremonies began, the cities of Detroit and Windsor and surrounding communities were preparing for the occasion. At eleven o'clock, acting upon the official request of John C. Lodge, the mayor of Detroit, sirens and whistles were sounded from factories and industrial plants in the city. The bells of churches could also be heard.[9] Planes droned overhead throughout most of that November day. In one of these, a Ford trimotor, Edward Austin, the son of J. W. Austin, and his University of Michigan companion, Jack Sumner, flew over the bridge and dropped balloons to mark the historic event.[10]

At a quarter past three on a gray November afternoon, the brief formal ceremony began after the respective military bands played "God Save the King" and one verse of "America." On the Canadian side, Charles McTague introduced the Honorable Charles McCrae, minister of mines for Canada, the featured speaker representing the Canadian government. McCrae cited the strong bond of friendship between the United States and Canada and then paid tribute to Joseph Bower: "Down through the ages," he proclaimed, "the world has acclaimed the bridge builder and his contribution to humanity and civilization. His work has ever been one of courage, perseverance, toil and skill."[11]

On the United States side, Governor Fred Green of Michigan, introduced by Congressman Clarence J. McLeod, the chairman of the day, captured the spirit of other speakers: "For more than 100 years this river has run as the only barrier between the people of Canada and the people of the United States along the most impor-

Wire fences at the center of the bridge separated the 150,000 American and Canadian spectators at the opening ceremonies. (Courtesy of the D.I.B. Archives.)

tant part of an international boundary unfortified and undefended save by the gracious and mighty power of friendliness and good will."[12]

Following speeches by McCrae and Green at the terminals, bronze plaques designed by Jonathan M. Swanson, an internationally known New York sculptor, were unveiled by Mrs. Joseph Bower on the United States side and by Mrs. Charles McTague on the Canadian side. While the bands entertained the audience, motorcades crossed the bridge carrying the main speakers to the opposite end where they, in turn, repeated their speeches.

The final part of the program was the ribbon-cutting ceremony at the terminals, administered by the spouses of the bridge officials—Mrs. James Fozard, Mrs. Joseph Bower, Mrs. James Austin, and Mrs. Charles McTague. According to the plan, this event was to mark the official opening of the bridge and signal the march of spectators to the center of the bridge. Here, a wire barrier marked the international boundary line and also kept pedestrians from marching to the other side.

Even before the ribbons were cut and the motorcades carrying the speakers and distinguished guests arrived back at the terminals, however, crowds in the tens of thousands broke the rope barriers and rushed headlong toward the center of the bridge. Police officers and soldiers tried to slow the rush but they were powerless. "Even those police mounted, or on motor-

The bronze plaque sculpted by Jonathan M. Swanson. (Courtesy of the D.I.B. Archives.)

cycles," noted one observer, "were like straw before a gale."[13] The crowd was so large that the motorcade was stopped near the middle of the bridge "and could not move backward or forward." There were many anxious moments for the dignitaries until the motorcades were able to slowly move back to the terminals.[14]

In the meantime, the thousands of pedestrians reached the center of the bridge, where they were restrained by police and a strong steel fence. Those hardy souls who could make no progress afoot or who wanted a more exciting and daring memory of the ceremony climbed the "rickety catwalks" which paralleled the cables "to the height of the piers until they resembled a myriad of monkeys in a gigantic monkey house."[15]

In retrospect, it was not difficult to understand why the bridge officials did not anticipate the actions of the unruly crowd.

November 11, 1929. *Front, from left:* Governor Fred M. Green, Judge Sherman D. Callender, and the Honorable Charles McCrae. (Courtesy of the D.I.B. Archives.)

Children of bridge officials at the ceremony: sons of Charles P. McTague and daughters of James L. Fozard. (Courtesy of the D.I.B. Archives.)

No one expected the huge crowds which assembled and the intensity of their desire to cross the bridge on foot—or, as it turned out, via the catwalks several hundred feet over the water. It was a miracle that there were no accidents or injuries. As one reporter on the *Border Cities Star* observed of the dedication ceremony, "It was an entirely different kind of an opening than the one that had been planned. But," he added, "no ceremony could have been half so impressive as the unbridled, uncontrollable rush of thousands upon thousands of people, turning out to see this new engineering marvel of the world."[16] At twilight, which arrived early in November, the red navigation lights on the main towers were turned on and slowly the thousands returned to the terminals and the exits. The Ambassador Bridge had been dedicated.

The official opening of the bridge to vehicular and pedestrian traffic was sched-

Opening day ceremonies. *From left:* Mrs. Charles P. McTague and Mrs. James L. Fozard. (Courtesy of the D.I.B. Archives.)

uled for the morning of November 15, four days after the dedication ceremonies. An informal affair took place on Thursday, November 14, when a parade of fifteen hundred Canadian motorists crossed the bridge and returned without leaving the U.S. terminal. This expedition was sponsored by the Border Cities Chamber of Commerce, a strong supporter of Joseph Bower and the Ambassador Bridge. The parade had been preceded by a luncheon at the Prince Edward Hotel in Windsor. E. Blake Winter, president of the Border Cities Chamber of Commerce, and Charles McTague, bridge official, presided at the luncheon which featured Sir Joseph Flavelle, Toronto financier, as the speaker. It took the caravan of cars about two hours to make the round trip.[17]

At half past ten on the following morning two small cannons signaled the opening of the gates on either side of the bridge. Hundreds of automobiles, some of which had been waiting all night, started across. Several thousand pedestrians had waited overnight also to make the two mile hike.

The first "official" automobile across the bridge, sponsored by the Detroit Automobile Club, was driven by Captain W. S. Gilbreath, prominent good roads promoter. Accompanying him on the trip, which took two minutes, were Edward N. Hines, director of the Detroit Auto Club and chairman of the Wayne County Road Commission, and other club officials—Dr. James W. Inches, Charles L. Weeks, John C. Burkhardt, and John Ramsey. A similar official car representing the Essex County Automobile Club rolled into the Detroit terminal a few seconds after Gilbreath's record trip. D. M. Eagle, president of the club and principal of the teacher's school in Sandwich, was the driver and was accompanied by other club officials—B. R. MacKenzie, V. Williamson, W. H. Adams, and J. D. McAlpine.[18]

The first American "customer" over

the bridge was R. L. Manning of Detroit, who had waited all night at the Detroit tollgate with his wife and daughters Helen, age five, and Gertrude, age fourteen. Their four-speed Graham-Paige led a line of autos across the bridge and for the honor, Manning was given a small bronze plaque of the bridge.[19] The first pedestrian to pass through the Canadian turnstile was Joseph A. Thibodeau of Windsor and his son, Eugene, of Chatham, Ontario.[20]

Other firsts were noted that day. Mrs. Georgie Hammond of Detroit was the first pedestrian in line at the United States tollgate, having arrived at five o'clock that morning. Another woman pedestrian, Miss Belle Zehorer, also of Detroit, had actually been at the tollgate since two o'clock but had stepped into the immigration office at ten. While there, the cannons boomed and she lost her first-place position to Mrs. Hammond. Mrs. Hammond won the prize, a miniature plaque of the bridge, presented by Joseph Bower for being the first through the tollgate. She also won the foot race across the bridge. Pat Collins of Detroit was the first to cross on a bicycle and was also awarded a plaque for this feat.[21]

The newspapers also played up the account of the first bride and groom to cross the span. On the evening of November 14, Miss Florestina Antaya of Tecumseh, Ontario, married Samuel Henderson of Detroit. Photographers and customs and immigrations officials met them at the Canadian terminal en route to their new home in Detroit.[22]

A steady stream of automobiles and pedestrians continued to cross the bridge in both directions during the weekend. There were more than fifty thousand automobiles which crossed during these three days, each averaging four to five passengers. An estimated twenty-five thousand pedestrians made the crossing during this time.

Three weeks later, the Detroit Interna-

Official car of the Essex County Auto Club, the first Canadian automobile to cross the bridge. Ross McKenzie pays the toll to Mr. Clark, bridge toll collector. Note the cash register in use before toll booths were completed. (Courtesy of the D.I.B. Archives.)

tional Bridge Company gave out more exact statistics on the use of the Ambassador Bridge. Between November 15 and December 6, 124,629 vehicles, including 3,413 trucks, crossed the span. Buses carried 20,218 passengers, and 196,767 passengers rode in automobiles. Pedestrians, totalling 53,049, paid five cents each to cross.[23]

There are no records about traffic tie-ups during this period although it was reported that it took automobiles about three hours returning to Detroit on Sunday eve-

ning, November 17. At peak times, four thousand cars and hundreds of pedestrians were handled each hour.[24]

The customs procedures, although relatively efficient, did not make the task easy. As money was collected from incoming cars at the tollgates, the driver of each car was given a license card and waved over the bridge. The customs officer at the other side took the driver's auto license and sent it by pneumatic tube to the excise building where it was filed by number. It was re-

The U.S. terminal, November 23, 1929. (Courtesy of the D.I.B. Archives.)

The Canadian approach from the tower. (Courtesy of the D.I.B. Archives.)

turned via pneumatic tube to the proper booth when the motorist returned. If the motorist did not choose to leave by the same route—for example, if ferry service was used for the return trip—he or she had to go through the slow and cumbersome formality of filling out a tourist permit, half of which was surrendered at the port of entry and the other half at the return port.[25]

The bridge tolls were similar to those charged by the Detroit-Windsor and Walkerville-Detroit ferries. An automobile driver paid fifty cents and an additional five cents for each passenger. A motorcycle and driver paid twenty-five cents; an ambulance, fifty cents; a bicycle, twenty cents; and a baby carriage, ten cents. A saddle, horse, and rider paid thirty cents toll, and horses and cattle on lead at specified hours under permit cost twenty cents per head. Buses paid from $1.75 to $3.00 each, plus five cents per passenger. Motor trucks, trailers, and tractors, which passed over scales, paid by hundred-pound units of gross weight. Commuters were able to buy books of tickets at reduced rates of one month of twenty-five tickets for ten dollars; book of sixty tickets, fifteen dollars; and an annual book of fifty tickets for twenty dollars.[26]

Despite the delays caused by defective cables and the embarrassment to the engineers who had approved their use, all parties connected with the building of the Ambassador Bridge were pleased with the outcome. It was completed nine months ahead of schedule and the initial volume of traffic during its first three months was interpreted as a good omen. It was heralded as the longest suspension bridge in the world, a claim that ended when the George Washington Bridge over the Hudson River was completed in 1931, at a length of thirty-

five hundred feet. The Ambassador Bridge continued, however, to hold the record as the longest international suspension bridge.

Under the provisions of the contract, signed in July 1927, McClintic-Marshall had been given authority to make changes in the design, plans, and specifications of the bridge "as should not materially vary the general scope and character of the structure," as long as such changes would have the written approval of Modjeski and Chase and appropriate government authorities.[27] The flexibility of the contract encouraged the engineering staff of McClintic-Marshall to constantly evaluate the project in order to improve the final product. Even more unique was the guaranty provided by McClintic-Marshall on the total cost of the bridge if it took more than three years to construct.

Under the contract, a number of changes were made in the original design and specifications, namely, those involving the substitutions of materials, certain structures, and techniques. For example, instead of inclined cylindrical struts, rectangular caissons were fastened into the rock, the stiffening trusses were decreased in depth, and overhead bracing was eliminated altogether. Concrete, instead of steel, was used at crossings over Lafayette and Fort streets, for architectural effect. The substitution of heat-treated steel wires for the traditional cold-drawn wires, as previously noted, was a serious mistake. It cost the contractors an additional one million dollars and delayed the completion of the bridge, although the problem did lead to new methods for testing steel wire and for setting specifications for heat-treated wire. Furthermore, removing the cable gave the engineers an opportunity to devise new methods for cable removal.[28] Another deviation from the plan was the spinning of cables in the saddles on top of the main piers, rather than spinning

The Ambassador Bridge, looking west. (Courtesy of the D.I.B. Archives.)

them first and then raising them to their positions. This was a new technique and created a precedent.[29]

The financial difficulties which were shortly to face the Ambassador Bridge ended the "boom period" of the toll bridge business in the United States. It soon became almost impossible "to finance any more privately owned toll bridge pro-jects."[30] Yet the Ambassador Bridge was to profoundly change the fortunes of the communities on either side of the Detroit River. It encouraged travel, tourism, and the economies of the two regions. Furthermore, it changed the skyline of Detroit and Windsor, and thus the perspective of millions of travelers who passed by and over it each year.

CHAPTER 9

The Crash of 1929 and the Depression

A decade of intensive effort by Charles Evan Fowler and Joseph A. Bower was required to build the international bridge across the Detroit River. Yet the first years of the Ambassador Bridge were profoundly affected by another event which occurred just two weeks before the bridge opened; the stock market crash. The result was a severe impairment of the financial stability of the bridge for ten years or more. Although the Great Depression created a fiscal slump throughout the United States and Canada, Michigan suffered more than most other states and the provinces because of its highly specialized industrial structure. Automobile production plummeted from 5 million units in 1929 to 2 million units in 1933. Moreover, in 1931, 20 percent of the state's nonagricultural workers were out of work; by 1933, the total unemployed had reached 50 percent.[1]

Ontario, and especially the Windsor area, also felt the blow of the depression. Canadian automobile production was centered in General Motors, Ford, and Chrysler plants which, like their American coun-

terparts, were forced to cut back production and make drastic layoffs. To make matters worse, more than ten thousand Windsor workers who commuted daily to work in Detroit lost their jobs because of the United States restrictions upon employment of noncitizens—a policy established to aid Michigan's unemployed.[2]

The massive unemployment and the fear, even among those who had jobs, that more layoffs were to come discouraged travel, recreation, and tourism. Even pedestrian traffic over the Ambassador Bridge dropped sharply after 1930. The anticipated industrial growth and real estate development in the Windsor area never materialized, and, of course, the profits that had been predicted by the traffic analysts were not forthcoming.[3]

During these discouraging years, Joseph A. Bower continued to take a strong leadership position in the management of the bridge. During the 1930s, indeed until 1959, Bower served as president of the board of directors of the Detroit International Bridge Company and its subsidiary, the Canadian Transit Company. Although his offices were in New York City in the financial district, he kept in constant contact with his general manager and the bridge's Detroit and Windsor legal counsel. Assisting Bower on the Detroit local scene were J. W Austin, Charles McTague, and Sherman Callender. Alfred A. Cook, Alfred C. Dent, and Jansen Noyes, all prominent business and financial leaders from New York City, also served on the board of directors of the International Bridge Company and the Canadian Transit Company.[4]

There were occasional changes in the governing boards during the 1930s. In 1931, following the resignation of J. W. Austin, who had moved to California, and of David Graham, two new members, Harry M. Bawden and John Edgar McAllister, both of Toronto, were elected to the board of directors, the former to represent the Debenture Holders Committee.[5] Charles McTague's resignation in 1935 created a vacancy which was filled by Stanley Springsteen as secretary-treasurer of the Canadian Transit Company. Robert A. Bower, the elder son of Joseph, served a single year in 1937; his significant contributions to the Ambassador Bridge were to come later. Finally, Frances M. Radford, a colleague of Joseph Bower at the Chemical Bank of New York, was elected to the board and served as assistant treasurer and assistant secretary of both boards.

The boards of directors met several times a year and in executive session as urgent business required. The day-to-day management of the Ambassador Bridge was in the hands of the general manager, who was appointed by the board of directors. The first to hold this position was James L. Fozard of Detroit, who served in this capacity from 1927 to 1930.[6] On November 1, 1928, he was joined by R. Bryson McDougald who was placed in charge of the Canadian operation of the bridge. In

1930, after Fozard resigned, McDougald was given full management responsibility for the Ambassador Bridge.[7]

McDougald had been recruited by Bower from the Canadian Customs and Excise Service. He was born in 1889 in Westville, Nova Scotia, and later was associated with the Continental Rag and Paper Company in Ottawa before joining the Customs Service in 1912.[8] McDougald's staff consisted of about thirty-five toll collectors, traffic guides, motorcycle police, and a small group of accountants, bookkeepers, and clerical personnel. A team of six men, three Canadian and three American, were responsible for the maintenance of the bridge, including painting, repair of curbing and roadways, and snow and ice removal.[9]

One of the first staff members hired was Elmer Paquette, who was associated with the Ambassador Bridge for more than thirty years, until his retirement in 1968. He had come to Detroit from Manchester, New Hampshire, in 1929 when he got word from a friend that there was an opening on the bridge staff. He was hired in October 1929 as a traffic patrol officer and later was appointed to the maintenance crew. He soon rose in the ranks to the head of bridge maintenance.[10]

The Ambassador Bridge also provided inspection and office space for about one hundred United States and Canadian customs and immigration officers on either side of the structure. They interviewed incoming motorists and passengers, and appraised the contents of trucks crossing the international border.[11]

At the same time that he managed the Ambassador Bridge, Joseph Bower continued to play a prominent role in financial circles in New York City. He continued as an officer at the Chemical Bank of New York, which had taken over the New York Trust Company. Furthermore, bridge building and other transportation projects continued to attract his interest and business investments. Bower invested in the Golden Gate Bridge project in San Francisco, which failed, and he served as a member of the port authority of New York City when it built the Lincoln Tunnel and the Triborough Bridge. He also proposed the construction of a high speed elevated expressway over the railroad tracks between Detroit and Pontiac, Michigan, but he could not obtain financial backing for this venture. The Ambassador Bridge was to be his single contribution to the automobile age.[12]

When the Ambassador Bridge was formally opened for traffic on November 15, 1929, there was still work to be done on the structure. The cables had to be wrapped with a wire covering to protect them from rain, snow, and pollutants. The foot-

R. Bryson McDougald. (Courtesy of the D.I.B. Archives.)

The bridge motor patrol during the 1920s. *From left:* Mr. White, Gustav Sinasac, and Elmer Paquette.

bridges, pilings, and cofferdams had to be removed, cracked tiles replaced, and sidewalks repaired. Some painting also remained, including the terminal interiors and some sections of the bridge spans. Both terminals were landscaped, ladders were constructed inside of the main towers, all bolts had to be tightened, and the areas under the anchorages were cleaned.[13]

Work also remained on the steel smoke stack adjacent to the Pere Marquette enginehouse over which the American viaduct approach was constructed. It was designed to carry smoke and other pollutants away from the bridge structure. McClintic-Marshall also had other contractual obligations, including the purchase and installation of a traffic counter system, the neon tower signs, cleaning and maintenance equipment, and typewriters, adding machines, and calculators.[14]

In the spring of 1930, as required by the contract, Ralph Modjeski, Clement Chase, and their staff of engineers made the final inspection of the Ambassador Bridge to determine if the work of the various contractors was satisfactory. Although there were a few minor changes recommended, the work was approved in large part and on June 26, 1930,[15] the Detroit International Bridge Company paid McClintic-Marshall the remainder of their fees, including a special award of $70,020.88 for completing the bridge nine months ahead of schedule.[16] The performance bonds and collateral held by the Mellon Bank of Pittsburgh were canceled, although McClintic-Marshall agreed to extend the guaranty on the bridge construction for an additional three years.[17]

During the following three years of the guaranty, several minor defects were discovered by the bridge consultants and their staffs. Some of the approach piers on the American side were found to have "slightly excessive settlements," and although no immediate remedial work was needed, the piers required periodic inspections. Several cable bands had to be tightened and expansion joints and a few sections of the pavement required repair. The most troublesome problem related to the condition of the paint on the superstructures and approaches, large sections of which showed extensive "blistering and rust."[18] Some of the paint had actually washed away, leaving the steel exposed to the weather. These areas were finally repainted to the satisfaction of the bridge staff, although not without some bickering between McClintic-Marshall and the bridge authorities. The final inspection was made in 1934, and the Ambassador Bridge was declared in excellent condition.[19]

The devastating impact of the depression upon the operation of the bridge is clearly reflected in the traffic statistics, although the impact was not evident during the first year of operation. In fact, Joseph Bower and his colleagues were optimistic during the first twelve months. For example, the first three weeks of business found 124,629 vehicles crossing the bridge, carrying a total of 196,767 passengers. An additional 3,413 trucks and buses carrying more than 20,000 passengers crossed the bridge during this period. More than 53,000 pedestrians also crossed the bridge during the first three weeks, although it was obvious to bridge officials that many of these simply wanted to witness the views of Detroit and Windsor and the river and would not be steady customers.[20]

During 1930, the total number of vehicles crossing the bridge was 1,622,730—the high point in the first fifteen years of the bridge's operation. From that point on, the traffic count dwindled steadily. In 1931, the vehicular count dropped to 1,044,805, down 35.8 percent from one year earlier. By 1934, traffic had plummeted to an all-time low of only 586,730 vehicles.[21]

When the economy of Canada and the United States improved in 1935, the bridge witnessed a slight increase in traffic—620,677 vehicles—for a 5.2 percent increase. By 1939, the tenth anniversary of the opening of the bridge, the vehicular traffic totaled 856,437, an improvement but still only about one-half of the 1930 traffic count. Significantly, the year 1939 witnessed the crossing of 37,262 trucks.[22]

The cause for the decline in vehicular traffic across the Ambassador Bridge is not difficult to explain. As noted earlier, the depression forced hundreds of thousands of Detroit and Windsor area citizens into the ranks of the unemployed, and they could little afford to travel. By 1933, the situation had become so desperate in Detroit that the city was forced to pay its employees in "paper script"[23] rather than money. Hunger and starvation soon became widespread on both sides of the Detroit River.

Form F-1 S. J. B. 11-29

AMBASSADOR BRIDGE TOLL RATES

Single Direction

Pedestrian, or passenger in vehicle—each 5c
Passenger automobile, with or without driver 50c
   Passenger automobile, with or without driver—Annual book 50 tickets $20.00
   Passenger automobile, with or without driver—Monthly book 60 tickets ... $15.00
   Passenger automobile, with or without driver—Monthly book 25 tickets ... $10.00
Motor Buses
   Up to and including 16 passenger capacity ..... $1.75 per bus and 5c per passenger
   Over 16 and up to 21 passenger capacity .... $2.00 per bus and 5c per passenger
   Over 21 and up to 30 passenger capacity .... $2.25 per bus and 5c per passenger
   Over 30 and up to 40 passenger capacity .... $3.00 per bus and 5c per passenger
Motorcycle and driver (with or without side car) 25c
Ambulance 50c
Baby carriage 10c
Bicycle, including rider 20c
Funeral car, and passengers $3.00
Hearse 50c
Saddle horse, including rider 30c
Horses and cattle on lead at specified hours under permit—per head . 20c
Vehicle including driver drawn by single horse or other animal 50c
Vehicle including driver drawn by more than one animal—per 100
   lbs. gross weight 2c
Live stock in vehicles—per 100 lbs. gross weight 2c
Motor trucks, trailers, tractors, fire apparatus—not on call—etc.
   When the gross weight does not exceed 10 tons per unit . 2c per 100 lbs. gross wt.
   When the gross weight exceeds 10 tons per unit and does not exceed 25 tons
    per unit the following schedule of parts shall apply—
    First 10 tons per unit .... 2c per 100 lbs. gross wt.
    Excess over 10 tons up to and including 15 tons ...... 3c per 100 lbs. gross wt.
    Excess over 15 tons up to and including 20 tons ...... 4c per 100 lbs. gross wt.
    Excess over 20 tons up to and including 25 tons ...... 5c per 100 lbs. gross wt.
   Loads in excess of 25 tons per unit require a special permit and may
    only cross at specified hours at rates quoted upon application.

Headlights must be turned down upon approaching terminals to permit
   reading number on front license plate.
No turning on bridge.
Slow moving vehicles must keep to the right.
Speed will be governed by traffic conditions—speeding or reckless driv-
   ing prohibited.
No freight accepted unless on vehicles and in care of custodian.

The management reserves the right to refuse admission to the bridge or
   terminals.

Rates subject to change by board of directors without notice.

For further information apply at office
     DETROIT INTERNATIONAL BRIDGE CO.

Bridge toll rates, November 1929. (Courtesy of the D.I.B. Archives.)

Five lanes of traffic were used in the 1920s. (Courtesy of the D.I.B. Archives.)

Vacations and leisurely shopping trips across the bridge were all but eliminated.

Furthermore, the Ambassador Bridge had to cope with other obstacles as well, mainly competition from the Detroit and Windsor Tunnel, which opened in 1930, and the Detroit-Windsor and Walkerville-Detroit ferries. In April 1930 the ferry companies slashed their tolls to twenty-five cents for an automobile and passengers and also expanded their dock facilities. Soon afterwards, the tunnel reduced its toll rates to match that of the ferries, twenty-five cents for an automobile and five cents for each additional passenger.[24]

Prior to the toll war, the ferries controlled about 27 percent of the vehicular traffic between Detroit and Windsor. The slash in rates increased their take to 41.5 percent. Bower and McDougald considered carefully the pros and cons of matching the toll rate reductions but finally decided against any major decreases in rates. They did cut the tolls for trucks in May 1930 from two cents to one and one-half cents per one hundred pounds and lowered the cost of commuter tickets to five dollars for a book of twenty.[25]

Additional reductions followed in order to meet the competition. In July 1931 the cost of commuter tickets was reduced to three dollars for a book of twelve, and the following year a commuter could purchase four tickets for one dollar plus five cents for each passenger. Children under twelve years of age were allowed to ride free of charge.[26]

In its traffic survey conducted in September 1930, Coverdale and Colpitts, the firm which had earlier conducted traffic surveys and projections for the Detroit International Bridge Company, acknowledged that the vehicular traffic had not reached its estimates made in 1927. They informed Joseph Bower that there was no cause for alarm; within a year the traffic would soar. They also discounted the potential competition of the Detroit-Windsor tunnel, and although they now admitted that the bridge would lose some customers to the tunnel, they predicted that the tunnel's "principal traffic will be derived from that now using the Windsor and Walkerville ferries."[27] Furthermore, according to Coverdale and Colpitts, the bridge would soon control at least 55 percent of the combined traffic of the Windsor ferry and the tunnel, or 50 percent of the total traffic, including that of the Walkerville ferry.[28] By 1931, 1935, and 1938, the traffic surveyors predicted that the Ambassador Bridge toll receipts would be $2,295,883, $3,597,000, and $14,573,000, respectively. It is not surprising that Joseph Bower and his colleagues misjudged the severity of the financial crisis based upon the report of the distinguished business firm.[29]

The Detroit and Windsor Tunnel also suffered from the depression. Although in its first full year of operation, 1931, tunnel traffic surpassed bridge traffic by 1,125,196 vehicles to 1,044,805, the total fell far below expectations. In the following year the tunnel traffic dropped sharply and continued to decrease through 1933. In 1934 tunnel traffic started to rise. In 1938, when the Detroit-Windsor ferry discontinued service, the tunnel picked up most of the ferry's customers; the following year 1,823,844 vehicles chose the tunnel over other means of crossing the Detroit River.[30]

The dismal traffic performance of the Ambassador Bridge during the first decade of its operation was matched only by its desperate financial situation. "The results of the Company's operation in 1930 are disappointing," stated Joseph Bower in his report to bond holders on January 28, 1931.[31] This bland understatement was repeated often in succeeding annual reports by Bower. Indeed, between opening day on November 15, 1929, and May 31, 1930, the bridge company lost $725,478. Although the company had sufficient funds to pay the interest on the first mortgage bonds, due February 1, 1931, Bower announced that it "will not be able to meet the interest due on that date on its debentures."[32] He confidently predicted, however, that "your management is firm in the belief that with the continued cooperation of the security holders of the Company and the exercise by them of a reasonable amount of patience, they will find that in due course appropriate return will be made to them on their investment." Furthermore, Bower concluded, "the outlook for the future is more encouraging."[33]

Despite Bower's optimism, the financial situation did not improve in 1931. In fact, not only was the company unable to pay the interest on its debentures due in February and August 1931, but it defaulted in the payment of interest on first mortgage bonds, due August 1, 1931. Bower still retained the backing of the bond holders, but they elected a new board member to direct a special bond holders committee to oversee the management of the Bridge.[34]

In the remaining years of the decade, Bower and McDougald not only had to struggle to help the bridge company survive, but also had to justify to the special bond holders committee routine management decisions. Questions were raised, for example, about the color and type of paint used to protect the bridge and whether it was better to keep a maintenance crew on the regular payroll or contract the painting and bridge upkeep to a private firm.[35] Despite the careful attention of Joseph Bower and the representatives of the bond holders, the bridge continued to show major losses. By 1938, the bridge had liabilities of $10,202,388, and except for 1930, had defaulted on all interest payments to bond holders.[36]

The Detroit and Windsor Tunnel and the Detroit-Windsor Ferry Company also suffered severe losses during the depression years. On April 30, 1932—following a fiscal year which showed a deficit of $861,054—the tunnel was placed in receivership in the federal court for the eastern district of Michigan.[37] The Detroit-Windsor ferry was forced to close its operation in 1938.[38]

Although the bridge and the tunnel were bitter rivals for motorists and often waged publicity campaigns against each other, the depression brought the two adversaries together on numerous issues. One such matter was property tax assessments levied against citizens and businesses of Sandwich, Ontario, Detroit, Wayne County, and the state of Michigan. In 1930, for example, the Ambassador Bridge was assessed taxes amounting to 53 percent of its gross earnings of $368,175. In 1932 the taxes continued to rise, and in this year captured 79 percent of the gross earnings of the company. In the following years, between 1933 and 1938, the ratio of taxes to gross earnings of the bridge amounted to 75 percent, 75.45 percent, 73.38 percent, 63.64 percent, and 53.56 percent, respectively. It reached an all-time high in 1938 with 82 percent. The tunnel suffered from the same property tax system.[39]

From time to time, Bower and his attorneys met with state and local tax authorities to plead their case for reduced assessments. Unless property taxes were slashed, the bridge company could not survive, claimed Bower. He won a minor victory in getting approval for the bridge to delay payment of its delinquent taxes on an installment schedule over a period of seven to ten years without penalty.[40]

Bower also criticized the method used in determining the "true cash value" of the Ambassador Bridge, charging that the tax system was not only erroneous, but grossly unfair, creating an "impossible burdensome situation."[41] In July, 1934, the law firm of Stevenson, Butzel, Eamon and Long, acting on behalf of the Ambassador Bridge, filed a formal petition to the Board of State Tax Commission requesting appeal of the tax assessment of 1934 by the state of Michigan, Wayne County, and the city of Detroit. The petition charged that the property assessment "was based solely on a preproduction basis and no wise took into consideration the income and earning capacity, power and experience of said bridge structure in fixing a true cash value of said property." The petitioners concluded thus: "The Bridge can be used for only one purpose, and one purpose only, and that was to earn income on vehicular traffic across it."[42]

Bower and his attorneys were upset and disappointed when their appeal was denied, and they immediately contemplated other legal action. They decided to await the outcome of a suit brought in the U.S. District Court in April 1932 by the Detroit and Canada Tunnel Corporation requesting a reduction of property taxes. In 1936 the Detroit court ruled in favor of the tunnel, and in the following year the decision was upheld by the U.S. Circuit Court of Appeals. The decision cut the tax assessment for the year 1938 and also reduced the tunnel's tax liability for the years 1932 to 1938.[43]

The Ambassador Bridge also benefited from the court's decision. In May 1938 the tax assessment of the bridge was reduced from $3,457,000 to $2,099,500. Bower also received a commitment that the bridge would receive treatment comparable to that given the tunnel.[44]

Later, the Detroit Common Council approved a tax assessment reduction and an adjustment in back taxes. All penalties and interest for 1933 and subsequent years were waived. A tax of $57,235.76, based upon a new assessment formula, was to be paid to the city of Detroit in installments at a 5 percent interest rate per annum. Similar tax adjustments were arranged with the state of Michigan and Wayne County, and with the cities of Sandwich and Windsor. Bower reported the results to the bond holders with justifiable pride, for the bridge company had saved $505,958.55 in back taxes.[45] The payment of the remaining tax bill of $349,107, however, nearly wiped out all of the contingency funds.[46]

Tax reduction was only one of Joseph Bower's objectives in dealing with the financial plight of the bridge. The salaries and fees of the officers and members of the board of directors, except for the position of general manager, were discontinued. The staff of the bridge was reduced to a minimum, and the salaries of the remaining employees were cut back. As a result of these actions, Bower announced a 63 percent decrease in administrative and operating expenses for 1932. In 1934, a further cut of 25 percent was made.[47]

The issue of toll rates was also considered carefully by Bower, McDougald, and the bridge directors as a means of maintaining the fiscal integrity of the bridge. When the Detroit-Windsor Ferry Company and the Detroit and Windsor Tunnel slashed tolls in an attempt to increase their traffic, some bridge board members wanted Bower to follow suit.[48] He resisted, and finally decided to maintain the existing toll schedule, even though it was higher than the competitors' rates. After a careful study of traffic patterns and an analysis of the typical user of the bridge, Bower concluded that a toll rate cut would not generate sufficient revenue to match the loss from reduced rates.[49]

Bower and McDougald made an all-out effort to attract additional business for the bridge. They developed a campaign to draw motorists from other parts of the United States and Canada. Advertisements extolling the beauty of the Ambassador

Roadside advertisements dotted highways in Michigan, Ontario, and midwestern states. (Courtesy of the D.I.B. Archives.)

This van advertising the bridge toured the Midwest. (Courtesy of the D.I.B. Archives.)

Bridge were carried in the local newspapers in Michigan and Ontario. Posters publicizing the bridge were placed in gasoline stations in Michigan, Ohio, Indiana, and Ontario. Finally, in 1934 Bower sent an advertising car on a trip through Michigan in the summer, and the western and eastern states during the winter, with the purpose of stimulating tourist trade across the bridge. Later, bridge officials cited the success of the campaign, although they lacked solid information to show the exact number of new customers.[50]

Bower also explored the possibility of creating a port authority of Detroit, similar to the one in Buffalo, New York, and Fort Erie, Ontario, which operated the Peace Bridge. Under such a plan, the state of Michigan and the Province of Ontario, with the appropriate approval of the U.S. Congress and Canadian Parliament, would issue tax-exempt bonds to acquire the assets of the Detroit International Bridge Company and the Detroit and Windsor Tunnel and reimburse all bond holders. The bridge and tunnel would be operated by a joint commission or port authority representing the United States and Canada.[51]

Bower finally abandoned the plan in 1934 because of the "financial condition of the Bridge and the Tunnel and the legal and constitutional limitations in Michigan and Ontario." Bower candidly appraised the plight of the bridge in 1934: "It just seems impossible for us to accomplish anything like that at Detroit but anything that may possibly improve our situation is worthwhile thinking about."[52]

Despite the serious financial problems facing Bower, his business associates, and his creditors, high priority was given to maintaining the bridge structure properly. A permanent staff of six to eight workers—mechanics, electricians, and painters—were employed to take care of every prob-

lem and contingency. In the winter, the maintenance crew kept the roadway clear of ice and snow and the expansion joints free from ice. From May until October, the crew was busy painting and making other repairs. Because of air pollution from nearby factories and railroads, the American side of the structure required more maintenance.

The work schedule of the repair crew was usually determined by the bridge inspector, who made annual examinations of the bridge. Under a parliamentary order-in-council in August 1927, this inspection was required along with a report to the minister of public works in Ottawa.[53] During the 1930s, and indeed until 1958, this inspection was made by Philip L. Pratley of Montreal, who had earlier served as consulting engineer to McClintic-Marshall during the construction of the bridge.

Pratley was ideally suited for the task. Not only was he familiar with the design and construction of suspension bridges, but he was intimately familiar with the Ambassador Bridge. Each year he made two trips to Windsor and Detroit and spent several days, usually in May or June, conducting a detailed inspection of the anchorages, substructures, towers, cables, suspenders, main stiffening trusses, roadway, toll plazas, terminal buildings, and approach spans. He gave special attention to the anchorages to determine if there was any evidence of rust, or excessive moisture, or corrosion. The wire cables and suspenders were checked carefully for breaks and corrosion, which required climbing the towers and cables. The condition of the paint also received Pratley's special attention. Finally, he checked the roadway carefully, noting any cracks or ruptures.[54]

On one such annual inspection in 1948, Pratley found "small patches of buff colored powder between the wires in a few of the cable strands." Samples of the pow-

Philip Louis Pratley. (Courtesy of Hugh Pratley.)

der were sent to a laboratory for chemical analysis where it was determined to be the result of "the interaction between two paints, namely the aluminum paint applied a few years ago and an earlier iron oxide and graphite paint." Pratley immediately gave instructions to have all the affected cables cleaned and carefully monitored.[55]

Pratley's annual inspection reports provided a schedule of priority work for the maintenance crews for the summer months. Each fall, Pratley returned to examine the maintenance work and to determine whether it met his standards.

Until 1933, most of the repair work and repainting was done by McClintic-Marshall under the terms of its performance guaranty. In that year, the bridge's maintenance crew took over and carried out the recommendations of Philip Pratley. In 1934 and again in 1935, for example, Pratley arranged to have certain sections of the bridge "spot painted" and the curbs and sidewalks re-

paired. In 1936 and 1937 a large portion of the bridge structure was scraped and repainted by the maintenance staff. In 1937 repairs were made to the paint on the suspender ropes as they passed over the main cables.[56]

Improvements were made on the terminal facilities in 1937. The board of directors authorized an expenditure of $35,000 to build on the Canadian side a new warehouse large enough to accomodate twenty trucks at a time. The plans were prepared and the construction of the facility was supervised by the bridge staff in order to keep costs down.[57]

The first decade of the Ambassador Bridge also witnessed numerous social occasions and news events. Weddings held at the international border at the center of the bridge were popular. For such occasions, the bride would stand in one nation and the groom in the other. On other occasions, the bride and groom stood astride the boundary line. Friends and relatives, often immigrants from Europe who could not obtain visas to cross the international border, met on the bridge to renew old friendships.[58]

Distinguished visitors to Detroit and Windsor were often taken to the Ambassador Bridge for a guided tour across the structure including a brief stop at the center of the span to view downtown Windsor and Detroit and the river below. In June 1934, the Norwegian International Golden Jubilee was held in Detroit and Windsor. It was highlighted by special ceremonies at the center of the bridge.[59]

The bridge was also the site of numerous publicity stunts. In May 1930 Dottie Reed, the blond-haired sixteen-year-old niece of the actor Wallace Reed, "toe danced" across the bridge from Detroit to Sandwich, accompanied by a five-piece orchestra. As she neared her destination at the Canadian terminal, the band struck up

New automobiles being transported across the bridge. (Courtesy of the D.I.B. Archives.)

A coast-to-coast bus tour, 1930s. (Courtesy of the D.I.B. Archives.)

A fleet of new Lincoln Zephyrs in 1939. (Courtesy of the D.I.B. Archives.)

the University of Michigan's "Victors." Miss Reed completed the jaunt by delivering a written message from Detroit mayor John C. Lodge to Mayor Ernest Thrasher, his counterpart in Sandwich. Judge Christopher Steen and Judge Henry Sweeney, representing the Recorders Court of Windsor, greeted Miss Reed amid the cheers of a large crowd gathered for the occasion. The wire services picked up the story and the young lady's photograph, which appeared in newspapers throughout the United States and Canada, bore the caption, "Dottie Tip Toes to Fame."[60]

Soon after the bridge opened, swimmers and high divers from all parts of Canada and the United States announced plans to dive off the span. The 160-foot dive had widespread appeal to such adventurers because it would exceed the existing record of 140 feet. Several actually came to Detroit and Windsor to consider such a dive. After measuring river currents and depths below the bridge, however, they decided against it. Bridge officials also discouraged the prospective record seekers.[61]

Others used the bridge for a tragic purpose—suicide. Shortly after the bridge opened, in April 1930, a Canadian immigration inspector jumped to his death from the center of the bridge.[62] Many others made similar suicide attempts, some successful. A few survived after jumping, and others were dissuaded by the bridge staff before they took the plunge.[63]

"Rum runners" also used the Ambassador Bridge and the Detroit and Windsor Tunnel to bring illegal liquor into the United States during Prohibition. This illegal traffic varied from motorists hiding a single quart of whiskey to those carrying several cases of contraband beverages. For the most part, the smuggling of liquor across the bridge was committed on a small scale. The more serious smuggling activities took place on the river below where

high-powered launches sped across the river in a matter of minutes, quickly unloading their cargoes into waiting trucks for shipment to Detroit and other cities. On one occasion, during the actual construction of the Ambassador Bridge, a worker on the Canadian tower discovered a truck below in twenty-five feet of water. It had broken through the ice during the winter. Its cargo consisted of two hundred cases of contraband liquor.[64]

By 1938 it was obvious to Joseph Bower, to the officers and directors of the Detroit International Bridge and Canadian Transit companies, and to the committees representing the bond holders and mortgage holders that the bridge's financial future was hopeless. As of June 30, 1938, the company was in debt in the amount of $10,202,388.62. Exclusive of penalty interest, the annual interest charge on the first mortgage bonds and the debentures was $1,338,570. The back property taxes had reached a total of $854,124.93 by December 31, 1938, and although there were prospects for lower assessments and revision of the tax assessments between 1933 and 1938, the tax bill would seriously deplete the company's treasury. Furthermore, even though the vehicular traffic across the bridge, especially motor trucks, had increased slowly since 1934, the prospects for further increases were not good. In addition, the opening of the Blue Water Bridge between Port Huron, Michigan, and Sarnia, Ontario, threatened to cut into the tourist travel between Detroit and Windsor.[65]

Bower, whose experience and past successes in saving financially troubled business firms had won him a national reputation, recognized that the Ambassador Bridge needed his expertise if it was to survive. Already he had explored ways to save the bridge, including, in 1934, the establishment of a Detroit-Windsor port authority. For most of the winter of 1937–38, Bower had been meeting with representatives of the committees representing the holders of first mortgage bonds and debentures to see what plan could be negotiated to save the company. All parties agreed that the existing arrangement was unworkable and that the company had to be completely reorganized. Other plans which had been considered and rejected included the issuance of a new fixed-interest obligation, the issuance to the holders of first mortgage bonds of a new mortgage obligation on a reduced basis bearing interest payable out of earnings, and the creation of a new corporation.[66]

At first, Bower and the committees decided to wait until the decision was rendered on the reassessment of the bridge property and a revision of earlier tax bills. The new valuation would determine the financial requirements and disposition of the funds of the bridge. These plans were changed suddenly in April 1938, however, when local newspapers ran advertisements that the Ambassador Bridge was for sale, for default of taxes. Although state, local, and county tax officials assured McDougald and the bridge attorneys that the newspaper notice was a mistake, Bower was skeptical and feared that sale of the bridge for taxes might gain popular support.[67]

On May 20, 1938, at a special meeting of the board of directors of the Detroit International Bridge Company, Bower and the chairman of the bond holders committee presented a plan to reorganize the company. The board approved the plan unanimously, with minor amendments, and authorized Bower to implement the plan at once.[68] On May 20, 1938, Bower's attorneys, acting on behalf of the bridge company, filed a petition in the United States District Court for the Eastern District of Michigan for relief under section 77(b) of the National Bankruptcy Act. Simultaneously, the Cana-

dian Transit Company instituted similar proceedings in the Supreme Court of Ontario under the Companies' Creditors Agreement Act of 1933. The courts accepted the petitions and authorized the companies to retain their property and the direction of the companies until the case was resolved.[69]

The Bower plan was based on the premise that the reorganization of the bridge "should leave the new company with a capitalization consisting solely of Common Stock."[70] Under this plan, 92.3 percent of the common stock would be issued to holders of the first mortgage bonds and 7.7 percent to holders of debentures—for a total of 191,648 and 16,000 shares, respectively. In addition, 7,027 shares of common stock would be reserved for issuance to holders of preferred stock, and 2500 shares would be reserved for the holders of the old common stock. A total of 217,175 shares made up the stock under the new plan. This reorganization plan was more generous than most business reorganizations of the period because the holders of securities of the junior rank were included. The action of the board of directors and the committee was approved, although not entirely on altruistic grounds. The company needed the concurrence of the holders of debentures to prevent them from being impounded and to prevent delay in the distribution of the cash reserves of the company which were being reserved for payment of delinquent taxes. Furthermore, under Canadian law, the cooperation of the holders of debentures in the Canadian Transit Company was needed to avoid delays and expensive foreclosure proceedings. The plan provided that the management of the reorganized company would be under a board of directors, six of whom would be nominated by the First Mortgage Bond Holders Committee and only one by the Debenture Holders Committee. The approval of the

The bridge at night. (Courtesy of the D.I.B. Archives.)

courts was also necessary. Other provisions of the plan set the value of the reorganized company at $2.6 million, provided that no assessment would be made on the holders of any securities, and finally, that a fund be reserved for the replacement and maintenance of bridge facilities.[71]

After a careful review of the reorganization plan and the bridge company's records, the U.S. Securities and Exchange Commission gave its endorsement. "The reorganization of the debtor (Bridge) by means of common stock appears to be the only feasible course." In conclusion, the report stated, "The plan is therefore feasible." The reorganization became effective on July 1, 1939, by order of the U.S. District Court, although court proceedings on the case did not close until June 3, 1940.[72]

The boards of directors of the Detroit International Bridge Company and the Canadian Transit Company were identical, consisting of Joseph A. Bower of New York, Harry N. Bawden of Toronto, Donald P.

Cameron of Poughkeepsie, William M. Donnelly of Detroit, Ezra H. Frye of Detroit, Charlton B. Hibbard of New York, Edward N. Munro of Detroit, T. Walker Whiteside of Windsor, and S. K. Young of New York. For both companies, Joseph A. Bower was elected president, R. Bryson McDougald vice-president, treasurer, and general manager, and Frances M. Radford assistant treasurer and assistant secretary. Edward Munro was elected as secretary of the Detroit company and Stanley M. Springsteen was elected secretary of the Canadian Transit Company.[73]

The first decade of the Ambassador Bridge's existence was the most difficult in its history. The deep and continuous depression, the property tax controversy, and the competition from the ferries and the Detroit and Windsor Tunnel seriously jeopardized the survival of the Ambassador Bridge, at least under the leadership of the

Detroit International Bridge Company. Despite these problems the bridge was properly maintained, inspected, and operated. Although the volume of automobile traffic over the bridge fell far short of expectations and declined during most years, the first ten years did see the steady growth of motor truck use of the bridge, a trend which was to have profound economic consequences for the bridge's future.

Joseph A. Bower's leadership abilities, business acumen, and financial expertise were also evident in the crisis of the depression years. Despite heavy financial losses, Bower was able to develop a plan of reorganization which won the unanimous support of the stock and bond holders. Even though he sustained heavy personal losses, Bower retained control of the management of the Ambassador Bridge. His reputation for "taking lemons and making lemonade" remained intact.

CHAPTER 10

World War II and Reconversion to Peace

After the successful reorganization of the Detroit International Bridge Company and a favorable settlement of the property tax dispute, Joseph A. Bower and his business associates on the board of directors had reason to be optimistic about the future of the Ambassador Bridge. There were sufficient funds in the treasury for operating expenses for at least one year and money to restore the salaries and wages of the bridge officers and employees. All salaries had been frozen or reduced during the depression. Furthermore, the bridge was found to be in excellent condition and needed only minor repairs, in addition, of course, to the periodic repainting of the towers, cables, and span, and the resurfacing of the roadway.

The traffic picture was encouraging. After dropping to a low of 586,730 in 1934, the number of vehicle crossings reached 856,437 in 1939. There were signs also that the economies of the United States and Canada were improving, and experts were predicting a healthy rise in tourism and travel. Important, too, was the steady rise of the use of the Ambassador Bridge by commercial traffic. This trend was most significant, for it demonstrated the ability of trucking companies to compete with railroads, and it reflected the competitive advantage of the Ambassador Bridge over the tunnel in attracting such business.

Suddenly the business outlook for the bridge changed. On September 3, 1939, England and France declared war on Germany. Canada soon joined her allies and established rigid controls over all aspects of its domestic economy. Travel within Canada and between its neighbors to the south was sharply curtailed, and the Canada Foreign Exchange Board severely limited the amount of currency which Canadian citizens could take across the border into the United States.[1]

The impact of the Canadian sanctions was felt by the Ambasssador Bridge immediately. In July and August 1940 the traffic declined 50 percent as compared to the corresponding period in 1939. Since the bridge conducted 35 percent of its business during these two months each year, the loss in profits would be felt throughout the year.[2]

Although there was a slight gain in traffic volume over the bridge in 1941, the introduction of gasoline rationing in 1942 by the United States after it had entered the war in December 1941 dealt a serious blow to travel-related business in America.[3] Predictably, vehicular traffic over the bridge in 1942 fell to 641,244, a loss of nearly 21 percent compared to 1941. The decrease continued in 1943, when only 486,472 vehicles used the bridge.[4] Fortunately, there was a steady build-up of commercial bridge use during the war, which helped, to some degree, to offset the loss of revenue from reduced automobile travel.[5]

As the war neared an end in Europe and the Pacific, travel restrictions were eased and automobile traffic increased once more. By the end of 1945, a count of vehicles using the bridge reached 1,187,327, the first time that the million mark had been reached since 1931.[6]

As peacetime economies were restored, new automobiles again became available and gasoline rationing ended. A great surge of vacation travel and tourism followed. In 1946, for example, a total of 1,363,517 vehicles crossed the bridge, stimulated in part by the influx of Detroiters and other Michigan residents into Windsor to buy gasoline and food items, both of which were in short supply in the United States.[7]

The cross-boundary trade would have been of even greater volume if the Canadian government had not introduced a new austerity program in November 1947. In order to strengthen its economy and preserve its United States dollar balances, Canada placed an embargo on a number of consumer goods. Thus Canadian citizens were not permitted to purchase items in the United States and return with them to Can-

ada. This was a temporary measure, however, and soon these restrictions were lifted.[8] By 1949, when the conversion to peacetime production was nearly complete, the traffic count had increased to 1,811,840 vehicles. Commercial truck use of the bridge also increased, rising steadily from 57,927 crossings in 1945 to 84,042 in 1949. Since the opening of the bridge for travel twenty years previously, 19,784,989 vehicles and 47,276,872 persons had crossed the Ambassador Bridge.[9]

During the war years there were other changes which affected the operation of the bridge. Indeed, security measures to protect the bridge from sabotage had been instituted immediately after Canada entered the war. For example, the bridge company hired guards to watch the anchorage housings and main piers on both sides of the Detroit River and increased their regular motor patrol as well. Floodlights were installed to illuminate the anchorages and towers. In addition, heavy chain-link fences, seven feet high, were erected beneath the approaches and viaducts "to prevent persons climbing upon the bridge steelwork."[10] As an added precaution, a private telephone system consisting of seven phones located in strategic places allowed the security patrol to report periodically to the toll offices. As a further effort to maximize the effect of manpower and communication, the bridge security patrol was connected by telephone and radio with the Windsor City Police, the Ontario Provincial Police, the Royal Canadian Mounted Police and the Detroit Police Department.[11]

Bridge security was given a tremendous boost in December 1941 when the United States entered the war. Guards from the United States Army stationed at Selfridge Field, near Mt. Clemens, Michigan, were posted at the bridge and the tunnel. At the same time, Canadian army personnel were assigned to guard the Canadian approaches to the bridge. As soon as the military units arrived at the scene, the bridge staff was relieved from patrol duty, except on the roadway of the bridge.[12]

Also of assistance were Home Guard units from Windsor and Detroit which joined the army patrols in protecting the bridge. These volunteers were billeted near the bridge on the United States side, in a building near Porter Street. It seems that the civilian patrols took their jobs seriously—so much so, in fact, that they left their mark in their living quarters. According to one bridge official, the walls of the Home Guard headquarters were punctured with bayonette holes made "by overzealous volunteers." The only civilian casualty during the war resulted from a case of mistaken identity. It appears that a member of the Home Guard was shot with his own weapon by a United States soldier assigned to the bridge patrol when he was thought to be an intruder.[13]

The bridge was well guarded, and there is no evidence that there were any attempts to sabotage the structure. There was no question, however, that the bridge was of utmost importance to the total Allied war effort, for Detroit quickly became one of the major manufacturing centers of war materials in the country. It produced tanks, jeeps, bombers, and airplane engines, as well as machine parts for shipment to other industrial centers. As trucks became the main means of transport for military equipment, the Ambassador Bridge became a well-traveled thoroughfare for shipments. Serious damage to the bridge not only would have interrupted this movement of weapons and equipment between Detroit and Windsor, but also would have disrupted the movement of vital war supplies and materials on the Detroit River.[14]

Security measures at the bridge were likewise justified when United States and Canadian authorities learned during the war that German saboteurs were operating in both the United States and Canada. Indeed, when a German agent was apprehended in Detroit, official concern for the safety of the bridge was intensified.[15]

A war-related action which disrupted the operation of the bridge was the restriction placed upon the transfer to the United States of tolls collected in Canada. The Canadian Foreign Exchange Control Board had established a policy at the outset of the war and refused to make an exception for the Ambassador Bridge, even though the majority of bridge stockholders were American citizens. By the end of 1945, the amount of restricted funds held by the Canadian Transit Company amounted to $619,424.17. Of this amount, $550,000 was invested in Canadian government war bonds. Even after the war ended, the restrictions continued as Canada struggled to convert from a wartime to a peacetime economy and to establish foreign trade markets.[16]

Finally, in 1946 the exchange board authorized the release of $128,000 in the form of a dividend to the Detroit International Bridge Company. It was not until 1951, however, when the total owed had reached $1,033,872 Canadian dollars, that the Canadian government removed the restrictions and allowed the money to be transferred to the Detroit International Bridge Company and its stockholders.[17]

The war had also brought to the forefront the controversy regarding the shipment through Ontario, from one American city to another American city, of trucks with goods "in bond." By traveling through Ontario, from Detroit to Buffalo, for example, about 125 miles and often a full day of time could be saved over the alternative route along the southern shore of Lake Erie. The principle of trucking "in bond" had been opposed since 1930 by Canadian railroad companies and Canadian customs authorities, who claimed that such traffic would lead to "unbridled smuggling."[18] The Canadian government did experiment briefly with a plan whereby a Canadian customs officer accompanied a truck or convoy of trucks across the Province of Ontario. The fees charged to the trucking companies for such service and the difficulty of scheduling such supervised trips made the plan impractical, and it was soon abandoned.[19]

The issue of trucking in bond was again raised during World War II, especially in the Detroit area, because of the gasoline shortage and the urgent need to transport war materials and equipment as quickly as possible to the eastern United States for shipment overseas. Bridge officials, who knew that commercial trucking business was necessary for the bridge to prosper, soon joined the trucking associations in supporting trucking in bond.[20]

Soon the trucking in bond issue gained political support. Stanley Springsteen, a prominent Windsor attorney and vice-president and board member of the Ambassador Bridge, lobbied for in-bond legislation in Toronto and in Washington, D.C. Springsteen's efforts, along with those of industrialists and trucking operators, finally met with success.[21] On July 16, 1942, the Canadian government issued an order-in-council under the War Powers Act providing that for the duration of the war, strategic war materials could pass through Ontario "from one point in the United States to another in the United States."[22] In order to qualify for the special exemption, a carrier had to be approved by the Dominion government and bonded by a guarantee company "acceptable to the Dominion Government." With such endorsements, trucks could pass through Ontario without unloading or inspection, and approved carriers were allowed to purchase a minimum of 350 single-trip tickets at a cost of one dollar each.[23]

Although the action of the Canadian government was well received by some carriers, Joseph A. Bower and officials of the Ambassador Bridge, joined by the Detroit Board of Commerce and some commercial carriers, urged that trucking in bond provisions be adopted for domestic freight as well as for strategic war materials. They argued that such provision would save gasoline, tires, truck parts, and manpower, and in this way would contribute positively to the Allied war effort. Moreover, they campaigned for equity between American and Canadian truckers, emphasizing that there were no restrictions placed upon Canadian truckers for shipping goods in bond across American territory.[24]

But the spirited campaign by the coalition of bridge, business, and trucking interests failed to sway the Canadian government on the issue of domestic trucking privileges. Railroad opposition to the measure was undoubtedly a factor, but the Canadians were saving such a concession as a bargaining chip in the critical postwar international trade meetings which were planned.[25] Nevertheless, the earlier action allowing shipment of war materials resulted in increased use of the bridge by commercial trucks. For between 1942 and 1945, 31,213 trucks, representing about eight commercial truck carriers, took advantage of the Trucking in Bond Plan and crossed Ontario enroute to another port of entry in the United States. Of these, 90 percent crossed the Ambassador Bridge. Another impressive statistic related to the contribution of the Trucking in Bond Plan to the war effort. It was estimated by one economist that between 1942 and 1945 the plan saved four million miles of wear and tear of tires and trucks, seven hundred thousand gallons of gasoline and thirty thousand days in transit time.[26]

The advantages of travel cost savings and equity with Canadian truckers, which the Trucking in Bond Plan offered, were not destined to last, however. When the measure expired on December 31, 1945, along with the Wartime Powers of Canada Act, American trucking through Canada came to a halt. In 1946 the Canadian authorities relented enough to allow 665 one-way inbond shipments through Ontario during the coal strike, but postponed further action on the matter.[27]

When the United Nations Conference on Trade and Employment met in Geneva, Switzerland, in October 1947, the issue of American trucking through Canada again surfaced. At this conference, where Canada, the United States, and twenty-one other countries participated, a treaty provision was adopted on December 23, 1947, providing "freedom of transit through each member country via the routes most convenient for international travel."[28] The government of Canada issued instructions and guidelines for the bond guaranties, but it insisted that "it will be the responsibility of operators [of trucks] to make their own arrangements for licensing of their trucks with the various Provincial Government Highway Departments."[29]

This is as far as the Trucking in Bond program progressed in Ontario. Strongly opposed by powerful railway companies and Canadian railroad brotherhoods, as well as by some Ontario communities which claimed that the trucks damaged county roads, the plan was doomed. The prime minister of Ontario and the minister of highways denied the applications of all American carriers to operate across Ontario's highways.[30]

Soon American trucking companies, business groups in Detroit and Buffalo, and officials of the Ambassador and Peace bridges lobbied the provincial government of Ontario and the Dominion government for approval of the Trucking in Bond Plan. Their efforts were not to meet with success

until 1952, however, when Canada finally began to accept and approve carrier applications from the United States.[31] The effect on truck traffic over the Ambassador Bridge was immediate. The volume of trucks rose by 23 percent in 1952, increasing from 126,850 in 1951 to 146,094 in 1952, and to 175,047 in 1953.[32]

The administration of the Ambassador Bridge continued under the strong control of Joseph A. Bower after the reorganization of the International Bridge Company in 1939. Although Bower never moved to Detroit from New York City, he kept in constant contact from his New York headquarters with the general manager of the bridge and legal counsel in Detroit and Windsor. He traveled often to Detroit and held frequent meetings with board members who lived in the New York area. All financial matters, including dividends, taxes, tolls, and salaries, with the exception of daily bridge operations, were under Bower's control. Day-by-day operations of the bridge, such as public relations, bridge maintenance, personnel, and Canadian and United States customs matters, were the responsibility of the general manager, R. Bryson McDougald.[33]

In 1942 there was a sudden change in management of the bridge when McDougald died unexpectedly after a brief illness. He had served as general manager for fifteen years during the difficult years of the depression and World War II. As general manager, McDougald had established sound operating procedures for toll collection and maintenance. He had also developed excellent relationships with civic groups and local government leaders in the Detroit and Windsor areas. As a former Canadian customs official, he understood the bureaucracy of the customs procedures and developed excellent working communications with the staffs of both the Canadian and United States customs services. He also

The first in-bond convoy of trucks enroute to Buffalo, New York.
(Courtesy of the D.I.B. Archives.)

recognized the importance of attracting commercial truck use of the Ambassador Bridge and expanded facilities for both trucking companies and customs brokers.[34]

To replace McDougald, the bridge board selected C. Clinton Campbell of New Jersey to serve, first, as assistant to the president. After Campbell won the confidence of Bower and the board, he was elected vice-president and treasurer in 1943. Then in 1945, when Bower stepped down and became chairman of the board, Campbell was elected president, a post he held until his retirement in September 1960.[35]

There were several changes on the board of directors of the bridge during the 1940s, caused, in part, by the action of special interests of stockholder groups. In 1942 Harry J. Mero of Windsor joined the board. One year later, Charles L. Morse, Jr., of New York was elected. Then in 1946 Sampson J. Scott was appointed treasurer of the bridge company and served one year before he was replaced by Arthur Shewman, who had been a member of the staff since the opening of the bridge in 1929. In 1948, after an absence of fifteen years, Charles P. McTague, Jr., of Windsor was elected to the board.[36]

As previously noted, McTague had been one of the prime backers of the bridge in the mid-1920s and had handled most of the legal work for the Canadian Transit

C. Clinton Campbell. (Courtesy of the D.I.B. Archives.)

Company. He had resigned as secretary of the Canadian Transit Company in 1934, when he entered government service in Toronto. But he continued to maintain a close personal relationship with Joseph A. Bower after he became judge of the Supreme Court of Ontario and a member of the Ontario Securities Commission.[37]

The staff of the bridge, made up equally of Canadian and American citizens, operated the tollbooths, directed traffic, patrolled the bridge and conducted routine daily inspection and maintenance. But during busy summer months and when traffic increased at other times, part-time employees were hired to assist with toll taking and painting. Outside firms were hired on contract to complete major repair work, such as resurfacing the roadway and painting the cables and main towers.[38] Although there was a constant turnover in the makeup of the staff, many employees remained with the bridge company most of their careers. In 1949, when the bridge celebrated its twentieth anniversary, four employees were honored for having served the bridge since the day of its opening. They were El-

mer Paquette and Earl Foley of the maintenance staff; John Nunn, toll supervisor; and Arthur Shewman, who had risen through the ranks to the position of treasurer of the company.[39]

The customs and immigration staff of the United States and Canadian governments increased steadily during the 1940s, especially during the postwar period, when automobile and truck traffic increased sharply. By 1948, 150 government employees operated the United States and Canadian customs. In that year, they handled more than 4 million motorists and passengers through the inspection lines and collected nearly $15 million in duty fees on items carried into the United States and Canada. Their offices issued 230,000 travel permits in that year, most of them for American citizens visiting Canada for extended vacations or business trips.[40] As customs work increased, the bridge provided additional office space and dock and truck inspection areas for the customs agencies.[41]

The staffs of the Ambassador Bridge and the United States and Canadian cus-

Charles P. McTague. (Courtesy of the D.I.B. Archives.)

Painting the main towers, 1946. (Courtesy of the D.I.B. Archives.)

The Canadian Customs office, 1940s. (Courtesy of the D.I.B. Archives.)

Painting the suspender ropes, 1947. *Upper left:* Elmer Paquette; *upper right:* Bill Murphy; *bottom left:* Earl Foley; *second left:* Louis Renaud. (Courtesy of the *Detroit News,* Burton Historical Collection of the Detroit Public Library.)

toms services enjoyed excellent working relationships during the depression and war years. A crisis arose in 1941, however, between the United States Customs Service in Washington, D.C., and the various international bridges over the issue of overtime pay for customs agents. For that year, the officials of the Ambassador Bridge, as well as those of the Detroit and Windsor Tunnel and other international bridges, were billed for "overtime and special services."[42] The share for the Ambassador Bridge was $31,910 for 1941. Acting upon the advice of counsel and following the decision reached by other international bridge companies, Bower and Campbell refused to pay the bill. Bower also reminded United States Customs officials that the United States Treasury Department had assured him in 1929 that "sufficient officers would be furnished to provide twenty-four hour service to operate the Bridge continuously, without cost for services of U.S. Customs officers."[43]

Bower's claim carried little weight with customs officials in Washington, for an additional bill of $40,000 was sent to the bridge company in 1942 and one for $52,000 in 1943—a total of $112,065.[44] When his efforts in trying to deal with the governmental bureaucracy in Washington proved futile, Bower turned to Congress for relief. With the support of officials of other international bridges, Bower persuaded Senator Arthur Vandenberg of Michigan to introduce legislation which would relieve international bridges from paying overtime for the services of United States Customs officers. The Vandenberg bill was passed by Congress in 1944, and the Ambassador Bridge and other international bridges were freed from a large financial liability.[45]

As previously noted, the bridge's earnings were down during the war years but they rose steadily during the postwar years. Net earnings, for example, rose from $14,816 in 1940 to $360,510 in 1945, and to

$435,922 in 1949. Notice of the bridge's financial solvency was given in 1944, when it paid its first dividend to stockholders since the structure opened in 1929—seventy-five cents per share. Since that first dividend, stockholders have received a continuous series of annual dividends. Another change in company finances occurred in 1946, when it increased capital stock from 217,175 shares of common stock to 373,232 shares, with the par value of one dollar per share remaining the same as before the increase.[46]

In 1940 another development affected the earnings for the bridge. The bridge company sought to hike its toll rates, the first upward adjustment since it had opened in 1929. But the city of Windsor, acting on complaints of some of its citizens who commuted daily to Detroit to work, objected to the increase, and took its case to the Board of Transport Commissioners of Canada. After a series of public hearings were held, the bridge toll rate increase was approved, as were similar toll raises requested for the Detroit and Canada Tunnel Corporation. Consequently, on February 5, 1941, the cost of bridge commuter tickets rose from four tickets for $1.00 to ten tickets for $3.50 and twenty-five tickets for $7.50. Commercial rates were also increased slightly and the rate for extra passengers was raised to ten cents.[47]

Another related change in operating procedures involved the collection of tolls. Beginning in 1941, all tolls were taken on the United States side of the bridge. In 1945 this change was made permanent and new tollbooths were constructed on the Detroit Plaza. In addition, the Canadian terminal facilities were enlarged in order to meet the needs presented by increased truck volume into Canada in 1942. The 1942 addition to the Canadian terminal cost $21,387, and by 1946 it was necessary to construct an even larger area at the terminal.[48]

During the 1940s, other bridge im-

Bridge paint crew with tower sign, about 1946. *From left:* John Loucks (*above "R"*), Louis Renaud (*above "G"*), Earl Foley (*at top*), Bill Murphy (*far right*). (Courtesy of the *Detroit News,* Burton Historical Collection of the Detroit Public Library.)

Bill Murphy, chief of maintenance for the Ambassador Bridge, July 17, 1947. (Courtesy of the *Windsor Star.*)

Checking suspender rope clamps on the main span, late 1940s. (Courtesy of the D.I.B. Archives.)

The Ambassador Bridge, from Windsor. (Courtesy of Schneider and
Associates, Detroit, Michigan.)

provements were undertaken as a result of the annual inspections and recommendations of Philip L. Pratley, who had been involved in the original construction of the Ambassador Bridge. For example, in 1945 the entire roadway of the bridge was resurfaced and the steel uprights, approaches, and cables were partially painted. A new sidewalk was constructed, the United States Customs island was enlarged, and trees and shrubbery were planted at the bridge's approaches as a part of a beautification program. In addition, the old lighting system was replaced on both the American and Canadian sides of the bridge.[49]

The annual inspections by Pratley failed to detect any major defects or problems in the Bridge structure during the 1940s. Although Pratley noticed a minor displacement of one or two strands of the west cable as it passed over the U.S. tower saddle in 1949, he concluded in his inspection report as follows: "There is no need for concern and a regular inspection of the saddles every summer should be ample protection unless some extraordinary windstorm should arise, after which it might be wise for your men to make a special inspection."[50] Pratley also reported that "only one wire seems to have been frayed during the 20-year life of the structure."[51] Among Pratley's inspection reports, a continuous complaint was made about juvenile vandalism. For example, in one report he said, "Stone throwing by school boys is a constant source of petty damage to the steel towers under the Canadian approach span and nothing much can be done about it."[52]

Joseph Bower and his colleagues had reason for pride in their accomplishments during the first twenty years after the Ambassador Bridge opened for travelers. After years of adversity and struggle for survival as a company, the bridge officials finally achieved sound financial standing. Bower expressed his own sentiments as he reflected upon the success of the bridge in 1949: "We have assuredly come a long way in attaining the hopes and objectives set for the Bridge when it was opened to the public twenty years ago. . . . We . . . can reflect with satisfaction on the progress made toward our ultimate goal . . . and face the future with confidence."[53]

CHAPTER 11

Coming of Age: The 1950s

The return of prosperity to the United States and Canada during the postwar period had a direct and almost immediate effect on the operation of the Ambassador Bridge. Millions of new automobiles and trucks rolled off the assembly lines, and Americans and Canadians took to the road for vacations and shorter recreational and shopping trips. The conversion of factories to peacetime automobile production in the Windsor and Detroit areas also led to increased vehicular traffic across the bridge, especially by commercial trucking firms.[1]

From the 1930s onward, the Ambassador Bridge was in direct and open competition with the Detroit and Windsor Tunnel for business. The location of the tunnel in the downtown districts of Detroit and Windsor gave it a great advantage in attracting motorists who traveled between the hotel and business districts of Detroit and Windsor.[2]

The bridge, on the other hand, captured most of the commercial truck traffic, and in this regard, it was able to maintain a competitive edge with the tunnel. In 1955, for instance, a single truck paid a toll equivalent to about eleven automobiles. Also, the majority of tourists passing through Detroit and Windsor enroute to vacation spots during the summer months preferred to use the Ambassador Bridge rather than contend with the heavy traffic in downtown areas of Detroit and Windsor.[3]

Regardless of the traditional traffic patterns and the preferences of motorists and trucks, the bridge and tunnel both sought to control a greater share of the total cross-river traffic. Advertisements in the news media stressed the advantages and attractions of each means of reaching the opposite side of the Detroit River. For example, in the 1950s the Ambassador Bridge ran a series of advertisements in Windsor newspapers citing the ideal location of the bridge for motorists seeking to reach the Ford Museum and Greenfield Village in Dearborn, Michigan, Tiger Stadium for Detroit Tigers games, and Olympia for Detroit Red Wing hockey games.[4]

In turn, Detroit newspapers featured advertisements citing the proximity of the bridge to scenic spots in Ontario, such as the historic British fort at Amherstburg, the nature center and bird sanctuary at Point Pelee, and a "pleasant drive along Lake St. Clair."[5] In advertisements aimed at its competitor, motorists were urged to use the Ambassador Bridge "to enjoy the fresh air and the wonderful view of the Detroit River and the shoreline."[6] The tunnel, which also utilized advertisements to attract customers, was hard pressed to match this claim.

The bridge also benefited from news coverage of special events and ceremonies taking place on its structure, not only in local newspapers but also on the international wire services. As in previous years, the bridge in the 1950s was a popular site for weddings. In one highly publicized ceremony in 1953, a thirty-year-old Yugoslavian auto worker from Windsor married a Detroit bank teller at the international boundary line at the center of the bridge, when neither could obtain visas to travel to the other country for the ceremony. The wedding received international coverage in the press and on radio news programs.[7]

The Ambassador Bridge continued to be used for suicide attempts, in some instances successful, and on other occasions thwarted by an alert bridge staff. On June 30, 1951, bridge workers noticed a man swinging back and forth on the top of a girder above the bridge sign on the main tower. After the alarm was sounded, several bridge workers rushed to the top of the tower and there found an unemployed factory worker laughing tipsily at the spectators 386 feet below. When he refused to come down from his perch, several bridge workers risked their own lives to climb to the top of the sign and put him in a harness to be lowered to safety.[8]

In 1955, a mother of seven tried to end her life by jumping off the railing of the bridge. She survived the plunge into the river below despite serious injuries.[9] An-

other tragedy was averted in 1956 when three fourteen-year-old boys were plucked from the cables high above the span. They had tried to sneak across the bridge after customs agents, suspecting that they were runaways, barred their entry into Canada. The boys decided instead to cross on the cables but became frightened when they were halfway across. They had to be removed by aerial truck operated by the Windsor Fire Department.[10]

On yet another occasion, in 1959 bridge workers had to rescue a freelance photographer who had climbed the cables to get some "exciting" views of the Detroit River. As he neared the main tower, he looked down to the river below and froze. Two bridge workers coaxed him to safety.[11]

The bridge also witnessed visits by famous world leaders. In 1954 Her Royal Highness the Duchess of Kent and her daughter, Princess Alexandra, visited the bridge and were met at the boundary line by mayors Arthur J. Reaume of Windsor and Albert E. Cobo of Detroit.[12] Later that year, Emperor Haile Selassie of Ethiopia was among the foreign dignitaries who visited the bridge.[13]

The bridge was the site of another public ceremony in 1954 when the Queens York Rangers of Toronto marched across the span and presented to the city of Detroit a replica of the United States flag which their famous regiment had captured during the War of 1812. These events were also widely covered in the public media.[14]

Traffic statistics, as well as the revenue collected by the bridge and tunnel, reflected the intense competition of the 1950s. The number of vehicles using the bridge rose steadily from 1950 to 1956, and then eased off slightly during the economic recession of 1957 to 1959. In 1950, 1,902,390 vehicles crossed the river on the Ambassador Bridge; in 1955, there were 2,765,207; and in 1959, the number was 2,637,150.

Michigan Governor G. Mennen Williams and Lt. Governor John M. Swainson speak at a ceremony to help the physically handicapped in 1954. (Courtesy of the D.I.B. Archives.)

Her Royal Highness of Great Britain, the Duchess of Kent, and her daughter, Princess Alexandra, visit the bridge in 1954. *From left:* Mayor Arthur J. Reaume of Windsor, Princess Alexandra, the Duchess of Kent, and Mayor Albert E. Cobo of Detroit. (Courtesy of the D.I.B. Archives.)

Congestion at Canadian Customs, July 4, 1952. (Courtesy of the D.I.B. Archives.)

U.S. Army maneuvers on the bridge, 1954. (Courtesy of the D.I.B. Archives.)

More significantly for revenue, the number of trucks using the bridge increased from 109,710 in 1950 to 262,491 in 1959.[15]

The competitive position of the bridge outside Detroit and Windsor is also noteworthy. By 1952 the Ambassador Bridge "led all similar crossings on the Canadian border in the field of international trade," and in that year it controlled 80 percent of the commercial truck crossings over the Detroit River.[16] By 1950 the bridge was gaining on the tunnel in total vehicular crossings. Of the total 4,453,085 vehicles crossing the river, the bridge claimed 43 percent. By 1955 the bridge's share had grown to 49 percent, but dropped to 45 percent in 1959.[17]

In comparing the bridge and the tunnel, a more significant figure is the percentage of total cross-river revenue from tolls. In 1950 the tunnel received $227,528 more than the bridge, but by 1954 the advantage of the tunnel had dropped to $80,233. Indeed, in 1955 bridge revenues exceeded those of the tunnel by $36,020.[18] Although the tunnel continued to surpass the bridge in total crossings, the steady increase in truck traffic over the bridge improved its competitive edge. In 1955, for example, commercial traffic contributed 37 percent of the total tolls of the bridge, almost $600,000 in revenue.[19]

The net earnings of the Ambassador Bridge were also impressive during the 1950s. At the beginning of the decade, the bridge showed net earnings of $492,364 and paid $1.37 per share to its stockholders. By 1958 the net earnings had risen to $635,378, and in 1959 reached $784,828.[20]

Closely related to the traffic statistics and revenues, especially in view of competition from the tunnel, was the issue of toll rates. The bridge had raised its tolls in 1941, and as operating and maintenance costs rose, C. Clinton Campbell, Joseph A. Bower, and the board of directors reviewed the matter again. The tunnel had raised its

tolls in November 1951 to sixty cents a passenger car, fifteen cents for a bus, and four dollars for a commuter ticket book of ten tickets. At this time, the bridge charged fifty cents per automobile with one driver and sold ten commuter tickets for $3.50.

There was strong sentiment on the board of directors of the Ambassador Bridge in 1952 to again raise the toll rates to match those of the tunnel, but Campbell expressed reservations about any toll increases at that time. He was concerned about the overall decline in tourist travel in 1952 because of the discounting of American money in Canada, the Canadian embargo on meat, and the rising unemployment in Detroit due to the steel strike. Campbell also believed that the bridge had benefited from the increase in tunnel rates and had won many more customers, especially among commuters. After heated debate on the board of directors, Joseph A. Bower backed Campbell, and action on the issue of toll increases was postponed.[21]

The issue was raised again in 1953 and again in 1955. On both occasions, Bower hired Coverdale and Colpitts to conduct a traffic survey of toll rates and passenger traffic patterns, including data on origin and destination of trips, purpose of trips, trip frequency, number of passengers, and method of payment. The survey included not only the bridge, but the tunnel and the Blue Water Bridge between Sarnia and Port Huron, as well. In addition to the annual reports of the bridge and tunnel companies, the 1955 survey involved personal interviews with 1,022 motorists at the Ambassador Bridge from August 24 to 29, 1956.[22]

On the basis of the survey, Coverdale and Colpitts recommended an increase in tolls for passenger cars from fifty cents per car and driver to sixty-five cents for a car and all passengers in the car; before, there had been a charge of five cents for each passenger. They also recommended the sale of a single book of tickets for commuters, twenty-five tickets for ten dollars, the tickets including all passengers in the car.[23]

Based upon the estimates of Coverdale and Colpitts, these toll rate charges would produce an increase of 10 to 15 percent in toll revenues and only a small decrease in traffic volume. They also cited other advantages of the proposed rate changes: namely, that they would be lower than the tunnel's rates, that the collection of tolls would be materially easier because there would be no need to determine the number of passengers per car, and finally, that the use of only one ticket booth would facilitate printing and sales.[24]

There was general support for the Coverdale and Colpitts recommendation among the bridge's board of directors, just as there had been several years earlier, but again, C. Clinton Campbell expressed serious reservations about a toll increase. Campbell was especially concerned that a major rate increase would cause the bridge to lose its favorable rate advantage over the tunnel, which was the main reason that the bridge had been able to "offset their favorable downtown location."[25] Campbell also cited the major traffic and revenue gains which the bridge had made between 1950 and 1955. Finally, he cautioned Joseph A. Bower and the board about the impact of fluctuating traffic caused by economic conditions, strikes, and bad weather and the resistance of motorists to higher costs.[26]

To determine the accuracy of the findings of Coverdale and Colpitts, Campbell also conducted a survey of his own of passenger car traffic in February 1957 by distributing 15,870 survey cards to motorists. After analyzing the 5,010 returns, Campbell moderated his position on toll increases, but strongly opposed the rates recommended by Coverdale and Colpitts and endorsed by several board members. "My feeling is," he wrote to Joseph A. Bower,

"that a 60 cent rate even without an extra passenger toll, is bad psychologically." In summarizing his views on the toll issue, Campbell concluded: "It is a very serious question and one which will have a far reaching influence on the company for many years to come."[27]

Because of the sharp difference between Campbell and board members, the toll rate issue was left to Joseph A. Bower to resolve. After hearing both arguments, he admitted that he was still uncertain as to which position to support. "I am annoyed at myself," he wrote to Campbell, "because I cannot reconcile two thoughts for which I have a good deal of respect. The first is your view that we must try and maintain a rate advantage or a sales promotion to induce traffic, the second is that we should take advantage of the psychology of the time to increase the rates."[28]

Bower held several meetings with Campbell and worked out a compromise rate schedule, which was approved by the board of directors in April 1957. It provided for an increase in passenger automobile rates, including driver, to sixty cents; for extra passengers over seventeen years of age, ten cents; books of twenty-five tickets for ten dollars; and pedestrians, ten cents. The rates for motor trucks remained at one cent per one hundred pounds gross weight.[29] The impact of the toll rates on the bridge is difficult to ascertain because of the recession which dampened the economy of the United States and Canada in 1957 and the tunnel's increase in toll rates for extra passengers riding in automobiles and buses.

Also, since the new toll rates went into effect on June 1, 1957, it is difficult to make comparisons between 1957 and 1958. There is information, however, that between 1956 and 1958 a loss of 170,000 passenger cars occurred in cross-river traffic on the bridge. Even more alarming to Bower and Camp-

The twenty-five-year-men, 1954. *From left:* Earl Foley, Elmer Paquette, and Arthur Shewman, treasurer of the bridge company. (Courtesy of the D.I.B. Archives.)

bell were the long-range implications of the toll increases.[30]

The general condition of the Ambassador Bridge in its third decade of operation remained excellent. In accordance with the recommendations of Philip L. Pratley, the main span roadway was resurfaced and new curbs were installed where needed. In 1959 the painting of the main span of the bridge was completed. The annual inspections during the 1950s found the towers, approaches, and cables in "splendid condition."[31] Only a few minor defects were discovered and promptly corrected. The major problem related to the nesting of grackles and pigeons on the United States side of the viaduct. Despite attempts to discourage nesting, such as stringing chicken wire on their favorite sites, the birds simply moved to another, less accessible location. The results were an eyesore, staining the piers and trusses and the houses, buildings, and street below. It caused one engineer to remark in 1959: "The plague of grackles will soon spoil the appearance of the American tower."[32]

The facilities of the bridge were enlarged during the 1950s, especially for the purpose of providing greater space for the steadily increasing fleets of commercial trucks using the bridge. In 1952 and 1953 the bridge's Canadian warehouse was en-

The board of directors, 1954. *From left:* Charles L. Morse, Jr., Harry B. Rottiers, secretary, Robert A. Bower, C. Clinton Campbell, Joseph A. Bower, Charlton B. Kibbard, Harry P. Schaub, and Charles P. Mc-Tague. (Courtesy of the D.I.B. Archives.)

larged and an addition was made to the Canadian administration building to provide offices for customs brokers doing business at the Ambassador Bridge. In 1955 the warehouse and customs inspection facilities on the Canadian side were enlarged to handle 500 trucks, a 50 percent increase in truck inspection capacity.[33] By the mid-1950s, there was sufficient office space for about 350 persons employed by the United States and Canadian customs agencies, customs brokers, and trucking companies, in addition to bridge staff of about 75 persons.[34]

A change in bridge inspectors also took place during this period. In 1958 Philip L. Pratley died after completing nearly thirty years of service to the Ambassador Bridge. He and his colleague, Colonel C. N.

Monsarrat, who died in 1940, had assisted McClintic-Marshall in building the bridge, and Pratley was hired after the completion to perform the annual inspections of the bridge. His reports not only gave a comprehensive account of the condition of the bridge but also served as a work plan for the bridge's maintenance.

Starting in 1958, H. Hugh L. Pratley, who took over his father's engineering firm in Montreal, conducted the annual bridge inspections. Like his father, Hugh Pratley had attained an international reputation as a bridge engineer. A graduate of McGill University in Montreal in 1947 and a student of Cambridge University in England from 1947 to 1949, Hugh Pratley joined his father's engineering firm in 1949. In addition to the annual inspections on the Am-

Joseph A. Bower resigned as chairman of the board in 1959. (Courtesy of the D.I.B. Archives.)

bassador and Blue Water bridges in Michigan and Ontario and other Canadian bridge structures, he was also involved in the construction of several major structures, including the Angus L. MacDonald and the Murray MacKay suspension bridges in Halifax, Nova Scotia, and the Champlain Bridge in Montreal. His thorough annual inspections have become a model of their kind and have helped keep the Ambassador Bridge in excellent condition.[35]

The most significant change in the management of the Ambassador Bridge in the 1950s was the election of Robert A. Bower to the board of directors. He had served briefly on the board in 1937 and was elected again in 1950. A native of Detroit and the son of Joseph A. Bower, the bridge's founder, Robert graduated from Yale University in 1934. He entered the business world and served on the managerial staff of Arthur Andersen Company, CIT

Corporation, and the Doehler-Jarvis Company. In 1952 he became vice-president and trust officer of the Ohio Citizen's Trust Company in Toledo, Ohio, a position which he held until December, 1972. Although his election to the board in 1950 was made at his father's request, Robert Bower soon demonstrated his sound business training, experience, and acumen. In 1955 he was elected vice-president of the Detroit International Bridge Company.[36]

Other important board changes in the 1950s involved the election of Harry Schaub of Newark, New Jersey, in 1954, to replace Donald Cameron, Jr., who resigned. Leonard W. Ryder was appointed treasurer of the Bridge Company in 1958, replacing Arthur Shewman, who became secretary of the company a year later.

The year 1959 marked the end of an era in the Ambassador Bridge's history when Joseph A. Bower stepped down as chairman of the board, turning the reigns over to his son Robert. He had suffered ill health and a serious eye problem for some time, and at the age of seventy-nine he asked to be relieved of most of the administrative duties of managing the bridge. He continued to serve as vice-president until 1963 when he was elected "honorary chairman and founder" of the Ambassador Bridge.[37]

For thirty-five years, Joseph Bower had directed the planning, financing, and operation of the Ambassador Bridge. He directed the company through the most difficult years of its history—the depression of the 1930s and World War II. His sound business judgment, his recruitment of talented and dedicated officers, and his careful planning served well the Ambassador Bridge and the communities which it touched on either side of the international border. Bower's philosphy was reflected in a letter he wrote to C. Clinton Campbell in 1953: "As you will appreciate, I am looking far into the future. That is what we Directors are supposed to do. I do not mean to infer that I am wise, but I am old enough with experience to know that you have to think and plan far into the future for all contingencies."[38] Bower demonstrated the wisdom of this philosophy in his management of the Ambassador Bridge.

CHAPTER 12

Lancaster Takes Over: The 1960s

The retirement of Joseph A. Bower as chairman of the board of directors of the Detroit International Bridge Company and the Canadian Transit Company created a dramatic change in the leadership of the Ambassador Bridge. Fondly known as "Father Bower" by the staff of the bridge, he had become an institution nearly as great as the bridge itself. But Bower's leaving was only the first of a series of events which would soon shape a new era for the bridge. For in the summer of 1960, C. Clinton Campbell announced that he planned to retire as president and general manager of the bridge company, effective on his sixty-fifth birthday, September 16, 1960. After having served the bridge for eighteen years, Campbell wanted to return to his family home in East Orange, New Jersey.[1]

The board tried to persuade Campbell to reconsider his decision or to defer it for a few more years, but he was resolute; he felt that he must retire. Campbell did agree, however, to assist the board in finding a replacement and, in addition, to remain in Detroit for one year to train and supervise the new candidate.[2]

After contacting business associates in the Detroit and Windsor area, Campbell soon identified one man who had the experience and credentials to replace himself. This prospect was Roy G. Lancaster of Windsor, one of the leaders in the commercial trucking industry of Ontario. After speaking with Lancaster's colleagues and friends, Campbell contacted Lancaster in September 1960 and arranged to meet with him. By all indications, the meeting was a success; Campbell arranged for Lancaster to be interviewed by Robert A. Bower, chairman of the board of directors of the bridge company.[3]

On November 29, 1960, Lancaster attended a meeting of the bridge's board of directors in New York City and was formally interviewed for the position, along with one other candidate. At this meeting, board members questioned Lancaster at great length about his business experience, his management ideas, and his knowledge of bridge and customs operations. Although the candidate readily admitted that he had no experience in "paying dividends or stock holder relationships," the board

Roy G. Lancaster. (Courtesy of the D.I.B. Archives.)

was favorably impressed with his "familiarity of customs on both sides of the border, his contacts with Teamster Local Unions and his experience in a highly competitive business."[4] As Lancaster was to recall many years later, immediately following the formal interview, Joseph A. Bower turned to him and asked, "Now that you are familiar with the duties of the position, do you think that you can handle the job?" "Yes, sir," Lancaster replied. So he was hired that day, to begin January 1, 1961.[5]

The selection of Lancaster was to bode well for the future development of the Ambassador Bridge. His predecessors had been recruited from various fields. The first manager, James L. Fozard, was an engineer; R. Bryson McDougald, a Canadian customs official; and C. Clinton Campbell, a public relations specialist. Roy G. Lancaster brought to the position years of experience as a trucking executive with extensive

knowledge of the business and transportation needs of the area. Moreover, he had excellent business connections in Windsor and Detroit.

Lancaster was born in Windsor, Ontario, the son of Edward W. and Anna Lancaster. After an early education in the Windsor public school system, he enrolled at Assumption College in Windsor, where he studied in the pre-engineering program. His college plans were interrupted, however, by two years' service in the Canadian Army, after which he entered the University of Western Ontario at London, Ontario. In 1947, he graduated with a B.A. degree in General Arts. He received his degree in business administration in 1964 from the University of Windsor after having attended its evening extension courses.[6]

After graduation in 1947, Roy Lancaster joined his father's firm, The E. W. Lancaster Company, of Windsor, a cartage, moving, and storage enterprise, on a full-time basis. He was already familiar with most of its activities, having worked there part-time during his high school years, "chasing parts, driving trucks and some office clerical work," as he later explained. Under Roy's leadership as general manager, the company, operating some ninety vehicles, soon became one of the leading steel haulers of Ontario and controlled much of the steel movement across the Ambassador Bridge into Canada.[7]

Although he enjoyed the work of managing the Lancaster Company, Lancaster became convinced that he did not wish to remain in the trucking business permanently. So in 1960, following the sale of the heavy freight division of his company's operations, the invitation to consider the executive position at the Ambassador Bridge came at a most propitious time.[8]

As planned, Lancaster started his new job as assistant to the president of the Ambassador Bridge on January 1, 1961. But he did not work under the supervision of C. Clinton Campbell, as he and the board had expected him to do. There were two reasons for this change in the working agreement—Campbell's confidence in Lancaster and Campbell's desire to break his ties with the bridge without delay. Indeed, Campbell stayed in Detroit only a few days each month, and it was Arthur Shewman, secretary and operations manager, who assisted Lancaster in learning the overall operations of the company. But this apprenticeship lasted only a few weeks, for Shewman, a faithful bridge employee since 1930, fell ill in February 1961. After a hospitalization of six months' duration, Shewman remained in poor health and was never able to resume full-time service to the bridge. Lancaster was virtually on his own during this time and in September 1961 he was made general manager when C. Clinton Campbell officially relinquished all active management responsibilities for the bridge. Campbell did, however, agree to continue as a member of the board of directors, a post he held until 1969.[9]

Although Campbell's absence from Detroit had placed Lancaster at a disadvantage, especially during the early months of 1961, it provided him with an opportunity and a challenge to learn quickly all aspects of the bridge's operations, including all ramifications of collection of tolls, reconciliation of vehicle counts and truck charges, as well as sales and promotion. In addition, with the assistance of Hugh Pratley, he was indoctrinated in the maintenance and engineering aspects of the Ambassador Bridge, especially the Canadian government's requirement for annual inspection of all sections of the bridge.

Although he kept in contact with board chairman Robert A. Bower, Joseph A. Bower, and other board members, Lancaster was given wide discretion in managing all bridge operations. In contrast to former

general managers, he quickly became involved in the actual proceedings of the meetings of the board of directors. He prepared the meeting agenda, took minutes of each session, and drafted the annual reports of the company in preparation for publication. Indeed, within a few years Lancaster was handling all of the details of the preparation and moderation of the stockholder meetings.[10]

The Bower family, as well as other board members, were well satisfied with Lancaster's management of the Ambassador Bridge. They showed their confidence and approval of his work in 1962 when they elected him secretary of the company, and in 1963 when they promoted him to vice-president and secretary. He continued his duties as general manager.[11]

Lancaster's tenure with the bridge differed from that of his predecessors in respects other than that of his relations with the board of directors. This difference was especially significant as it related to the relationship between the bridge and the tunnel. For, unlike C. Clinton Campbell and R. Bryson McDougald, Lancaster sought to establish a good working association with the officials of the Detroit and Canada Tunnel Corporation. He was fully aware of the intense competition between the bridge and the tunnel, but he also recognized that both companies had many interests in common, particularly as they related to customs and immigration. One of his first steps was to establish a personal relationship with W. S. Burton, president of the Detroit and Canada Tunnel Corporation. Soon the two men collaborated on a number of projects, including the "Trailblazer Sign" program, a display of attractive markers which directed motorists to both the bridge and the tunnel. The signs were installed at key locations on major thoroughfares throughout Detroit and Windsor.[12]

The greatest challenge facing Lancaster in 1961, and for the remainder of the decade, was the promotion of automobile and truck use of the bridge. Since the year 1956, when a total of 2,801,528 vehicles had crossed the bridge, to 1961, there had been a steady decline in traffic. By 1960, the total annual tally was 2,625,763 vehicles.[13]

The causes for the decline in bridge traffic were beyond the control of Lancaster and previous bridge officials. For example, the severe economic depression between 1957 and 1960 had curtailed tourist and commercial travel, but an even greater factor was the impact of a new expressway feeding directly into downtown Detroit. When the John C. Lodge Expressway was completed in 1959, it diverted a significant number of motorists from the bridge to the tunnel. Fortunately for the Ambassador Bridge, commercial truckers did not abandon the suspended span across the Detroit River; in fact, the volume of truckers remained stable during the recession years. Although there was a slight decline of less than 5,000 commercial crossings between 1957 to 1958, the years that followed showed an increase in trucks using the bridge.[14] As in the past, a single truck brought in more total revenue to the bridge than did twelve automobiles.[15]

It was obvious to Lancaster and his associates that the future growth and profits of the Ambassador Bridge depended upon attracting an increased volume of commercial trucking. So he used his previous business associations to contact firms in the Detroit and Windsor areas and to offer them office space at the bridge. Chrysler Corporation of Canada took advantage of Lancaster's offer and opened offices on the Canadian terminal of the bridge, where Chrysler staff soon expedited the clearance of Chrysler trucks through customs.[16] Soon General Motors and Ford Motor Company of Canada both maintained customs offices at the bridge.[17]

The facilities of the Ambassador Bridge were also enlarged and renovated to accommodate increased business trade, especially that of commercial trucking. In 1964, for example, the terminal office buildings and warehouse on both sides of the bridge were renovated to provide more space; and in 1966, the Canadian Customs facilities were enlarged. One year later, the United States plaza area was also enlarged for truck examinations.[18]

From the outset, Lancaster strove to make the plaza areas attractive to motorists. The dismal black and orange toll plazas were repainted "highway" green and white in 1961. At one point, Lancaster considered having the bridge superstructures painted a lighter color, but abandoned the plan when he was advised that a lighter shade of paint would soon darken when exposed to the high level of air pollution from riverfront factories in Detroit.[19]

It was soon evident that Lancaster's efforts to improve the appearance of the Ambassador Bridge were successful. Motorists, as well as bridge and customs employees, were impressed with the changes. But there were other developments beyond the control of bridge officials which would have an even greater impact upon the use of the bridge. In 1965, as a result of a formal agreement between the governments of Canada and the United States, an auto pact was signed by Prime Minister Lester Pearson and President Lyndon B. Johnson. Under the terms of the agreement, signed on January 16, 1965, and named The Automotive Products Trade Agreement, all new automobiles and trucks manufactured in Canada, as well as automobile parts, could be shipped into the United States duty free. In turn, similar duty-free arrangements were approved for American-made automobiles and new parts shipped to Canada. This duty-free arrangement eliminated the duplicative manufacturing of some

The *Montrose,* after it sank at the U.S. pier of the bridge during the summer of 1962. (Courtesy of the *Detroit Free Press.*)

model cars in both countries. Prior to the new agreement, a 17.5 percent tariff was charged on cars and trucks and as much as 25 percent on auto parts brought into Canada. Moreover, an 8.5 percent duty on parts and 6.5 percent on automobiles was charged to all Canadian manufacturers shipping into the United States.[20]

The new auto pact, which had been enthusiastically promoted by automobile manufacturers, stimulated the sale and interchange of Canadian- and American-made automobiles and trucks by reducing the cost of the vehicles to consumers. But the continuation of the pact was threatened by certain controversial features. One of these was the "Built-in-Canada, Sold-in-Canada" provision, designed to protect the

interests of Canadian automobile manufacturers and the jobs of Canadian workers. This provision required that the "Built-in-Canada, Sold-in-Canada" ratio be maintained at the 1964 level. In effect, this policy made it necessary for Canadian manufacturers to produce four cars for every seven sold in Canada. It further required that Canadian parts and labor must account for 60 percent of the value of automobiles produced in Canada.[21]

Other criticism leveled at the pact came from American business leaders, many of whom viewed the agreement as a "blatant form of protectionism," a conviction shared by some influential members of the U.S. Congress. Indeed, a typical expression of congressional opposition to the pact was

The Canada-U.S. auto pact facilitated the shipment of automobiles and parts across the bridge, 1965. (Courtesy of the D.I.B. Archives.)

given by Senator Albert Gore from Tennessee, who charged that the auto pact "was probably the most disastrous bilateral agreement in U.S. history," and he further demanded that it be eliminated.[22]

Actually, the pact had benefited automobile production in the United States, as well as in Canada. For example, trade in the automotive sector increased from $800 million in 1964 to $4 billion in 1968. Accordingly, Canadian automobile manufacturers increased their production by 76 percent between 1964 and 1968. Although there was some interest in renegotiating the pact in 1969, this movement was blocked by the powerful coalition of automotive interests.[23]

The auto pact had a dramatic effect upon commercial truck traffic crossing the Ambassador Bridge. The number of truck crossings increased by 53 percent from 1964 to 1966. Moreover, by the end of the decade in 1969, the total truck crossings had more than doubled to 628,000.[24] This was a significant, albeit unexpected, boon to the Ambassador Bridge.

Other events which contributed to the financial success of the bridge during the 1960s were the opening of the St. Lawrence Seaway in 1959 and the development of a new harbor facility at Windsor, which became operational in 1962. According to Roy Lancaster, these two shipping improvements contributed substantially "to the movement of freight to and from the central areas" of Detroit and Windsor, greatly benefiting the Ambassador Bridge.[25]

Another stroke of good fortune for the business operation of the Ambassador Bridge was the opening of the Windsor Raceway in 1965. Located in Ojibway, about five miles west of the bridge, the raceway attracted thousands of Detroiters during the winter months. According to Lancaster, "One would almost think that we had a hand in it. It started during our low fall season and came at a time of day after our commuters had crossed the Bridge," he observed.[26] During the eight weeks when the raceway was open between October and December, 1965, an estimated additional

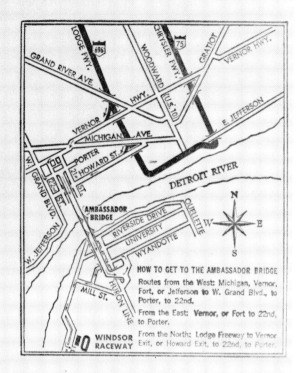

Bridge advertisement of the Windsor Raceway. (Courtesy of the D.I.B. Archives.)

70,000 vehicles crossed the Ambassador Bridge.[27]

Although the completion of the John C. Lodge Expressway in 1959 had benefited the tunnel, rather than the bridge, the construction of the larger interstate highway system in southern Michigan was a significant factor which contributed to increased volume of traffic on the bridge during the 1960s. In addition, Ontario Highway 401, the 585-mile MacDonald-Cartier Freeway between Windsor and Montreal, coupled with the Michigan system, boosted travel and, consequently, the bridge's profits.

By 1966, Interstate Highway 75 was being quickly constructed between Toledo, Ohio, and Detroit. On December 28, 1966, a new nine-mile section of I-75 was opened, leading up to a point only five miles from the bridge.[28] Then one year later, on December 12, 1967, the final section of the Toledo-Detroit freeway was opened, passing within a few hundred yards of the bridge plaza.[29] Although the disruption in traffic caused by the construction contributed to a temporary sharp decline in automobile crossings—a loss of 61,000 cars in 1967—once it was completed, the expressway facilitated the flow of traffic from southeastern and northern Michigan to the bridge. The announcement of plans to build Interstate 96, the Jeffries Freeway, westward, parallel, and north of the Edsel Ford Freeway and connecting the Ford and Lodge expressways to the bridge, was acclaimed by Lancaster and bridge officials.[30]

Although the new Michigan interstate highway system provided a great advantage for the bridge, the procedures followed by the Michigan Highway Department prior to construction caused consternation to Roy G. Lancaster and his business associates. A critical problem was the lack of communication between Highway Department officials and those of the bridge prior to Lancaster's tenure. Bridge officials were still smarting from losing a large part of their traffic in 1959 to the tunnel as a result

of the location of the Lodge Freeway, when they learned about final plans for Interstate 75 from articles in local Detroit newspapers.[31] Since I-75, as proposed, would pass within a few hundred yards of the entrance to the bridge, it is conceivable that the Highway Department could have worked together with the bridge company in planning that part of the project.

When Lancaster heard of the plans, he immediately contacted local and state highway officials in order to corroborate the newspaper story. As a consequence, the bridge hired a traffic engineering consultant, Lloyd B. Reid, a former director of traffic engineering for Detroit and a former commissioner for the Michigan State Highway Department, to review the location and impact of the new highway on bridge traffic. The results of Reid's investigation

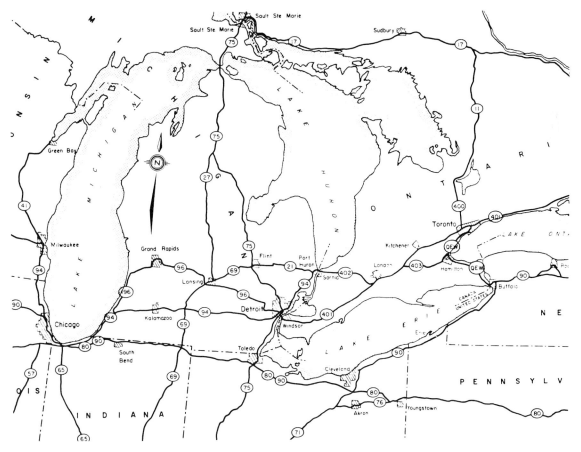

The Ambassador Bridge is a hub for Michigan and Ontario freeways.
(Courtesy of the D.I.B. Archives.)

Interstate 75, adjacent to the U.S. plaza, created traffic problems at the plaza. (Courtesy of John Sullivan, Aerial Associates, Ann Arbor, Michigan.)

did nothing to endear the State Highway Department to bridge administrators. They learned, for example, that the highway engineers had prepared and considered seven different plans for the entrance to the bridge from the freeway before making its final decision. And although the final plan called for a route immediately adjacent to the bridge's entrance and exit, no bridge officials were ever contacted or consulted regarding the plan.[32]

From the outset, Lancaster and his associates knew that the proposed location of the exit ramp from the freeway to the Porter Street entrance would create a serious and dangerous bottleneck for motorists crossing to Canada as well as to those entering the United States. There was no allowance made in the plans for trucks and autos waiting in line on entry to the toll plaza. Similarly, those vehicles leaving the toll plaza would be subjected to the same traffic congestion. For example, motorists exiting the United States plaza from several lanes would find themselves almost immediately on Porter Street. Thus, drivers would have to maneuver across lanes of traffic to exit in the direction desired. Furthermore, the traffic signal at the Vernor Highway, three short blocks north of the bridge exit, frequently caused vehicles to line up all the way back to the toll islands on the plaza during peak traffic periods.[33]

Confronting the problem, bridge officials urged the Highway Department to redesign the route of the freeway farther from the bridge and to realign Porter and Lafayette streets near the bridge plaza. The Highway Department refused to alter its plans, although department officials promised Lancaster that they would consider other alternatives if they felt the increase in bridge traffic justified it at a later time.[34] Following the completion of I-75, the fears and concerns of bridge officials proved well founded within a few years. Although the expressway undoubtedly stimulated traffic using the bridge, "the lack of an adequate approach," maintains Lancaster, "has crippled us since that time."[35]

As previously noted, the completion of Ontario Freeway 401 in the early 1950s, connecting Windsor with Toronto and Montreal, was also a catalyst to enlarging the volume of bridge traffic. Although 401 ended at Windsor's city limits, a four-lane highway, Huron Church Road or Route 3, led directly to the bridge. As in the case of I-75 on the American side, the widening and improvement of Huron Church Road in 1969 disrupted bridge traffic for several months, but once it was completed, the expressway proved a boon to bridge travel.

In addition to the auto pact and improved highway access to both sides of the bridge, other developments had a significant effect upon the fortunes of the Ambassador Bridge. The devaluation of the Canadian dollar by 7 ½ percent in 1962 discouraged many Windsorites from traveling to Detroit to shop; on the other hand, it caused an increase of American tourists to Canada.[36] Overall, the bridge profited from this financial situation.

As one might expect, the Detroit race riot of 1967 had a negative effect upon bridge use, at least during the remainder of 1967. In fact, within a few hours after the eruption of violence on Sunday, July 23, 1967, Windsor policemen began to stop all Canadian citizens from entering the United States, either via the Ambassador Bridge or the Detroit and Windsor Tunnel. Although United States citizens were allowed to return to their homes in Detroit, they were cautioned about the seriousness of the situation in Detroit. At Mr. Lancaster's request, United States National Guard forces were assigned on Monday evening, July 24, to protect the bridge, and they immediately took up stations at the toll offices on the United States plaza. The bridge remained open but traffic came to a virtual standstill for several days, until the violence was brought under control. For the rest of the year, especially during the usually busy summer months, traffic use of the bridge was down sharply.[37]

The activities of the bridge were also affected by labor problems during the 1960s. In the early summer of 1962, the Teamsters International Union conducted a strike against the Ontario trucking industry.[38] In 1956, bridge employees in Canada and the United States, including toll collectors, scale operators, and maintenance workers, had been organized by Teamsters Local 880 in Windsor and Teamsters Local 299 in Detroit.[39] United States Teamster Local 299 called a strike in August 1962, and bridge employees were required to withdraw their services for the first time since the bridge opened in 1929. The strike lasted approximately six weeks, at the end of which a three-year contract settlement was reached by Local 299; Canadian workers settled soon afterwards.[40]

In 1968 Teamsters Local 299 in Detroit again went out on strike for three weeks before a new settlement was reached. During

Bridge maintenance crews repairing bolts on suspender clamps. *From left:* John Laucks, Earl Foley, and Elmer Paquette. Below, a railway ferry enroute to the Windsor dock. (Courtesy of the D.I.B. Archives.)

both disputes, supervisory and office employees manned the toll booths and kept the bridge in operation. The existence of Teamster picket lines caused truck traffic to decline during the duration of each strike, but with the absence of the trucks, auto traffic increased significantly.[41]

Automobile manufacturer strikes in the United States and Canada in 1960 caused further disruption of the use of the Ambassador Bridge. The shipment of new cars, trucks, and auto parts was curtailed, and thousands of workers postponed travel plans when they went on strike. The decrease in revenue was felt immediately at the bridge's tollbooths.[42]

The annual inspections of Hugh Prat-

ley, consulting engineer to the company, found the bridge to be in excellent condition throughout the 1960s. His examinations continued to provide priorities for maintenance work on the span and other parts of the bridge. In addition to the renovation and enlargement of the Canadian customs inspection facilities, recommended and supervised by Mr. Lancaster, work was also undertaken on the traditional and ongoing maintenance projects. The main towers and the main span were painted on a continuous basis as recommended by Mr. Pratley.[43]

In 1969, when replacement of the outmoded original lighting system became a priority, the entire system was removed and new mercury vapor lamps, transformers, and automotic photocell switches were installed after the entire bridge was rewired. As in the past, the lights on one side of the roadway were controlled by a Canadian power source and the other side drew power from a source in the United States. Thus, if the power on either circuit failed, there would be adequate illumination of the roadway at night.[44]

Roy Lancaster provided yet another change in the lighting at this time which was to prove important more than a decade later. He recommended to the board of directors that it was an appropriate time to consider adding lights to the cables of the bridge. Although the cost of such decorative lighting for the Ambassador Bridge was beyond the financial resources of the company in 1969, Lancaster arranged to have the lead wiring installed for the future installation of a necklace of lights on the main cables.[45]

Another innovation during the 1960s was the opening of a duty-free export store on the United States plaza in October 1963. Operated by the Ammex Warehouse Company, this facility, like similar ones installed at other bridge outlets along the United

States and Canada border, was warmly received by tourists and has proved a financial advantage to the bridge over the years.[46]

The expanding volume of automobile and commercial truck traffic across the Ambassador Bridge during the 1960s brought about by the upswing in the economy, the stimulus of the auto pact, and the opening of the Windsor Raceway, made it clear that the customs and immigration facilities on the United States plaza were completely inadequate. Bridge officials had been confronted with the problem since the end of World War II. Since the original inspection lanes had been designed for automobiles of the 1930s and not for the wider cars of the postwar era, there was room for only one car to be served at a time in each lane, instead of two, as intended. Thus, inspection lanes were cut by half, creating a long back-up of cars at times, especially during peak commuting hours.[47]

When truck traffic increased, especially during the 1960s, the problem became even more serious. All trucks, except for those which were empty and, after 1965, those carrying new autos or parts, had to stop for a thorough inspection by customs officials. The procedure required trucks to pass through the customs primary inspection lanes adjacent to the terminal buildings, turn left, cutting at right angles across all traffic lanes, and park, awaiting secondary examination. When the necessary paperwork was completed, the driver backed his truck across all lanes of traffic to the inspection dock. Finally, after being cleared by customs, the trucks entered the main traffic exit lanes.[48]

Lack of space as truck use of the bridge increased during the 1960s also created noise and congestion at the United States terminal plaza areas, and traffic snarls developed as the trucks blocked exit lanes. The requirement by customs officials that a driver stay with his cargo until it was fully inspected added to the burden of costs to the trucking companies.

Another related problem was that the United States Customs and Immigration posts were at most times undermanned, causing even further delays. On some days, traffic came to a standstill as trucks exiting on the American side were backed up in a line from Canada a distance of at least two thousand feet on the bridge itself.[49] Roy Lancaster observed that it was not uncommon for single commodity loads to take from one to ten hours to clear customs, and some multiple shipments were delayed in excess of ten hours.[50]

Lancaster, on behalf of the Ambassador Bridge, constantly appealed to U.S. Customs to increase its staff of examiners and to extend its hours of the examination of commercial goods. Finally, in 1965, U.S. Customs responded to his request and extended regular closing hours from 5:00 P.M. to midnight. Canada Customs had instituted such hours years before, and eventually both agencies provided twenty-four hour service.[51]

Canada Customs officials were more receptive to other changes requested by bridge officials. As a result of lengthy negotiations in 1968, Canada Customs expedited the clearance of commercial goods, particularly auto parts, at primary inspection, "thus eliminating a great deal of the parking and storing of semi-trailers which hithertofore awaited inspection in the customs compound yard," stated Lancaster.[52] Canada also relaxed regulations, effective January 1, 1970, covering the importation of personal goods by Canadian residents returning from visits to the United States, in order to encourage the travel of tourists.[53]

Negotiations with United States Customs and Immigration officials, which began in 1966, proved difficult, not because both agencies at Detroit failed to realize that

Truck congestion at U.S. Customs. (Courtesy of John Sullivan, Aerial Associates, Ann Arbor, Michigan.)

additional office space and clearance facilities were necessary in order to reduce traffic congestion, but because they did not have the power to authorize such renovations. It was the United States General Services Administration (GSA) which exercised authority over all government buildings, including customs and immigration facilities, and this federal agency was better known for creating than for solving problems.[54] The GSA became the major stumbling block for any expansion plans proposed by the

bridge company for larger inspection facilities.

Starting in 1966, bridge officials made a series of proposals to expand the customs facilities and inspection booths on the Detroit plaza. Because of constraints in the size of the plaza, Lancaster, in 1968, recommended the establishment of a permanent off-site customs secondary truck examination facility some six blocks east of the bridge. Such a plan had not been considered before, but the successful utilization of a similar operation during the Teamster strike in 1968 had demonstrated its feasibility.[55] As a result, the bridge company hired the firm of Smith, Hinchman and Grylls Associates, the same architectural engineering firm which had originally designed the buildings and terminals of the bridge, to undertake a feasibility study for such an off-site truck clearance center.

In its report, issued on May 29, 1969, the firm strongly confirmed the bridge's recommendation that a large United States Customs clearance center was necessary. Although adequate space for such a facility immediately adjacent to the bridge was not available at that time, bridge officials accepted the plan provided by Smith, Hinchman and Grylls for the site approximately six blocks distant. Furthermore, the proposal became a major goal of the Ambassador Bridge in dealing with U.S. government officials during the following fifteen years.[56] This concept was before its time, however. Such an off-site customs examining warehouse was never established at the bridge, but the idea was implemented at the tunnel several years later.

The 1960s were also a time when attempts to change the control and administrative structure of the Ambassador Bridge were undertaken. In 1963, the board of directors and the stockholders proposed to the Canadian Transport Commission that the Canadian Transit Company, the fully owned subsidiary of the Detroit International Bridge Company, be merged with its parent company. Although the Transport Commission approved the merger, the Canadian Cabinet or Governor-in-Council denied the petition. It notified the bridge company on January 28, 1965, that the proposed merger "would not be sanctioned," on the grounds that it would be of "no advantage to Canada."[57]

There was also an attempt in 1960 to change the ownership of the bridge. During that year, a New York financier promoted a plan to have the state of Michigan buy the Ambassador Bridge and the Detroit and Windsor Tunnel and place them under the authority of a state public commission. The motivation for the proposal was that it would provide funds to repay debts incurred by the construction of the Mackinac Bridge. Much to the satisfaction of Joseph A. Bower, who opposed the sale of the bridge, the plan failed.[58]

There were important changes in the board of directors, as well. In 1963, Joseph A. Bower resigned from the position of vice-president and also from the board, but the directors elected him "Honorary Chairman of the Board of Directors."[59] One year before, on March 12, 1962, Charlton B. Hibbard had resigned after serving twenty-five years on the board. Then, on November 6, 1966, the board lost one of its most valued members when Charles P. McTague, formerly of Windsor and later of Toronto, died. A highly respected Canadian lawyer, McTague had been associated with the bridge and Joseph A. Bower since the mid-1920s, except for a number of years when McTague took a leave of absence while serving on the bench of the Supreme Court of Ontario.[60]

Several new members were added to the board to fill the vacancies. In 1962 Victor Klein, U.S. counsel to the bridge company, was elected; Blancke Noyes and H. Peter Schaub, Jr., in 1963; Arthur H. Lamborn in 1964; and Charles J. Clark joined the group in 1969.

There were changes in the staff of the bridge as well. The retirement of Arthur Shewman as secretary of the board of directors in 1963 ended a career of thirty-five years of dedicated service to the company. Then, in May 1966, Leonard W. Ryder retired as treasurer of the company, after more than twenty years' association with the bridge. In his place, the board ap-

Board of Directors, 1964. *From left:* Charles P. McTague, C. Clinton Campbell, Joseph A. Bower, Blancke Noyes, Robert A. Bower, chairman, Victor W. Klein, Philip L. Carret, Harry P. Schaub, and Harry L. Derby. (Courtesy of Jack Landress Co., Inc., New York, New York.)

pointed Frank V. Kefalas as assistant treasurer in 1966.

Kefalas, a native of Granite City, Illinois, had graduated from the School of Commerce and Finance at St. Louis University in 1952. He had come to Detroit in 1954 and was employed as a public accountant with the firm Plante and Moran, C.P.A.'s. In 1958 he became secretary and controller of Aggregate Surfaces of Dearborn, Michigan. He brought to his new bridge job fourteen years of experience as a C.P.A. One year after his appointment to the bridge administration, he was promoted to the position of treasurer of the Detroit International Bridge Company.[61]

Another long-time employee who rose through the ranks of the bridge staff was John L. Hannan, who began work for the Canadian Transit Company in June 1947. After serving with the bridge's painting and maintenance crew, he was promoted to toll supervisor and then, upon Arthur Shewman's retirement, he was promoted to the position of superintendent of operations in January 1963. He assumed charge of personnel, scheduling, toll traffic, and relations with customs personnel. In 1968 Hannan became operations manager of the bridge, a position which he held until his retirement on December 31, 1985.[62]

Recognition was given also to the work of Roy G. Lancaster. In 1966 he was elected to the board of directors, and the following year he was elected president of the company, replacing Robert A. Bower, who continued as chairman of the board of directors. The high regard shown for Lancaster by Joseph A. Bower and the board might best be described by the following excerpt from a letter from Joseph A. Bower to C. Clinton Campbell on the occasion of the latter's retirement in 1969. It reads as follows: "I am grateful for all the help and assistance

Expansion of the University of Windsor campus, adjacent to the
bridge, 1962. (Courtesy of John Sullivan, Aerial Associates, Ann Arbor,
Michigan.)

you have given me in the past, and I am not unmindful of your having done two very important things for the Bridge Company. . . . One is that you got Lancaster for us."[63]

Although formidable problems faced the Ambassador Bridge during the 1960s—the 1967 Detroit race riot, labor strife, construction of I–75, and the acute shortage of customs staff and inspection space—the decade was the most successful financially since the bridge opened in 1929. The total traffic volume had increased sharply from 2,625,763 in 1960 to 3,329,346 in 1965 and 4,204,805 in 1969. Even more significant was the growth of commercial truck use.

In 1960 truck crossings had increased to 253,000; by 1965 the count had reached 360,000 and by 1969, 628,000. By 1969 truck traffic provided 45.5 percent of the total revenue of the bridge.[64]

The net earnings of the bridge mirrored the significant increase in traffic. From 1960 to 1964 the net earnings averaged $705,000 per year; and from 1965 to 1969, $1,189,000, an increase of $484,000 per year. The total earnings for the decade was $9,468,865. This success fulfilled Joseph A. Bower's prediction that the Ambassador Bridge would be a profitable venture, after about forty years of struggle and adversity.[65]

CHAPTER 13

Changing with the Times: The 1970s

The sharp increase in the use of the Ambassador Bridge during the first four decades of its operation was indeed impressive. Joseph Bower's original expectations of the use of the Detroit-Windsor bridge were finally materializing. By the end of 1969, 77,298,033 vehicles and many more millions of passengers had crossed the bridge between Canada and the United States.

Of the total number of vehicles, an increasing percentage were trucks, a boon in terms of operating revenues, but a source of wear and tear on the span and approach viaducts.[1] Fortunately, the bridge was designed for a capacity far in excess of the projected traffic of the 1930s. Also, as commercial trucks increased in length, their overall weight was spread over a greater area and caused less damage to the roadway. Nevertheless, the bridge required constant attention and continuous maintenance. As a result, Roy Lancaster and bridge officials gave highest priority to the upkeep of the structure. In 1970, the electrical work on the bridge, which had commenced one year earlier, was completed.[2]

During 1970 and 1971 Roy G. Lancaster, president, and the board of directors undertook significant rehabilitation of the roadway, the first such work since the bridge opened in 1929. Extending the life of the deck for ten years, a major rehabilitation was started; the repairs involved stripping the wearing surface off both approaches (viaducts and truss spans). Curbs and sidewalks were rebuilt on both approaches, and some concrete slab was replaced because of the deterioration that had taken place. Each approach was then waterproofed and repaved with asphalt.[3]

During the reconstructive repair, the granite blocks on the American approach were removed. Although they were originally installed to give greater traction to vehicles climbing the 5 percent grade, by 1970 the heavy traffic flow had caused the blocks to loosen and move out of position. The granite blocks were to be removed and disposed of at a site downriver, but Roy Lancaster had a better idea. He arranged with Canada Customs to give the blocks to the city of Windsor, free of duty. Since that time, the Parks Department has used the

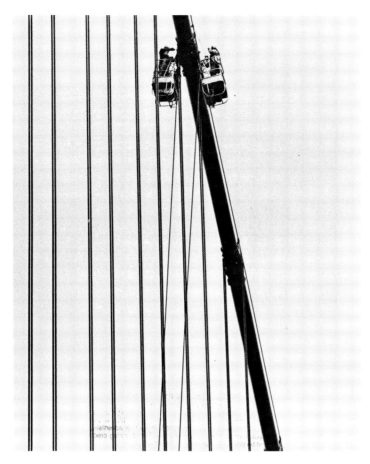

Crews replace bolts in clamps holding suspension wire cables, June 18, 1977. (Courtesy of the *Windsor Star.*)

granite blocks throughout the city for the attractive development of parks and malls.[4]

In addition to the rehabilitation of the roadway, the bridge was repainted on a continuous basis during the 1970s. Based on the annual inspections and recommendations of Hugh Pratley, the main towers, approach, and stiffening trusses and viaducts were carefully scraped and repainted between 1971 and 1973.[5] New six-foot-high tower signs were erected in 1973, replacing the second set of signs installed twenty years earlier.[6]

Canadian and American plaza areas were also renovated as part of the bridge maintenance program, in order to meet the needs of the increased truck and automobile traffic. To lessen the disruption to vehicular traffic using the bridge, the plaza sections were improved in phases. The terminal buildings were also repaired and, in

1972 and 1973 four seventy-five-ton truck scales were installed, two on each side. The scales not only facilitated truck toll collection but also provided a means to control weight of individual vehicles prior to their crossing the span.[7]

The modernization of the tollbooth plazas also facilitated the movement of traffic. In 1972 the tollbooths located at the entrance of the U.S. plaza were removed and eight new ones were constructed several hundred feet toward the bridge itself. In 1973 new tollbooths and canopies were erected on the Canadian plaza, returning the collection of tolls in Canada, which had not occurred since 1942.[8]

In 1976 the six original primary inspection booths for Canada Customs and Immigration were razed and eleven new ones were constructed. The outdated and inefficient original booths were designed to handle automobiles on both sides and placed inspectors alternately on the passenger side of the vehicle. The new lanes reflected the increased width of modern automobiles and provided driver-side inspections.[9]

The completion and opening of two new retail sales buildings, leased to the Ammex Duty Free Warehouse Company, complemented the renovation of the Detroit plaza.[10] In addition, in 1979 the bridge company installed a computerized toll collection system, which facilitated the collection of tolls, provided better accountability over the collection of toll revenues, and gave bridge officials up-to-date information on traffic statistics.[11]

In addition to the annual inspections conducted by Hugh Pratley, the board of directors of the Ambassador Bridge decided in 1974 to hire the engineering consulting firm of Howard, Needles, Tammen and Bergendoff (HNTB) of Cleveland, Ohio, to undertake a comprehensive inspection of the entire bridge structure. During 1974,

HNTB began a thorough examination of the bridge, including a physical inspection, engineering tests, and computations of the load-carrying capacity of the span.[12]

As a part of the bridge inspection, HNTB decided to remove the "shroud at the point of entry of the east cable [American side] and also to remove the wrapping wire between the splay point and a position just outside the anchorage for inspection of the [interior] cable wire." The wire was found in excellent condition—a tribute to the original cable construction—but "considerable difficulty was experienced when an attempt was made to replace the wrapping wire" It was decided finally not to attempt to rewrap the portion under the shroud or inside the anchorage, but rather to replace the shroud and cover the "disturbed area" with a heavy coat of red lead paste and paint.[13] In looking back on the cable inspection, Roy Lancaster later said, "We're sorry in a way that it was done; it was in perfect condition." At least, all doubts about the condition of the original cable were laid to rest.[14]

In its report, issued in 1974, HNTB acknowledged that the "forty-five year old Ambassador Bridge was found to be in good condition" but announced also that "over a long period of time the bridge deck or parts thereof will require rehabilitation or replacement."[15] The firm advised bridge officials that such work should be started by 1976. The total cost would be approximately $13 million.[16]

The consultants' report, especially the cost estimate, took the board of directors by surprise. Although they were aware of the age of the bridge and the increasing volume of traffic crossing it, they had not anticipated the reported potential cost of repairs. After further meetings with Roy Lancaster, Hugh Pratley, and the board members, HNTB clarified parts of its report, stating that neither the consultants nor Mr. Pratley

recommended that such renovations be undertaken immediately. They observed also "that with continuing maintenance, the life of the original parts of the Ambassador Bridge can likely be extended for about ten years, and possibly as much as fifteen years, without permanent repair."[17] The revised cost estimates for the "permanent repair of the deck . . . (in September, 1976 dollars)" was reduced to $4.5 million "depending upon whether or not deck joints were replaced."[18]

It was decided not to undertake immediately any of the major roadway renovations recommended by the HNTB consultants, but the board did approve one of the firm's recommendations—the adoption of a corrective and preventive maintenance program. This program, similar to the one which Hugh Pratley had followed, was declared official board policy in 1976.[19]

The HNTB consultants also recommended that the cable band bolts be replaced. Hugh Pratley had discovered during an inspection earlier that a slight slip of one cable band bolt existed but it was not until the later comprehensive inspection by HNTB that some loss of tension in the cable band bolts was discovered. After discussion with the American Bridge Division of U.S. Steel, it was decided, with Hugh Pratley's concurrence, that it would be cheaper to replace all of the bolts rather than to tighten them. The work was completed by fall 1977.[20]

The completion of the interstate freeway system in Michigan and the improvement of the highways connecting Ontario's Route 401 continued to stimulate traffic flow over the Ambassador Bridge. In September 1970, Interstate 75, named the Fisher Freeway south of Detroit, was completed and provided a 1,776-mile connection between Sault Ste. Marie, Michigan, and Miami, Florida. The construction of Interstate 96, the Jeffries Freeway, was also completed in the 1970s. Constructed in sections which began at the Ambassador Bridge, the first installment of I-96 opened in July 1971; the freeway was completed in 1978. This major roadway, which started at the entrance of the Ambassador Bridge, ran 25.6 miles northwest via the Davison corridor, then west to Livonia and north to the existing I-96 which had already been completed to Muskegon. When the Jeffries was completed, the bridge was linked directly with all major freeways in southeastern Michigan, I-75, I-94, and I-96—which in turn led to all other parts of the state.

The widening and improvement in 1971 and 1972 of Huron Church Road, or Route 3 in Windsor, connected the bridge with Ontario Route 401 and also facilitated traffic flow to the bridge. New exit and entrance ramps and connectors were constructed at the bridge at the same time under an agreement with the city of Windsor, with the Ambassador Bridge bearing the latter costs.[21]

The completion of the Ontario and Michigan limited access freeway systems was a major factor in increasing bridge traffic overall and in giving the bridge a competitive advantage over the tunnel. The freeways also created new problems, however, for bridge operations, especially in the form of traffic congestion, delays, and safety problems. As noted earlier, little, if any, consideration was given to the traffic problems of the bridge by the Michigan State Highway Department during the planning of the interstates, nor were bridge officials consulted regarding the location of the freeway exit and entrance ramps in the vicinity of the bridge. The bridge plaza, designed in 1929, was based upon then-existing needs and traffic projections for the 1930s. Given the limited plaza area, there was only minimal space for vehicles to await passage through the toll gates during peak traffic periods. Furthermore, for auto-

mobiles and trucks exiting from the inspection booths on the American side, there was inadequate space for vehicles to maneuver into the proper lane to enter the desired interstate route—either I-75 south or north, I-96 west, or a local thoroughfare. For motorists, especially tourists or travelers unfamiliar with the exit directions, getting off the Detroit plaza was often confusing and somewhat dangerous.[22]

Officials of the Ambassador Bridge were aware of the traffic problems long before the freeways were completed. After a series of studies of traffic patterns, the traffic engineering consulting firm of Reid, Cool and Michalski recommended in July 1970 a renovation and revision of the Detroit plaza area and the adjoining arterial connections. This plan would have extended the U.S. plaza north beyond Porter Street, separated truck and passenger car movements through customs and immigration areas, increased primary and secondary inspection areas, and increased the exit area between the inspection booths and freeway and sidestreet systems.[23]

Although it initially received the "conceptual approval" of the Michigan Highway Department, the city of Detroit, and local neighborhood groups, the plan never received the federal governmental support necessary for implementation.[24] Without such support, there was little the Ambassador Bridge could do to eliminate the traffic congestion at the American end of the bridge. The transfer of toll collections to the Canadian plaza and the relocation of U.S. tollbooths farther distant from the Porter Street entrance to the bridge was a minor improvement but did not resolve the bulk of the problems. Even the eventual acquisition of a customs inspection area adjacent to the U.S. plaza did not provide a solution. As of 1987, the horrendous bottleneck still exists and awaits resolution by the Michigan Highway Department and the city of

Improved access to the bridge along Huron Church Line Road, May 1984. (Courtesy of John Sullivan, Aerial Associates, Ann Arbor, Michigan.)

Detroit, both of which are actively working with bridge management towards a compatible solution.

The haphazard locations of the interstate highway system adjacent to the Ambassador Bridge caused serious traffic problems for Lancaster and the bridge staff. More serious, however, was the traffic tie-up created by a shortage of U.S. Customs and Immigration officers and the lack of adequate inspection space for trucks on the U.S. plaza. At peak travel times during the months of June, July, and August, when more than one thousand vehicles per hour crossed the bridge into the United States, automobiles and trucks were often backed up across the bridge. Some trucks, after reaching the customs inspection area, were delayed for hours, awaiting clearance.[25]

Despite the entreaties of business leaders and bridge officials, U.S. Customs did next to nothing to alleviate this intolerable situation. In 1969 the U.S. Bureau of Customs conducted a survey of the traffic situation at the port of Detroit to determine if the complaints of bridge and tunnel officials and other interested groups were valid. In its findings, the bureau acknowledged that a "shortage of inspectional personnel did exist at Detroit" and that the situation had worsened on "a gradually increasing basis over the past few years."[26] The agency also announced that it had requested additional inspector positions for the port of Detroit and that it was recommending "more overlapping tours of duty, especially to meet the needs during peak periods."[27] The need to assign customs officers to ship-related duties when the navigation season opened each spring was also cited as an explanation of the personnel problem in Detroit.[28]

Although Roy Lancaster and tunnel authorities, joined by the Greater Detroit Chamber of Commerce, took issue with the Bureau of Customs over the need for additional staff, there had never been a dispute over the need for additional customs inspection facilities.[29] As early as 1966, bridge officials sought to locate and acquire land near the bridge plaza for an off-site truck inspection facility. In 1968, Lancaster contacted the city of Detroit about purchasing vacant Housing Commission property six blocks from the bridge, bounded by Fourteenth, Howard, Sixteenth, and Porter streets, for use as a customs clearance center.[30] At the same time, Lancaster notified local trucking companies, automobile manufacturers, customs brokers, and U.S. Customs and General Services Administration officials about his proposal to acquire off-site property.[31] Frequent meetings were initiated by Lancaster to keep the interested parties informed and especially to secure the support of U.S. Customs officials.[32] In 1969, the bridge company financed a feasibility study by Smith, Hinchman and Grylls, architectural engineers, to plan the site for a customs clearance center.[33]

Although the plan was sound and the need for such an off-site center was justified, Lancaster and bridge officials met opposition from a number of sources. The city of Detroit refused to sell the Housing Commission property and the Hubbard-Richard Community Council, a local neighborhood group, actively campaigned against the proposed use of the site because of their fear that additional truck traffic in the area would compromise "the residential nature of the area."[34] The U.S. Customs Service also voiced its disapproval of the Housing Commission site for use as a customs clearance center because of a lack of security in its operations.[35]

The U.S. General Services Administration (GSA) was also deeply involved in the issue because it controlled the construction, leasing, and maintenance of all federal buildings, including customs facilities. In a separate venture, Lancaster proposed in October 1970 that GSA trade its vacant and

Overland Western Company to the left of the U.S. plaza, 1973. (Courtesy of John Sullivan, Aerial Associates, Ann Arbor, Michigan.)

unused nine-acre property eight blocks from the bridge at Trumbull and Labrosse streets for the Detroit Housing Commission site.[36] The following year, the Simon Realty Company proposed to purchase the nine-acre site, develop the customs clearance center, and lease it back to GSA for customs purposes.[37] Despite backing of the plan by the mayor, the city controller, and the Detroit Housing Commission, GSA adamantly refused even to consider the proposal. An attempt to persuade the U.S. Bureau of Roads to acquire needed property by eminent domain also failed.[38]

In 1973, Lancaster pursued another alternative, the acquisition of property owned by Overland Western, a Canadian trucking company located immediately to the east of the bridge terminal building. This two-and-one-half-acre parcel, on the site of the old Webster School, had been acquired by Overland Western in 1963, but a decade later had become too small for the company's operation. Lancaster opened negotiations for the property which led to an agreement on October 26, 1973, whereby the bridge would buy the Overland site conditional upon the trucking company purchasing the Detroit Housing Commission property at Sixteenth and Porter streets, then being negotiated by Overland with the city.[39] Based upon this conditional contract, Lancaster then contacted GSA officials to offer the property for lease as a truck clearance facility on behalf of U.S. Customs. When Lancaster could not guarantee that the property would "be available in 180 days," GSA refused to consider negotiating a lease.[40]

In the meantime, Overland Western was having difficulty acquiring the Fourteenth-Sixteenth-Porter-streets site. Neighborhood groups petitioned the city against selling the property for use by trucks. Even after the Detroit Master Plan was amended in April 1974, designating the area as industrial, community opposition continued. On December 31, 1974, the agreement between Overland Western and the Detroit International Bridge Company expired, and, at the time, Overland was not interested in extending the agreement. Thus, another plan to ease the unyielding access bottleneck was defeated.[41]

By this time, the Ambassador Bridge was not alone in its campaign to develop an off-site customs clearance center. Other business and public groups, concerned about the traffic congestion at the U.S. plaza, joined the fight for the center. Initiated by Roy G. Lancaster and supported by the Greater Detroit Chamber of Commerce, major bridge carriers, and automotive companies, a special Customs Clearance Terminal Committee was formed on behalf of the commercial carriers of the bridge.[42] It raised funds for an updated feasibility study by the Washington, D.C., firm of Linton, Mields and Coston; it met with local, state, and federal officials on behalf of the customs clearance center; and it publicized the need for additional customs facilities.[43] A series of meetings was arranged with regional and national officials of General Ser-

vices Administration, U.S. Customs, and the Michigan congressional delegation in order to demonstrate the widespread community support for the project.[44] The committee, which was supported by the Greater Detroit Chamber of Commerce, assisted Overland Western in its attempt to relocate from its existing site. The new feasibility study recommended the Overland Western site as the logical location for the clearance center.[45]

Despite this groundswell of support for a new customs center, GSA once again blocked the bridge's efforts to secure additional truck inspection facilities, and successfully thwarted the efforts of the Chamber of Commerce and the Customs Clearance Terminal Committee as well. Instead, GSA contacted the Overland Western Company directly in 1975 with an offer to purchase the Overland site. Overland rejected the offer, stating its preference to deal with the Detroit International Bridge Company, whose ownership, in its opinion, was of greater benefit to the trucking industry.[46] General Services Administration officials continued to pursue the matter, taking the position that "Government ownership and operation of a facility is the most practical long-range solution."[47] The federal agency eventually sought congressional approval to purchase the Overland property.[48]

Lancaster was not opposed to this new GSA approach. In fact, he applauded it because he hoped it would result in eventual construction of the much-needed customs facility. Lancaster continued, however, to negotiate with Overland Western, and on November 30, 1976, he executed an unconditional agreement whereby the bridge would purchase the property for $1.2 million and take possession of the Overland Western property on July 1, 1977.[49] U.S. Customs and GSA were notified of the purchase agreement, and Lancaster immediately offered to negotiate a lease to be effective on the same date. General Services Administration replied, "We are not about to change our course of action."[50]

GSA officials continued to delay and create obstacles to progress by refusing to permit customs officials to use the former trucking terminal for truck clearance purposes even though the latter had agreed with Lancaster to do so. On August 2, 1977, GSA gave the bridge company ten days to submit final specifications for the reconstruction and renovation of the property for customs use.[51] Because of the impossibility of meeting such a deadline, Lancaster offered to sell the property to GSA at reimbursible cost so that the federal government could proceed with its use for customs purposes.[52]

Again, GSA delayed. It notified the bridge company that it must first secure congressional approval and an appropriation for the purchase as well as secure an appraisal of the property.[53] When the appraisal was completed in the spring of 1978, GSA offered the Ambassador Bridge $800,000 for the property, $400,000 less than the price that was paid by the bridge. The offer was rejected.[54]

In December 1978, in an attempt to have the property used, the Ambassador Bridge offered the Overland Western property to U.S. Customs Service without charge, including the required renovation, with the proviso that the bridge company would seek reimbursement through a service fee from carriers, a great many of whom sanctioned the agreement.[55] On June 8, 1979, GSA rejected this proposal and prohibited the U.S. Customs Service from using the property.[56]

Furious at this action, Lancaster lashed out at the General Services Administration in a letter to the Congressional Committees on Public Works and Transportation as follows: "In its protracted endeavor to satisfy its own ill-contrived and self-serving determination to purchase the property, GSA has placed one impediment after another to both U.S. Customs Service and our Company."[57]

The local news media joined the conflict, citing the problem of traffic congestion at the Ambassador Bridge. In an editorial on August 27, 1978, the *Detroit News* charged that poor service by U.S. Customs and Immigration officers caused the waste of thousands of gallons of gasoline each weekend as cars and trucks were forced to wait halfway across the bridge for clearance. The newspaper insisted that the traffic jams "increase trade deficits" and drive "the value of the dollar down."[58]

In January 1980, after the Overland Western property had remained vacant for two and one-half years, GSA took possession of the property under the provision of eminent domain.[59] One month short of another three years, on December 1, 1982, the new customs inspection terminal, having been renovated under GSA jurisdiction, opened and received its first trucks for inspection. Thus, after approximately sixteen years of agitation, much-needed customs facilities were finally available, but were very shortly to be proven used far short of their capacity because of inefficient and inappropriate design. Once again, the customs facilities, as well as the bridge itself, was the cause of heavy congestion in clearing trucks.[60]

At the same time that Roy Lancaster and the bridge company were fighting GSA for a customs clearance center on the American side, the bridge company was having some difficulties with Canada Customs, although on a smaller scale. The issue in Canada, which affected all international bridges on the Canada–United States border, related to the reimbursement for services provided by the bridges to Canada Customs. Unlike those of the United States, Canadian laws provided that international bridges

The new U.S. Customs facility (*shown in center*), which opened in January 1985. (Courtesy of John Sullivan, Aerial Associates, Ann Arbor, Michigan.)

must provide such services as office space, inspection facilities, warehouses, heat, light, and maintenance free of charge. This policy, which was based upon the premise that bridges were considered "revenue producing transportation facilities," put a severe burden upon many international bridges, especially the Ambassador Bridge, which provided in 1974 $118,000 in unreimbursed services.[61] Starting in 1973, the Ambassador Bridge, along with the United States–Canada Bridge-Tunnel Operators Association, undertook a lobbying campaign to change Canadian government policy to provide for reimbursement of customs and immigration services.

A consulting firm was hired to evaluate the governmental requirements of all border crossings throughout Canada, and its report, submitted by Roy G. Lancaster, president of the association, to the ministers for customs and immigration, brought about a change in policy which provided for all future alterations to be accomplished at government expense.[62]

Although the problems created by the location of Interstate 75 and the battle for additional U.S. Customs facilities required the constant attention of Roy Lancaster and bridge officials, there were other developments over which the company had little control but which nevertheless had a profound effect upon the fortunes of the Ambassador Bridge. Actually, some of these developments caused a significant short-term decline in vehicular use of the Ambassador Bridge. For example, the economic recessions in 1970, 1975, and 1978 had a serious impact upon traffic crossings, especially by tourists and commercial trucking interests. Although there was a recovery of business following each recession, the bridge suffered an overall loss during these troubled economic periods.[63]

The strike by the UAW against General Motors, which lasted for two and one-half months in the fall of 1970, also caused a decline in traffic across the Ambassador Bridge. Not only did the strike curtail the shipment of new automobiles, trucks, and parts between the United States and Canada, but the work stoppage also discouraged workers and others affected by the strike from vacationing or traveling for shopping or sightseeing purposes.[64] The illegal strike or walkout of Canada Customs employees and other Canadian civil servants also caused a disruption in traffic in 1970. Later in the decade, a brief nationwide Teamsters strike in April, 1979 resulted in a decrease in commercial truck use of the Bridge and other border crossings between the United States and Canada.

More serious to the bridge's operation were strikes called during the 1970s by the Teamster unions representing both Canadian and American bridge employees. During a three-week period in August and September 1972, Canadian bridge employees of Teamsters Local 880 withheld their services from the bridge.[65] In the summer of 1978 the Teamsters Union again called both United States and Canadian employees out on strike.[66] Supervisory and office employees manned the toll booths during these work stoppages, and although there was a substantial decline in truck traffic, automobile traffic increased considerably.[67]

Other events which affected bridge business included the extension of the race track season at the Detroit tracks in 1970, although, to be sure, a great deal of the race track business was recovered in 1972 when the Windsor Raceway season was extended to provide a six-week summer session of harness racing.[68] The discovery of extensive and dangerous mercury pollution in Lake Erie in 1970 discouraged hundreds of Michigan fishermen from making their annual smelt fishing expedition into Ontario.[69] The crackdown on drug smuggling by U.S. Customs in 1970 and 1971 caused traffic congestion and delays, and undoubtedly discouraged motorists from crossing the border to shop and sightsee.[70]

In the fall of 1971 the Ambassador Bridge was the site of a huge protest march by Canadian students who walked across the bridge in opposition to the U.S. nuclear weapons tests at Amchitka, British Columbia. Traffic was stalled for nearly four hours while protesters milled about on the roadway listening to speakers. Thirty trucks were stuck among the crowd until the protesters dispersed peacefully. The episode, which was also witnessed at the Blue Water Bridge between Port Huron, Michigan, and Sarnia, Ontario, caused John Nichols, police commissioner of Detroit, "to wonder outloud" as he stood at the Detroit plaza of the Ambassador Bridge, "if the Canadians are getting even with us for the War of 1812."[71]

Motorist fears of the shortage of gasoline during the energy crisis of 1973 and 1974 caused a temporary downturn in automobile traffic across the bridge, but it did not last long. By the last half of 1974, auto traffic returned to its normal levels.[72] The Bicentennial celebration in the United States during 1976 also had a minor negative impact on tourist travel into Canada when Americans visited Revolutionary War battlefields and other historic sites in the United States, rather than crossing the border into Canada for their vacations.[73]

Despite these impediments to bridge business, there were other developments which served to balance the loss of vehicular traffic, most notably the continuation of the Canada-U.S. auto pact. The agreement continued to stimulate trade between the two countries, much to the benefit of the Ambassador Bridge, which was located directly between the centers of the automobile manufacturing industry in Michigan and Ontario. Nevertheless, the pact came under criticism from American and Canadian business leaders and politicians during the 1970s.[74] Some American business leaders, for example, lobbied the government to discontinue the special transitional protective features of the pact which were designed to prevent the Canadian auto industry from being swamped as trade barriers were partially removed. Politicians also called for changes in the pact. Congressman Wilbur Mills, the powerful chairman of the House of Representatives Ways and Means Committee, demanded in 1972 that the U.S. International Trade Commission alter the agreement so that Canadian citizens could buy automobiles directly from American auto manufacturers, rather than having to buy through Canadian dealers.[75] In the same year, John Connally, the secretary of the treasury under Richard Nixon, also took a hard line on the trade agreements, arguing that the auto pact caused a major trade deficit with Canada.[76]

Canadian leaders, in return, voiced sharp criticism, charging that the auto pact made it easy for the United States automobile manufacturers "to export unemployment to Canada" by moving production of low production models to Canadian auto plants.[77]

On the other hand, the auto pact also had its advocates who lobbied effectively for its continuation. General Motors, Ford, and Chrysler were steadfast in their support for the pact.[78] Their position was endorsed finally in 1975 by the U.S. International Trade Commission. In its report, the commission acknowledged that the auto pact had worked more to the advantage of Canada than the United States, but it claimed "that the comparative advantages to Canada have not been so great as some U.S. sources have charged."[79] Although the Ambassador Bridge was not involved in the discussions, it was one of the main beneficiaries of the auto pact, so its representatives monitored the controversy with vested interest. From 1965, when the pact was first approved, the volume of trucks crossing the Ambassador Bridge rose sharply from 286,000 in 1964 to 628,000 in 1969, 895,000 in 1974 and 988,000 by the end of the decade.[80]

Automobile and related traffic also increased steadily during the 1970s. In 1970, for example, there were three and one-half million crossings, excluding trucks. By 1974, the count had risen to four million. Five years later, in 1979, the traffic count, excluding trucks, was 4,361,000 with an overall total, including trucks, of 5,349,000 vehicle crossings.[81]

Also impressive during the 1970s was the comparison of vehicular traffic between the Ambassador Bridge and the Detroit and Windsor Tunnel. In 1969, for example, the bridge controlled forty-two percent of the total Detroit River crossings. But by 1974 the bridge's percentage had risen to forty-

The Ambassador Bridge, February 27, 1976. (Courtesy of the *Windsor Star*.)

eight percent; and by 1979 the bridge was capturing fifty percent of the river crossings.[82]

A significant contributing factor in the competition between the bridge and the tunnel was the bridge's dominant control of truck traffic between Detroit and Windsor. Furthermore, by the 1970s the bridge was becoming directly connected to the major interstate highways in Michigan and had convenient access to the MacDonald-Cartier Freeway or Route 401 in Ontario. Although the tunnel had a higher weight limit than the bridge—it also had a height restriction of twelve feet, eight inches. The bridge had the added advantage of providing four traffic lanes, as compared to two in the tunnel. Truck toll rates in the 1970s favored the bridge significantly—$.01 per one hundred pounds versus $.0125 for the tunnel.[83]

Although inadequate custom inspection facilities at the United States end of the bridge were a problem, the bridge was favored by an increasing number of commercial operators. The control of truck traffic had direct economic consequences for the Ambassador Bridge. Although the ratio between tolls for trucks and automobiles did not maintain the early twelve-to-one standing, the difference was substantial. In 1976, for example, the average toll for a truck was $4.38, as compared to $.69 for an automobile.[84]

During its fifth decade of operation, the bridge continued to gain financially. Although there were recessions and labor problems which undoubtedly decreased profits for the company, there was an overall increase in revenue from $4,824,208 in 1969 to $6,756,718 in 1978. The net earnings of the bridge increased from an average of $1,682,714 during the period 1969 to 1973, and $2,106,723 for the years 1974 to 1978. During the same time periods, the earnings per share averaged $1.33 and $1.66, respectively.[85]

A change in the toll rates in July 1971 also improved the financial status of the bridge. The rate for a passenger car was increased from sixty to seventy-five cents per car, but the ten-cent charge for each passenger was abolished. This toll change simplified collections procedures and facilitated motorist travel across the bridge.[86] There was no further toll adjustment until January 1, 1981, when the fee for autos and other passenger vehicles, including the driver and all passengers, was increased from $.75 to $1.00. Tolls for automobile trailers and motorcycles were raised at the same time to $.50 and $.75, respectively, and bus tolls were raised from $3.50 to $5.00. The commercial rates for trucks were increased for the first time since the bridge opened, from $.01 to $.0125 per one hundred pounds gross weight.[87]

Meanwhile, the decade of the 1970s also witnessed changes in the board of directors of the Detroit International Bridge Company. In 1975 Joseph W. Bower, another son of the bridge's founder, Joseph A. Bower, was elected to the board. A former partner in the certified public accounting firm of Coopers and Lybrand of New York and a resident of Connecticut, the young

Bower continued the interest of the Bower family in the Ambassador Bridge.[88] Two years later he replaced his brother, Robert, as chairman of the board of directors, although the latter continued to serve as a director and consultant to the company. Later in the year, on August 15, 1977, Joseph A. Bower died at the age of ninety-six, ending more than fifty years of close association with the Ambassador Bridge.[89]

Two other key board members left the board of directors in 1976—Arthur H. Lamborn of New York, who had served since 1965, and Victor W. Klein of Detroit, who had been a director since 1962 and for several decades before had been associated with the Detroit International Bridge Company as a member of the company's general counsel. In place of Klein, Harold A. Ruemenapp of St. Clair Shores, Michigan, a member of the law firm of Butzel, Long, Bust, Klein and Van Zile of Detroit, was elected as the general counsel for the Ambassador Bridge. Ellis Merry, formerly chairman of the board of the National Bank of Detroit, after only two years, also retired from the board of directors in 1976. The following year, Charles T. Munger, chairman of the board of Blue Chips, was elected to the bridge company's board of directors.[90]

The Bower era ended in March 1979 when Joseph W. and Robert A. Bower retired from the board of directors. For the first time since the bridge opened, a Bower was not among the leadership of the Detroit International Bridge Company.[91]

As the Detroit International Bridge Company increased its business from commercial trucking and automobile traffic and improved its financial condition, there were numerous attempts to buy out the stock of the bridge and later control the bridge company. In 1960 a New York promoter tried to arrange the purchase of the bridge and the Detroit and Windsor Tunnel by a sale of revenue bonds, with the bridge and tunnel to be operated by a Detroit port authority.[92] In the fall of 1971 another New York group formed the IPEX Group for the purpose of buying out the bridge's stockholders. Led by four New Yorkers, IPEX proposed to acquire all of the assets of the bridge with minimal capital investment of its own. Although the proposed price of $32.50 per share was four dollars above the September market price, there was immediate opposition to the proposed sale by the Harry T. Schaub Investment Firm of New York, which had for years been associated with the bridge. Schaub claimed that the asking price of $32.50 was too low and advised the stockholders that the price should be at least $39.50 per share.[93]

By February 1972, IPEX had modified its offer to provide for a merger with the Detroit International Bridge Company. The new terms provided that the shareholders of the bridge would receive thirty-four dollars for each share of stock in cash and a half share of IPEX for each share in the Detroit International Bridge Company.[94]

The IPEX merger proposal was subject to the approval of the bridge company stockholders and a favorable ruling by the U.S. Internal Revenue Service and the Canadian government for the sale of the wholly-owned Canadian Transit Company. Although the proposal, which required a two-thirds vote of the stockholders, passed by 72 percent, the Canadian government failed to give its approval for the merger.[95]

After the failure of the IPEX proposed merger, the board of directors received inquiries from other investment groups interested in acquiring ownership and control of the bridge. After careful consideration of the proposals, the board notified bridge stockholders that because the new proposals were similar to the IPEX plan "the Board does not believe that it would be in the present interest of the Company or its stockholders to pursue such inquiries."[96]

According to Roy G. Lancaster and Robert A. Bower on March 1, 1973, "the Bridge is not being offered for sale."[97]

The IPEX proposal did result in the announcement in 1973 by the Canadian government of new requirements for any change in ownership of the Ambassador Bridge. These announcements included provisions that any effort to purchase bridge assets shall include a commitment to convey the Canadian portion of the bridge to the Canadian or Ontario government at no cost in twenty-five years; that resident Canadians participate in the management of the bridge; that tolls subject to Canadian control be collected on the Windsor end; that the company continue to provide accommodations for customs and immigration personnel; that land not needed for the operation of the bridge be conveyed to the Canadian government at no cost; and finally, that a fair portion of maintenance labor and materials be obtained from Canadian sources. The Canadian Foreign Investment Review Agency (FIRA), formed in 1973, was given authority to determine whether any proposed sale was in the best interests of the Canadian government.[98]

The death of Joseph A. Bower in 1977 and the decision of the members of the Bower family to withdraw from participation in the management of the bridge led to renewed interest in the sale of the bridge. During 1977, several investment firms expressed interest in acquiring the bridge company. The WESCO Financial Corporation of California made a cash tender offer for the bridge and increased WESCO's common stock holdings in the company from 10.6 percent to 25 percent. A Detroit business, The Central Cartage Company, whose application to FIRA had been rejected in 1975, increased its investment in the bridge by over-the-counter market purchases and, by January 1, 1978, it owned approximately

22 percent of the Bridge's common stock. Moreover, by March 1, 1979, Central Cartage held about 24.6 percent of the common stock.[99]

Two weeks later, on March 13, 1979, the Detroit International Bridge Company was notified that Central Cartage had arranged the purchase of the shares of common stock held by WESCO interests in the bridge company for a purchase price of twenty-four dollars per share, representing another 24.9 percent of the outstanding common stock. Shortly thereafter, the Central Cartage Company, now owning 49.5 percent of the bridge, offered to buy the remaining stock at twenty-five dollars per share. Under the proposal, the bridge company would become a wholly-owned subsidiary of the Central Cartage Company.[100] On July 31, 1979, the plan was approved by the bridge company's shareholders. Thus the ownership of the Ambassador Bridge changed hands just three and a half months before the bridge celebrated its fiftieth anniversary.[101]

The change in ownership resulted in a major turnover in the directors of the Ambassador Bridge. At the stockholders' meeting, held March 23, 1979, Ronald W. Lech and Larry Mason, executive officers of Central Cartage Company, and Bert Mendelson and Don Rafelman, of Toronto, Ontario, were elected to the board of directors. Roy G. Lancaster and Charles J. Clark of Windsor were reelected and Lancaster was reelected president and designated chief executive officer.[102]

The Central Cartage Company, with headquarters in Sterling Heights, Michigan, is a family-owned firm under the direction of Manuel J. Moroun. Associated with Moroun have been his father, Tufeck J. Moroun, and three sisters: Florence Moroun McBrien, Agnes Ann Moroun, and Victoria Moroun Baks.

The management of the Ambassador Bridge during the 1960s had fallen gradually into the control and direction of Roy G. Lancaster. As he demonstrated his ability to manage the bridge operation, he was given more responsibility by the board, fully supported by Joseph A. Bower and his family and, later, by the Moroun family. Battles with the General Services Administration were waged almost exclusively by Lancaster, without interference or involvement by the bridge company's board of directors. Although he had not had a role in the passage or renewal of the Canada-U.S. auto pact, Lancaster recognized the importance of the trade agreement, which resulted in a sharp increase of truck traffic over the Ambassador Bridge. His campaigns to improve truck inspection facilities, to increase U.S. Customs and Immigrations staffs, and to resolve the freeway traffic congestion problem at the bridge were all aimed at attracting even greater use of the bridge. If traffic statistics, net earnings, and stockholder dividends bear any testimony to his skill and management of the Detroit International Bridge Company, the decades of the 1960s and 1970s were a resounding success for Lancaster and the bridge.

CHAPTER 14

The Challenge of the Future:
A Necklace of Lights

In 1979 Roy G. Lancaster and bridge officials made plans for special ceremonies to commemorate the fiftieth anniversary of the opening of the Ambassador Bridge. The continued public interest in the span led to widespread coverage of the event by the news media. Local television and radio stations, newspapers, journals, and magazines featured stories and accounts of the building of the bridge and its achievements over five decades. Charles Evan Fowler, Joseph A. Bower, and Roy G. Lancaster were given special recognition for their individual contributions.[1]

On November 7, 1979, the Detroit International Bridge Company hosted a fiftieth anniversary reception at the Cleary Auditorium in Windsor. Speakers extolled the accomplishments of the Ambassador Bridge and the important role that it had played in the recent history of the Windsor and Detroit areas. Roy Lancaster, who chaired the ceremony, gave tribute to Joseph A. Bower and his role in bridge affairs for more than fifty years.[2] The unveiling of an oil painting of the bridge by a young De-

troit artist, Robert Gniewek, and the showing of the original Movietone news film of the 1929 opening day ceremonies were highlights of the affair.

Among the special guests at the anniversary celebration were Robert A. Bower, recently retired chairman of the Detroit International Bridge Company, and the new owners of the bridge company, the Moroun family of Grosse Pointe, Michigan. Former bridge directors, Victor Klein, Philip L. Carret, H. Peter Schaub, and longtime bridge employee Elmer Paquette were cited for their contributions to the bridge. Also featured were C. G. Russell Armstrong of Windsor, Ontario, who had conducted the original survey work on the bridge and the Honorable Paul Martin, also of Windsor, Canada's high commissioner to Britain, who fifty years earlier was one of the young lawyers who assisted Joseph Bower in acquiring the property on which the bridge was built in the old town of Sandwich, Ontario. Mayor Bert Weeks of Windsor and Philip Meathe, president of the Greater Detroit Chamber of Commerce and president of Smith, Hinchman and Grylls of Detroit, who had been architectural consultants to the bridge, also participated in the ceremony.

On November 10, members of local vintage car clubs crossed the Ambassador Bridge in a caravan of forty-four cars from the 1920s and 1930s, commemorating a similar crossing of automobiles fifty years before. The tour ended with a luncheon banquet at the University of Windsor.[3]

The fiftieth anniversary ceremony, in a real sense, marked the end of an era in the management of the Ambassador Bridge. The Bower family, so prominent in the development, construction, and leadership of the span, had retired completely from all involvement in its operation. The Central Cartage Company of Sterling Heights, Michigan, under Manuel Moroun and his

The fiftieth anniversary. *From left:* Hugh Pratley, bridge inspector, Roy Lancaster, and Chester Comstock of Modjeski and Masters, consulting firm. (Courtesy of the D.I.B. Archives.)

Unveiling the painting of the bridge at the fiftieth anniversary, November 7, 1979. From left: Charles Clark and Roy G. Lancaster. (Courtesy of the D.I.B. Archives.)

The fiftieth anniversary. *From left:* Frank V. Kefalas, vice-president and treasurer, Roy Lancaster, Elmer Paquette, and John L. Hannan, operations manager. (Courtesy of the D.I.B. Archives.)

Bridge staff at the fiftieth anniversary ceremony. *From left:* Margarita (Besieris) Kaiafas, Patricia Fredley, Dorothy Saull, Janet Goralski, Sandra Boucher, Elvia Martinez, Dorothy Togalski, Elaine (Shindel) Klaus, and Elaine Contreras. (Courtesy of the D.I.B. Archives.)

The Ambassador Bridge

family, now owned the Detroit International Bridge Company. Roy G. Lancaster, who had been reelected president of the bridge company earlier in the year, retained the key management position which he had held since 1967.[4]

The year 1981 witnessed a magnificent change in the appearance of the Ambassador Bridge, at least during the nighttime hours, when a necklace of lights was hung on the cables of the span. As early as 1969, when the bridge roadway lights were completely rewired, a plan to light the cables of the bridge was considered by bridge directors on the recommendation of Roy Lancaster. The cost of installation in 1969 was estimated at $69,000, with an additional $9,600 for the lead wiring. Because of extensive renovation of the roadway planned for the following year, the lead wiring was installed at that time.[5]

In the summer of 1981, the lighting project was revived by the inquiry of Diane Edgecomb, president of the Detroit Central Business District Association, who had been asked by Detroit Mayor Coleman A. Young "to add some spark to the city this season as it hosts the National League of Cities Convention and the Super Bowl."[6] Mrs. Edgecomb approached Roy Lancaster regarding lighting the cables of the bridge and was surprised to learn that such lighting had been considered earlier and the necessary lead wiring had already been installed. Lancaster contacted the Motor City Electric Company of Detroit and Tucker Electric of Windsor, the two firms which had accomplished the rewiring of the roadway lighting on the bridge in 1969. The mayors of Detroit and Windsor heartily endorsed the project.[7]

The cost of installing the new lights, which had risen to approximately $150,000 in 1981, was shared by a number of groups, including contractors, public utilities, the Windsor City Council, and private dona-tions. The Ambassador Bridge contributed half the cost of the project and agreed to assume the annual maintenance cost of electrical power for the high-pressure sodium vapor lights.[8]

The laying of the light cables was carefully planned and involved the cooperative efforts of Canadian and American electrical workers. After carefully determining the length needed, the wire was coiled onto huge spools which were raised by a helicopter above the span. On October 19, 1981, the huge helicopter hovered seventy-five feet above the span, dangling a six-foot, round, two-hundred-pound reel, with an electrical brake attached, and carrying thirteen hundred pounds of cable about two miles long. Slowly, it lowered the wire to electricians and bridge employees who were stationed atop the main cables. It took only thirty-five minutes to lay each wire of the two spools on each cable of the bridge. The wires were immediately fastened to the bridge cables. It took several weeks more "to install the supports and insulators needed to fasten the new electrical wire, then mount and connect the sixty-pound lamps every sixty feet along the suspension cables."[9]

On November 23, 1981, at the annual "Detroit Aglow" ceremony, Mayor Bert Weeks of Windsor and Mayor Coleman Young of Detroit jointly threw the switch for the lights, kicking off the holiday season in both communities.[10] Since that time, the lights have been controlled automatically, turning on at dusk and off again before dawn.

The "necklace of lights" was, from the beginning, a great success and was heralded by citizens and motorists on both sides of the Detroit River. People driving west from Chatham, Ontario, or north from Toledo on Interstate 75, as well as ship captains, sailors, and airline pilots approaching Detroit and Windsor, now view the lighted

Ambassador Bridge as a landmark. Thousands of tourists and convention visitors at the Joe Louis Sports Arena, Cobo Convention Hall, and the Renaissance Center in downtown Detroit, as well as in the hotels and business district of Windsor, have seen and no doubt admired the necklace of lights against the evening sky. It remains one of the unique architectural features of the Detroit-Windsor area.

The recognition attracted by the new lighting of the bridge was well received by Lancaster and city officials. Also a source of great satisfaction to the bridge leadership were the traffic statistics recorded between 1979 and 1985. The total vehicular crossings rose during those five years from 5.35 million to more than 6.25 million. Automobile traffic increased by 7.5 percent. Even more impressive was the rise in truck crossings, from 1 million to 1.55 million, a 26.5 percent increase. Since 1984, the ratio of an average truck toll compared to a single automobile was 7.5 to 1. The increased use of the bridge by trucking companies was therefore especially significant.[11]

The relative traffic use between the Ambassador Bridge and the Detroit and Windsor Tunnel reflects motorist and carrier preference for the span over the river. The bridge had a slight edge in 1979—5,350,000 to 5,285,000. The tunnel led in vehicle crossings until 1975, when the bridge took the lead for two years. Because of the bridge employee strike in 1978, the bridge lost the lead for that year, regaining it in 1979. Traffic was comparatively equal until 1983, when the bridge took a significant lead, which it has maintained since that time. Even more important, in terms of income, was the bridge's dominance in commercial truck crossings. Truck traffic crossing the span is approximately ten times that using the tunnel. By 1984 the Ambassador Bridge was second only to the Peace bridge between Buffalo, New York, and Fort Erie,

Ontario, in total border crossings between the United States and Canada.[12]

In looking back upon the history of the Ambassador Bridge and its operation during the first fifty-eight years, the management of the bridge looms large as a reason for its success. Despite the difficult financial crises of the depression years and the restraints of World War II, the bridge was always properly maintained and kept in excellent condition. Fortunately, McClintic and Marshall had designed and constructed a bridge capable of handling far more than the traffic of 1929. As a result, the bridge was able to accommodate a steadily increasing volume of traffic, especially in the years following World War II.

The manner in which the management responded to the various problems facing the bridge was essential to the bridge's survival. Under the leadership of Joseph A. Bower, R. Bryson McDougald, C. Clinton Campbell, and Roy G. Lancaster, as well as key members of the board of directors, including Robert A. and Joseph W. Bower, the Ambassador Bridge was able to overcome these obstacles and prosper, unlike the countless business enterprises which failed during this period.

The challenges facing the bridge leadership began the day the span was opened on November 11, 1929. The stock market crash had occurred only two weeks earlier and within one year the company had defaulted on its bond and interest payments. Joseph A. Bower provided the leadership to win the support of the stockholders until he was able to reorganize the company in 1938. Bower also successfully fought the local, county, state, and provincial governments to win more equitable tax treatment for the bridge during these trying times.

The bridge also survived the restrictions of World War II, with its gasoline rationing, curbs upon the purchase of foreign goods, foreign exchange controls, and

Installing the necklace of lights. (Courtesy of the D.I.B. Archives.)

Sikorsky helicopter hovering over the bridge with a spool of wire, October 20, 1981. (Courtesy of the *Windsor Star*.)

Electricians Walter and Mike Warden look up at the helicopter, November 7, 1981. (Courtesy of the *Windsor Star*.)

Bart Tucker installs wires for lights, November 7, 1981. (Courtesy of the *Windsor Star.*)

shortage of automobiles. The company provided adequate security for the bridge until Canadian and U.S. military forces were available to guard the structure. The bridge leadership also led an effective campaign for "in bond" shipment of goods by commercial trucks across southern Ontario between Detroit and Buffalo and won the battle with U.S. Immigration over the issue of overtime pay for weekend duty for customs and immigration officers.

The postwar period likewise witnessed a myriad of serious problems for the bridge management. The difficulties of conversion to a peacetime economy in the United States and Canada and a series of economic recessions plagued the bridge. Labor unrest in the auto and truck industries during the 1960s and 1960s and a major controversy with U.S. Customs and Immigration over

Electricians attach lights to the main Canadian tower, November 7, 1981. (Courtesy of the *Windsor Star.*)

adequate staffing and provision of increased facilities for Canada Customs without capital reimbursement required the constant attention of bridge officials and interrupted the normal day-to-day operation of the bridge.

Competition from the Detroit and Windsor Tunnel, the Detroit-Windsor railroad tunnel, and U.S. and Canadian railroad companies taxed the energies of the bridge administrators, as well. The Ambassador Bridge had to compete constantly in the early years for motorists and commercial trucking and to fight for legislation on the federal, state, and provincial levels designed to allow the bridge to retain a competitive position. Although the eventual location of the interstate freeway system in southeastern Michigan and the proximity of the MacDonald-Cartier Highway 401 in Ontario gave the Ambassador Bridge a logistical advantage over its competitors, bridge managers had to campaign vigorously and continually to maintain and increase the bridge's share of the growing market.

The lengthy controversy between the bridge and the General Services Administration over the issue of acceptance of an off-site customs clearance facility to be provided by the bridge company cost the management of the bridge considerable time and resources. Eventually, the problem was temporarily resolved by the opening of the customs cargo clearance facility at the former trucking terminal immediately adjacent to the U.S. plaza. It is not the final solution to the truck customs inspection problems.

At the same time, the congestion at the U.S. plaza was another major and long-standing problem which has faced the bridge since the mid 1960s. Even without a sharp increase in traffic crossings, there would have been a serious and hazardous traffic problem at the plaza. The location of Interstate 75 and Interstate 96 immediately

adjacent to the bridge plaza has compounded the problem. The traffic bottleneck and the inadequate customs staffing remain as unfinished business for the bridge management.

The problems facing the bridge in the coming decade do not end with those of providing adequate inspection facilities and easing traffic congestion. Other challenges, as serious as any faced by the bridge in its first fifty-eight years, are surfacing. For example, the Detroit-Windsor railroad tunnel may challenge the competitive position of the bridge. Since it opened in 1909, this railroad tunnel has attracted a constant volume of railroad freight traffic.

In December 1984, after years of negotiations, the Detroit River Tunnel Company and the Canada Southern Railway were acquired from the Consolidated Rail Corporation of Philadelphia by the Canadian National and Canadian Pacific railways of Montreal. As a part of the purchase agreement, the latter company acquired the "1,146 foot double track bridge near Niagara Falls and 225 miles of track linking Buffalo and Detroit along the north shore of Lake Erie."[13] The new owners took immediate steps to study the feasibility of enlarging the walls of the Detroit-Windsor rail tunnel "to accommodate specially designed railroad cars which would carry automobiles, semi-trailers and other over-sized loads."[14]

The implications of the proposed tunnel were obvious to railroad and Ambassador Bridge officials. A larger tunnel, capable of handling large loads, would allow diversion of railroad traffic between Canada and the United States from Sarnia, Ontario, and Port Huron, Michigan, to Detroit. Other plans called for the development of a new "laser piggyback service that would link Toronto and Cincinnati" via the Detroit-Windsor railroad tunnel, thereby saving about fifteen hours of travel, as com-

Traffic backed up to the Canadian side, May 29, 1984. (Courtesy of
John Sullivan, Aerial Associates, Ann Arbor, Michigan.)

pared to the Port Huron–Sarnia route.[15] A new railroad freight service between Montreal and Chicago, starting in September 1985, has also been announced. Although these plans are directed to new trade markets, the potential competition with commercial trucking firms which now serve as the profitable backbone of the users of the Ambasssador Bridge is a source of some concern to bridge officials.[16]

A more serious potential challenge to the competitive position of the Ambassador Bridge is the Blue Water Bridge, connecting Sarnia and Port Huron over the St. Clair River. Recent engineering studies, conducted jointly by the Ontario Ministry of Transportation and Communications, Transport Canada, the U.S. Federal Highway Administration, and the Michigan Department of Transportation formed the basis for a state of Michigan announcement in 1983 of plans to improve the plaza on the American side of the Blue Water Bridge. The plans call for new facilities for primary and secondary customs inspections, toll collection, bridge administration, and maintenance and access roadways. The estimated $25 million cost of these renovations will be borne by the state of Michigan from public tax revenues.[17] The Michigan Department of Transportation has also announced provision in the future for the construction of a second bridge just south of and adjacent to the Blue Water Bridge.

Yet another development which will have a direct bearing on the future fortunes of the Ambassador Bridge, and over which the bridge has little control, is the fate of the Canada-U.S. auto pact. Since the pact was signed by Prime Minister Lester Pearson and President Lyndon B. Johnson on January 16, 1965, it has provided a phenomenal stimulus to the use of the Ambassador Bridge by commercial trucking transport of new automobiles and auto parts. Truck crossings over the Ambassador Bridge, for example, increased from 286,000 in 1964 to 895,000 in 1974, and to 1,457,000 in 1984, an overall gain of 67.2 percent. Figures for 1985 and 1986 show this increase continuing.[18]

Although the auto pact has received the continuous support of auto manufacturers, prominent business and labor leaders, and public officials on both sides of the border, there has also been strong opposition to it. Some free trade advocates in the United States have sharply criticized the pact for its alleged preferential treatment of Canadian auto and parts manufacturers, especially the provision which established a ratio governing Canada's share of the automobile market, calling for it to build cars in the same ratio as it consumes them. They argue that these conditions, imposed upon the auto producers by the Canadian government, "were meant to be 'transitional' safeguards only" and should be removed in order "to achieve unrestricted free trade in the North American automotive industry."[19] The prohibition against Canadian consumers buying automobiles directly from American dealers has also been a target of opponents of the pact ever since it was signed.[20]

With its twenty-year history, it is unlikely that the auto pact will be altered substantially in the near future. Some experts, however, have raised serious questions about the long-term survival of the pact. In addition to political considerations, they cite such vexing problems as the recent division between Canadian and American automobile workers, the establishment of Japanese and other foreign automobile plants in the United States, and the relocation of auto plants in Mexico and Korea.[21] Management of the Ambassador Bridge, like that of other businesses, is sure to be affected by changes in, or abandonment of, the pact, but will have to await the outcome and live with the ensuing results.

Meanwhile, new developments in

trans-Atlantic ship transportation have had an effect on railroad transport and commercial trucking between the East Coast and western Ontario and the Midwest. This will undoubtedly have a major impact upon the use of the Ambassador Bridge. During the past twenty years, new super vessels have been built to travel between ports in Europe and North American ports such as Philadelphia, New York, Boston, Montreal, and Quebec City. The introduction of innovations such as containerization and intermodal services has revolutionized ship transportation. Standard-size containers for storing goods not only fit on the ships, but can be easily transferred to trucks and railroad cars. Increasingly, larger ships have been off-loading at Montreal and Quebec City, transferring containers to rail and truck, rather than the usual course, sailing up the St. Lawrence Seaway and across lakes Ontario, Erie, and Michigan to their destinations. Not only does the transfer to rail and truck save several days' time, which can be critical in the preservation of some goods, but during the winter months when the St. Lawrence Seaway and upper Great Lakes are closed to shipping, the "overland-bridge" system provides a continuous and reliable flow of goods from Europe to inland North America.[22]

The increasing shipment of cargo by air will also affect traditional means of rail, ship, and truck transportation. Many large metropolitan centers in Canada and the United States are enlarging their airport facilities to handle such commerce. During the spring of 1985, for example, the Detroit Metropolitan Airport improved its air cargo center, adding three new warehouses and adopting an aggressive plan to attract more air freight business.[23]

Bridge officials are well aware of the long-range impact these trends will have upon the commercial use of the Ambassador Bridge. A comprehensive study is underway of the transportation facilities needed in the Detroit-Windsor area and the changes and future trends of commercial goods shipment from eastern seaports to the upper Great Lakes business centers.

Also among the plans of bridge officials designed to keep pace with the changing transportation and tourism industries is a new travel information center adjacent to the Detroit plaza of the bridge. Such a facility has been high on the agenda of Roy Lancaster since the idea was first introduced by him to the Federal Highway Administration during Mrs. Lyndon Johnson's beautification program and later initiated by the Detroit City Council in 1974. In that year the council petitioned the Michigan Department of Transportation to develop a travel center in Detroit, noting that Detroit was "the only major access point into the United States and Michigan which does not have state supported Tourist Information facilities." It recommended two sites for consideration by the state—the Detroit and Windsor Tunnel and the Ambassador Bridge.[24]

The Michigan Department of Transportation responded promptly and favorably to the council's petition and approved a detailed study of the two sites. When the findings were complete, the State Highway Commission, on October 22, 1975, voted to locate the proposed tourist information center at the Ambassador Bridge.[25] According to highway officials, the decision was based upon "the need for the information center to be readily accessible to the inter and intra state travel, as well as the international travellers."[26] An important factor in the commission's decision was the availability of federal aid for the project because of the bridge's location near Interstates 75 and 96.[27]

In 1976 the Highway Department established a project development team to gather data about possible sites for the travel center and to elicit information from the residents of the area near the bridge. One year later, in August 1977, a policy committee was formed "to guide the subsequent detailed study for the development of a Travel Information Center", consisting of representatives of the Hubbard-Richard District Community Council, the Detroit International Bridge Company, the Detroit Department of Transportation, the Detroit Community and Economic Development Department, the Michigan Department of Transportation, and, as an ex officio member, the U.S. Federal Highway Administration. A site area near or at the Ambassador Bridge had already been determined but the policy committee had the task of locating specific sites, preparing a design, protecting local community interests, and identifying proper access routes to the center.[28] Toward these ends, the policy committee selected and considered three sites near the bridge, held a public hearing, and analyzed the advantages and disadvantages of each. When their findings were reported in 1983, a site directly across and north of the bridge plaza on Porter Street was selected.[29]

Lancaster and Bridge officials were pleased with the recommendations of the policy committee of the Department of State Highways. The site selected would be convenient for motorists, and at the same time it would provide a reasonable solution to the long-standing traffic problems at the Bridge entrance and exit areas. In fact, bridge officials predict that the travel center will "resolve one of the major obstacles to a more efficient Bridge operation."[30] Furthermore, such a facility will complement the appearance of the plaza area and improve the entrance to the United States.

Even more promising are developments taking place in 1986 and 1987 involv-

ing the expansion of the U.S. Customs facilities for the clearance of trucks. Bridge officials, working with representatives of the Detroit Community and Economic Development Department, the Michigan Department of Transportation, the U.S. Customs Service, and the Hubbard-Richard District Community Council, have developed a proposal to establish a twenty-eight-acre area south of the bridge plaza for the clearance of trucks and other bridge-related activities. This plan is now undergoing an environmental impact study being conducted by the city of Detroit, which should be completed by mid-1987. Bridge officials feel confident that the expanded customs facilities could be available within two years.

The fact that the service of the Ambassador Bridge has expanded tremendously since it opened in 1929, without major reconstruction, is a tribute indeed to those with the vision to plan for its future usefulness. Its fifty-seven years of history are marked by the leadership of men who planned the structure; the expertise of engineers who built and maintained it; and the competence and resourcefulness of those who managed it. Although the success of the enterprise has, too often, been measured in terms of profit and revenue margins, the benefits from the bridge extend far and wide. It has done more than facilitate crossing of the Detroit River for people and vehicles. Reaching skyward, its magnificent towers give the populace of Detroit and Windsor, as well as traveling newcomers, a sight perhaps as awe-inspiring as that witnessed by Father Louis Hennepin, the Jesuit priest, who reported on the remarkable beauty of the natural Detroit River scene more than two hundred years ago.

Bridge Statistics   *Note:* All statistics are from *The Detroit River Bridge: An Engineering Record* (Pittsburgh: McClintic-Marshall Co., 1930).

General Dimensions

Length main piers	1850 feet
Length main pier to anchorage—United States	973 feet
Length main pier to anchorage—Canada	817 feet
Length approach viaduct—United States	1431 feet
Length approach viaduct—Canada	1419 feet
Length abutment to abutment	7490 feet
Total distance entrance to exit	9200 feet
Clear height at mid-span	152 feet
Clear height at harbor lines	135 feet
Maximum grade	5% for 777 feet
Roadway width	47 feet
Sidewalk width (one only)	8 feet

Roadway—reinforced concrete slabs on steel joists

Pavements—2½-inch sheet asphalt, except
    (1) on United States approach (5% grade), granite block
    (2) in terminals, concrete

Steelwork

Main Towers—shafts (silicon)	3605 tons
—bracing (carbon)	736 tons
Anchorages—eyebars (carbon)	570 tons
—grillage, girders, etc. (carbon)	219 tons
Cables (2 @ 8066, no. 6 galvanized wire)	3097 tons
Cast steel fittings	214 tons
Suspenders and hand rope (67,000 linear feet)	167 tons
Wrapping and miscellaneous	85 tons
Suspended span—trusses (silicon)	1547 tons
—floor (carbon)	2490 tons
Truss spans—columns and trusses (silicon)—United States	991 tons
—columns and trusses (silicon)—Canada	800 tons
—floor and bracing (carbon)—United States	690 tons
—floor and bracing (carbon)—Canada	568 tons

Approach viaducts (carbon)—
United States   2016 tons
Approach viaducts (carbon)—
Canada   3042 tons
Total steel and wire   **20,837 tons**
Total number of field rivets   **479,000**

Miscellaneous Quantities

Main piers—concrete   15,500 cu. yds.
        —granite   290 cu. yds.
Anchorages—substructure
        concrete   40,000 cu. yds.
        —superstructure
        concrete   14,150 cu. yds.
Subordinate piers—concrete   10,550 cu. yds.
Terminal walls—concrete   7,518 cu. yds.
Pavement slabs and sidewalks   8,790 cu. yds.
Total masonry   **96,798 cu. yds.**
Total excavation   **77,000 cu. yds.**
Pavements—granite block   13,007 sq. yds.
        —asphalt   26,292 sq. yds.
        —sheet concrete   21,603 sq. yds.
        —one-course
        concrete   30,867 sq. yds.
        —macadam   8,083 sq. yds.
Buildings—limestone and
        reinforced concrete   540,000 cu. ft.
Earth fill in terminals   192,300 cu. yds.

Chronology

Contract signed   July 20, 1927
Contract in effect   Aug. 16, 1927
Subcontract let for main piers
and anchorage substructures   Sept. 20, 1927
Tower base steel set on
main piers   Mar. 30, 1928
Anchorage steelwork erected
complete   June 22, 1928
Main tower completed—
United States   July 15, 1928
Main tower completed—
Canadian   July 27, 1928

Cable footbridge ropes placed
(celebration of first contact
shore to shore)   Aug. 8, 1928
Cable erection (heat-treated wire)
commenced   Sept. 24, 1928
Cable erection (heat-treated wire)
completed   Dec. 11, 1928
Cable and appurtenances
completed   Dec. 27, 1928
Footbridge ropes removed
complete   Feb. 7, 1929
Suspended span steel erection
commenced   Jan. 23, 1929
Erection discontinued   Feb. 28, 1929
Removal of main cables
(wire) commenced   May 16, 1929
Removal of main cables (wire)
completed   June 6, 1929
Cable erection (cold-drawn
wire) re-commenced   June 14, 1929
Cable erection (cold-drawn wire)
completed   Aug. 15, 1929
Cable compacted (main span)   Aug. 17, 1929
Suspended span steel erection
re-commenced   Aug. 29, 1929
Suspended span steel erection
completed   Sept. 27, 1929
Suspended span concreting
commenced   Sept. 27, 1929
Suspended span concreting
completed   Oct. 15, 1929
Approach steel in place—
United States   Mar. 17, 1929
Approach steel in place—
Canadian   Mar. 13, 1929
Approach concrete slabs
completed—U.S.   May 4, 1929
Approach concrete slabs
completed—Canadian   June 11, 1929
Terminal paving commenced—
United States   July 18, 1929
Terminal paving completed—
Canadian   Aug. 13, 1929

Terminal paving completed— United States	Aug. 27, 1929
Terminal paving completed— Canadian	Oct. 10, 1929
Terminal administration bldg. occupied—U.S.	Oct. 1, 1929
Terminal administration bldg. occupied—Canadian	Nov. 15, 1929
Granite block pavement completed—U.S. approach	Nov. 3, 1929
Asphalt pavement completed— Canadian approach	Oct. 29, 1929
Asphalt pavement completed— suspended span	Nov. 6, 1929
Dedication exercises (letter of preliminary acceptance dated)	Nov. 11, 1929
Bridge opened to traffic	Nov. 15, 1929
Elapsed time from effective date of contract	2 yrs., 3 mos.

Introduction

1. Louis Hennepin, *A New Discovery of a Vast Country in America* . . . (London: M. Bentley, 1698).

Chapter 1

1. Neil F. Morrison, *Garden Gateway to Canada* (Windsor: Herald Press, 1954), 30–37.

2. Silas Farmer, *The History of Detroit and Michigan*, 2 vols. (Detroit: Silas Farmer and Co., 1889), 1:890. For an account of the operation of railroad and other ferries between Detroit and Windsor, see J. J. Holton, D. H. Bedford, and Francis Cleary, "History of the Windsor and Detroit Ferries," *Ontario Historical Society Records and Papers*, 16 (1918): 40–51; Miriam M. Stimson, "From Shore to Shore," *Inland Seas*, 28 (Fall, 1972): 171–82; *Michigan Central Railroad Annual Report*, 1867, 23, and 1873, 14–15. In addition, the Local History File at the Burton Historical Collection, Detroit Public Library, has numerous citations and newspaper accounts relating to the Detroit-Windsor ferry service during the nineteenth and twentieth centuries.

3. Farmer, *History of Detroit*, 1:890.

4. U.S. Corps of Engineers, *Report of the Chief of Engineers, U.S. Army, 1874*, 597.

5. Corps of Engineers, *Report, 1874*, 607.

6. Ibid., 605–7.

7. For an account of James F. Joy, see Farmer, *History of Detroit*, 2:1059–62; and Milo Quaife, "Guide to James F. Joy," Biographical File, Burton Historical Collection.

8. For an account of the construction of the Detroit-Windsor tunnel, see Corps of Engineers, *Report, 1874*, 598. Also in this report is a copy of a paper on the tunnel by E. S. Ches-

brough, presented at the Society of Civil Engineers at Louisville, Kentucky, pp. 631–32; and a letter to the editor of the *Detroit Post* by D. D. McBean, superintendent of the tunnel works, pp. 619–20.

9. For the articles of association, see James F. Joy Papers, 25 and 29 Aug. 1871, Burton Historical Collection, Detroit Public Library. Among the directors, in addition to Joy, were Christian Buhl, Allen Sheldon, George N. W. Lothrop, William B. Wesson, N. W. Brooks, and Chauncey Hurlburt, all prominent Detroit businessmen. Of the total 5,000 shares, Joy controlled 4,994, representing a capital stock of $500,000.

10. Farmer, *History of Detroit*, 1:891; Detroit Common Council, *Journal, 1871–1872*, 82–83.

11. *Border Cities Star*, 6 Oct. 1925.

12. For additional accounts of the tunnel construction, see George Catlin, *The Story of Detroit* (Detroit: Detroit News Co., 1923), 553–54; Farmer, *History of Detroit*, 1:891. See also historical accounts from "Old Times in Windsor," *Border Cities Star*, 3 and 7 Oct. 1925; *Detroit Free Press*, 9 Nov. 1930 and 2 Nov. 1980. In addition, the James F. Joy Papers contain correspondence from E. S. Chesbrough to Joy, relating to the construction. See letters of 15 Jan. 1869 and 10 May 1873. See also Lake Carriers Association, *Annual Report, 1909*, 39–40.

13. For Chesbrough's and McBean's position on the issue, see Corps of Engineers, *Report, 1874*, 619–20, 631–33.

14. Ibid., 598.

15. Ibid., 594, 599–603; *Michigan Central Railroad Annual Report, 1872*, 9.

16. Farmer, *History of Detroit*, 1:891; *Toledo Blade*, 30 Jan. 1873, 8 Feb. 1873; *Border Cities Star*, 3 Oct. 1925.

17. *Michigan Central Railroad Annual Report, 1873*, 20–21.

18. *Detroit Free Press*, 1 Feb. 1873.

19. Corps of Engineers, *Report, 1874*, 588.

20. Ibid., 587–636.

21. Ibid., 604–9.

22. Among those who testified in favor of the bridge were Franklin Moore, Russell A. Alger, B. W. Gillett, Michael B. Kean, Allen Shelden, George B. Dickenson, Duncan Stewart, and Willard S. Pope.

23. Corps of Engineers, *Report, 1874*, 617.

24. Ibid., 616–18.

25. Ibid., 613.

26. Ibid., 616.

27. Ibid.; Catlin, *The Story of Detroit*, 552–53.

28. The three plans were described in detail in Corps of Engineers, *Report, 1874*, 600–602.

29. Corps of Engineers, *Report, 1874*, 604–5.

30. In his statement to the board of inquiry, Alger cited the captains of his two large tugboats, the *Torrent* and the *Vulcan*, William H. Rolls and Edward E. Hackett, respectively. Although the captains acknowledged that there were navigational problems on the Detroit River below Detroit at the "Limekilns" point, they stated that a "bridge with 160 foot would be no serious problem." When concluding his remarks, Alger offered a disclaimer that he had no interest in railroads and that he had "never received a dollar from them nor a pass in my life." Corps of Engineers, *Report, 1874*, 604–5.

31. Corps of Engineers, *Report, 1874*, 601, 604–9, 630–31; Lake Carriers Association, *Annual Report, 1907*, 40. A. B. Maynard, counsel for Michigan Central Railroad, and E. W. Meddaugh, counsel for the Canada Southern Railroad, notified the board of inquiry on Nov. 13, 1873, of their compromise "for the purpose," they stated, "of harmonizing as far as possible, the apparently conflicting interests between the vessel-owners and railroad companies."

32. Lake Carriers Association, *Annual Report, 1909*, 40–41. The Lake Carriers Association did not limit their lobbying efforts against the proposed Detroit-Windsor bridge to the U.S. Corps of Engineers inquiry. They also sent representatives to Washington, D.C., to pressure congressmen to oppose the plan. Led by William Livingstone and Captain J. T. Whiting of Detroit and Captain Henry Judson of Cleveland, they testified before several congressional committees.

33. All of the data gathered, including detailed statistical tables, were published in Corps of Engineers, *Report, 1874*, 590–600.

34. Ibid., 602–3.

35. Corps of Engineers, *Report, 1874*, 603.

36. Farmer, *History of Detroit*, 1:891; Lake Carriers Association, *Annual Report, 1909*, 41. According to Catlin, *The Story of Detroit*, 553, vessel owners denounced those who endorsed the bridge "as a lot of grafters and deadbeats who had come to Detroit on free passes, authorized by Mr. Joy, to put over a grab game for the railroads."

37. Corps of Engineers, *Report, 1874*, 633.

38. For accounts of the Trenton-Stony Island Railroad during the 1870s, see "Ambassador Bridge," E and M File, Burton Historical Collection, Detroit Public Library. In articles clipped from the *Detroit Free Press, Detroit Post-Tribune*, and *Detroit News*, the role of Cornelius Vanderbilt and other eastern financiers is described. See also *Toledo Blade*, 25 June 1872.

39. Catlin, *The Story of Detroit*, 554; Corps of Engineers, *Report, 1874*, 598, 633–34; Lake Carriers Association, *Annual Report, 1909*, 13; Farmer, *History of Detroit*, 1:891; *Detroit Free Press*, 9 Nov. 1930.

40. During the 1870s representatives of the board of trade campaigned throughout southern Michigan for support of the bridge. They formed a "Citizens Committee for a Bridge" in numerous cities and towns and submitted petitions to the U.S. Congress on behalf of the bridge. Among those involved were Ann Arbor, Chelsea, Dexter, Onondega, Centerville, Ypsilanti, Otsego Lake, and Detroit. On the other side of the issue, vessel interests solicited petitions against a bridge from groups in Wisconsin, New York, Ohio, and Minnesota. *U.S. Congressional Record, Index, 1874–1879*.

41. Farmer, *History of Detroit*, 1:891.

42. Ibid.

43. For an account of a meeting of Windsor citizens in April 1879, see "Ambassador Bridge," E and M File, Burton Historical Collection, Detroit Public Library. In Windsor, as in Detroit, there was a strong sentiment against a Belle Isle location as being "detrimental to the interests of the town." The mayor of Sandwich recommended his village as the site for the bridge. Farmer, *History of Detroit*, 1:891.

44. Corps of Engineers, *Report, 1880*, 1852–53.

45. For an account of the hearings and testimony presented by various interest groups, see Corps of Engineers, *Report, 1880*, 1852–61.

46. Ibid., 1854, 1857.

47. Ibid., 1854–55.

48. Lake Carriers Association, *Annual Report, 1909*, 41–42.

49. "Ambassador Bridge," E and M File, Burton Historical Collection, Detroit Public Library, 28 Mar. 1879.

50. Morrison, *Garden Gateway to Canada*, 123–24.

51. Corps of Engineers, *Report, 1890*, 3461; *U.S. Congressional Record, Index, 1880–1889*.

52. For a summary of the hearings, see Corps of Engineers, *Report, 1890*, 3456–64.

53. In 1879 Beecher had presented a proposal to finance the construction of a tunnel from Belle Isle to Walkerville, Ontario. He offered to give the entire income from his property for a period of from ten to thirty years at an estimated annual rate of $50,000. *Detroit Post-Tribune*, 1 Apr. 1879. Beecher was later involved in the development of a real estate venture in Windsor, "The New Bridge Subdivision," located on London Street and the riverfront area.

54. Corps of Engineers, *Report, 1890*, 3458.

55. Ibid., 3456–64.

56. Ibid., 3459–60.

57. Ibid.

58. Ibid., 3459.

59. Ibid.

60. Ibid.

61. Ibid.

62. Ibid.

63. Ibid., 3461; The bridge proposal also received the endorsement of the Detroit Common Council, which urged support by the Michigan state legislature and U.S. Congress. Detroit Common Council, *Journal*, 19 Feb. 1889.

64. Corps of Engineers, *Report, 1890*, 3462–64.

65. Lake Carriers Association, *Annual Report, 1890*, 42.

66. David P. Billington, *The Tower and the Bridge* (New York: Basic Books, 1983), 122–28.

67. *Detroit Free Press,* 17 Dec. 1895, 18 Dec. 1895, 14 Jan. 1896, 26 Jan. 1896, 31 Jan. 1896, 4 Feb. 1896, 12 Feb. 1896, 13 Feb. 1896; *Detroit Evening News,* 9 Dec. 1895, 29 Dec. 1895, 2 Jan. 1896, 3 Jan. 1896, 13 Jan. 1896, 16 Jan. 1896, 2 Feb. 1896, 4 Feb. 1896, 5 Feb. 1896; *Detroit Post-Tribune,* 17 Dec. 1895, 4 Jan. 1896, 13 Jan. 1896, 15 Jan. 1896, 31 Jan. 1896, 3 Feb. 1896, 15 Apr. 1896.

68. James F. Joy, who was no longer associated with the Michigan Central Railroad, and his son, Richard, announced their opposition to the bridge proposal, charging that it was introduced "entirely in the interest of the Michigan Central Railroad Company to the exclusion of all the roads." *Detroit Free Press,* 18 Dec. 1895.

69. Lake Carriers Association, *Annual Report, 1909,* 42.

70. *Detroit News,* 2 Feb. 1896.

71. *Detroit Post-Tribune,* 15 Apr. 1896. Senator McMillan "withdrew from placing the bill to a vote," because of a three-to-one estimated majority against the measure with the U.S. Senate.

72. Morrison, *Garden Gateway to Canada,* 186–87; *Detroit News,* 18 Apr. 1903; *Border Cities Star,* 15 Aug. 1919.

73. Morrison, *Garden Gateway to Canada,* 186–87; Detroit Board of Commerce, *Annual Report, 1904,* 13.

74. Morrison, *Garden Gateway to Canada,* 186–87; Detroit Common Council, *Journal, 1903–1904,* 26 Mar. 1903.

75. *Detroit Post-Tribune,* 10 Apr. 1903; Detroit Common Council, *Journal, 1903–1904,* 30 June 1903; *Detroit News,* 19 Apr. 1903.

76. For an account of the construction of the tunnel, see "Ambassador Bridge," E and M File, Burton Historical Collection, Detroit Public Library; Lake Carriers Association, *Annual Report, 1906,* 26; Lake Carriers Association, *Annual Report, 1909,* 42–45. Lake Carriers Association, *Annual Report, 1910,* 49; Rich Ratliff, "The Secret of the Tunnel," *Detroit Free Press,* 12 June 1983.

77. Lake Carriers Association, *Annual Report, 1909,* 46.

78. Catlin, *The Story of Detroit,* 558.

Chapter 2

1. "An International Bridge," *Detroit Saturday Night,* 14 June 1919.

2. *Detroiter,* 21 July 1919, 11; *Border Cities Star,* 23 July 1919 and 1 Aug. 1919.

3. The Waddell plan is described in *Border Cities Star,* 1 Aug. 1919.

4. *Detroit Saturday Night,* 27 Sept. 1919.

5. *Detroiter,* 21 July 1919, 11. In an editorial 5 July 1919, *Detroit Saturday Night* opposed the construction of another tunnel: "To us there is nothing inspiring about a ditch. It assuredly has its utilitarian features, but that is saying all." Mayor Couzens advised Mayor Winter of Windsor that he had received approval of W. E. Livingstone of the Great Lake Carriers Association for the construction of a "high bridge" over the Detroit River. *Border Cities Star,* 23 July 1919.

6. Charles Evan Fowler, "Progress Report of the Detroit-Windsor Bridge," July 1920, in the official files of the Detroit International Bridge Co. (hereafter cited as the D.I.B. Archives). According to the report, "Previous to this time or

beginning in August 1919, Mr. Fowler had made several trips to Detroit to obtain a general idea of the traffic conditions across the river and as to the desirability and feasibility of a bridge."

7. For a brief account of Lindenthal's career, see Billington, *The Tower and the Bridge,* 122–28.

8. Billington, *The Tower and the Bridge,* 125.

9. Billington, *The Tower and the Bridge,* 128. Ammann was associated with Lindenthal from 1912 to 1923 as chief engineer on both the Sciotoville and Hell Gate bridges. Ammann was perhaps best known for his design of the George Washington Bridge over the Hudson River and the Bayonne Bridge, both completed in 1931. For an account of Steinman, see Billington, *The Tower and the Bridge,* 141–46, and William Ratigan, *Highways over Broad Waters* (Grand Rapids, Mich.: William B. Eerdmans, 1959).

10. For a brief biography of Fowler, see *Who's Who in Engineering* (New York: Who's Who Publications, 1925), 725; *Detroiter,* 12 Jan. 1920, 19 July 1920, 6 Sept. 1921; *Michigan Manufacturer and Financial Record,* 29 Nov. 1919 and 10 Apr. 1920; and *Detroit River International Bridge* (Detroit: Douglass Printing, 1921). Fowler's proposed design for the San Francisco–Oakland Bay Bridge was not the one adopted in the 1930s, nor was Fowler involved in the design of the Lake Ponchartrain Causeway, built in 1955–1956.

11. Fowler, "Progress Report," 1–2.

12. In Fowler's "Progress Report" of 1920, a handwritten statement in the margin, p. 2, reads: "Lindenthal dropped out." It is undated.

13. Fowler credited Steinman with the work on computations on the structure. See Charles E. Fowler, *The Detroit-Windsor Bridge over the Detroit River* (New York: Douglass Printing, 1928), 14. According to David Steinman's official biography, Steinman, unemployed, called on Fowler at his New York office in March 1921 looking for work. Steinman had known Fowler in Seattle. Later, Steinman recalled that although Fowler had no work to offer him, he did suggest that Steinman rent "part of [Fowler's] office and hang out your shingle and start your own private practice." Steinman also remembered that Fowler bragged, "I've got Steinman in my office, working for me." Ratigan, *Highways over Broad Waters,* 129. Regardless of Steinman's disclaimers, he was identified with the project. See, for example, "Bridging the Detroit River," *Scientific American,* 126 (Feb. 1922): 88, where Steinman was cited as "chief assistant" to Fowler.

14. *Detroiter,* 12 Jan. 1920 and 25 Sept. 1920. *Michigan Manufacturer and Financial Record,* 10 Apr. 1920. Fowler, "Progress Report," 13–16.

15. Ibid., 15. Fowler also gave this traffic estimate to the Detroit-Windsor Bridge Committee of the Border Chamber of Commerce, 10 Aug. 1920; Minutes, Border Chamber of Commerce Collections, Series II, Subseries F, Box 12, File 117, University of Windsor Archives.

16. Fowler, "Progress Report," 16–17.

17. Livingstone to Fowler, 11 Nov. 1919, in Fowler, "Progress Report," 6. See also Fowler, *Detroit-Windsor Bridge over the Detroit River,* 1.

18. Fowler, *Detroit-Windsor Bridge over the Detroit River,* 2; Fowler, "Progress Report," 6–7.

19. *Detroit News,* 3 Aug. 1921; Fowler, "Progress Report," 1920, 6–7.

20. Fowler, *Detroit-Windsor Bridge over the Detroit River,* 14; Fowler, "Progress Report," 4–5, 8–11.

21. The Articles of Incorporation of the American and Canadian transit companies are in the D.I.B. Archives.

22. This agreement is in the D.I.B. Archives.

23. The statements of Pegram, Burr, Monsarrat, and Young of 10 and 15 Aug. 1921 were published in Fowler, *Detroit-Windsor Bridge over the Detroit River*, 15–16; "Fundamentals of Design" (1921), files of Hugh Pratley, Montreal.

24. *Detroiter*, 17 July 1920, 3–4; 16 Oct. 1920, 5; 3 Dec. 1921, 5; Fowler, "Progress Report," 1–2; *Detroit Times*, 16 July 1920. The board of commerce also provided lobby space for Fowler to display cable sections from the Manhattan-Brooklyn suspension bridge. *Detroiter*, 25 Sept. 1920. The Border City Chamber of Commerce assisted Fowler in his bridge campaign. Fowler, "Progress Report," 3; Border City Chamber of Commerce, Minutes, 20 Oct. 1920, University of Windsor Archives.

25. Fowler, "Progress Report," 1–2.

26. *Detroiter*, 16 Oct. 1920, 5 and 2 May 1927.

27. "Detroit and Border Cities United by Bridge," *Detroit River International Bridge*.

28. Typical of the numerous newspaper accounts of Fowler's speeches on behalf of the proposed bridge was the one to the second annual banquet of the Border Cities Real Estate Board. He was warmly received by the audience and received a standing ovation at the end of the meeting. *Border Cities Star*, 28 Jan. 1920.

Fowler not only received widespread publicity for his bridge proposal in the local press, but also attracted the attention of national journals and magazines. See, for example, C. R. Young, "Characteristics of Long-Span Suspension Bridges," *The Canadian Engineer*, 39 (4 Nov. 1920): 483–86; "Work on the Detroit River Bridge to Begin in 1922," *Railway Age*, 71 (20 Aug. 1921): 343–44; "Eight-Cable Suspension Bridge of 1803 Feet Span for Detroit," *Engineering News-Record*, 87 (29 Sept. 1921): 524–26; "Bridging the Detroit River," *Scientific American*, 126 (Feb 1922): 88–89; "Huge International Bridge Across the Detroit River," *Popular Mechanics*, Apr. 1922; and "Detroit River Bridge Project Again Under Discussion," *Engineering News-Record*, 94 (21 May 1925): 868.

29. Fowler, "Progress Report," 18–22.

30. Ibid., 18.

31. Ibid., 18; "Meeting of Detroit-Windsor Bridge Committee," Border Cities Chamber of Commerce, Minutes, 10 Aug. 1920, University of Windsor Archives.

32. Fowler, "Progress Report," 19; House of Commons of Canada, Fifth Sess., 13th Parliament, 11–12 George V, 1921, Bill 32, passed 8 Apr. 1921.

33. *Detroiter*, 12 Mar. 1921, 7, and 9 Apr. 1921, 4.

34. Fowler, "Progress Report," 21. Not all Canadian officials endorsed every aspect of Fowler's plan. Premier Drury of the Province of Ontario favored the bridge project, but he recommended that it be built by "Province of Ontario, the State of Michigan and federal governments," not by private capital. Border Chamber of Commerce, Minutes, 20 Oct. 1920, University of Windsor Archives.

35. For a copy of the Harding letter, see Fowler, *Detroit-Windsor Bridge over the Detroit River*, 5.

36. *Detroiter*, 23 July 1921, 4.

37. *Detroit Times*, 23 Jan. 1922.

38. *Michigan Manufacturer and Financial Record*, 11 Nov. 1921; *Detroiter*, 23 July 1921, 9 Feb. 1922; *Detroit News*, 3 Aug. 1921;

Detroit Free Press, 23 Oct. 1927; *Toronto Star*, 27 Dec. 1921; *Border Cities Star*, 9 Nov. 1929; and *Detroit Times*, 10 Oct. 1927.

39. *Michigan Manufacturer and Financial Record*, 29 Apr. 1922; *Border Cities Star*, 8 Apr. 1922. See also Border Chamber of Commerce, Minutes, 8 Sept. 1921, University of Windsor Archives.

40. *Detroit Free Press*, 21 June 1925 and 11 Oct. 1927; *Border Cities Star*, 9 Nov. 1929; *Detroit Times*, 10 Oct. 1927; *New York Times*, 27 Oct. 1927.

41. Arthur Woodford and Frank B. Woodford, *All Our Yesterdays* (Detroit: Wayne State University Press, 1969), 280–81.

42. McClintic-Marshall, the construction firm which built the Ambassador Bridge, gave credit to Fowler for his contribution. *Detroit International Bridge* (New York: Detroit International Bridge Co., 1928), 8.

Chapter 3

1. J. B. McMechan, "How Mr. Bower Built the Ambassador Bridge," *Detroiter*, May 1973, 18, 20. *Spanning Half a Century* (Detroit: Detroit International Bridge Co., 1979), 1. See also Helen Austin Sumner, interview with author, San Marcos, California, 12 Mar. 1983, D.I.B. Archives.

2. For an account of the meeting between Austin and Bower, see J. W. Austin, News Release, 3 Sept. 1925, Publicity File, D.I.B. Archives. See also *Detroit Free Press*, 21 June 1925; *Border Cities Star*, 29 June 1927. For an account of the McClintic-Marshall firm, see "Data Relative to the Fair Market Value of McClintic-Marshall," Schwab Information Center, Bethlehem Steel Corp., Bethlehem, Pennsylvania.

3. *Detroit Free Press*, 24 Aug. 1915.

4. *Detroit Free Press*, 10 Mar. 1918; McMechan, "How Mr. Bower Built the Ambassador Bridge"; and *Detroit Journal*, 12 Dec. 1916.

5. *Detroit News*, 5 Oct. 1902.

6. *Burton Scrapbook*, 81:109, Burton Historical Collection; *Detroit Journal*, 23 Dec. 1916; and *Detroit Free Press*, 24 Aug. 1915.

7. *Detroit Free Press*, 24 Aug. 1915.

8. *Detroit Free Press*, 10 Mar. 1918.

9. McMechan, "How Mr. Bower Built the Ambassador Bridge," 18.

10. *Detroit Free Press*, 21 June 1925.

11. Ibid.; *Detroit News*, 4 June 1925.

12. *Detroit Free Press*, 21 June 1925. Fowler's survey is cited in Fowler, *Detroit-Windsor Bridge over the Detroit River*, 11–12.

13. *Border Cities Star*, 29 June 1927.

14. *Detroit Free Press*, 21 June 1925.

15. The option agreement and assignment are in the D.I.B. Archives.

16. *Border Cities Star*, 9 July 1925 and 6 Aug. 1925.

17. *Border Cities Star*, 9 July 1925.

18. *Border Cities Star*, 13 June 1925 and 27 Nov. 1925.

19. *Border Cities Star*, 13 June 1925 and 23 Aug. 1926.

20. *Border Cities Star*, 10 June 1925 and 23 Aug. 1926.

21. For accounts of the meetings, see *Border Cities Star*, 10 June 1925, 13 June 1925, 16 June 1925, 19 June 1925, 7 July 1925, 8 July 1925, 9 July 1925, and 5 Aug. 1925; *Detroit News*,

28 June 1925; *Detroit Free Press,* 13 June 1925 and 8 July 1925.

22. For copies of Bower's speeches and news releases, see Publicity File, D.I.B. Archives.

23. *Border Cities Star,* 9 July 1925.

24. Ibid.

25. For accounts of the campaign for a Detroit-Windsor tunnel, see *Border Cities Star,* 15 June 1925, 27 June 1925, 30 June 1925, 2 July 1925, 9 July 1925, 11 July 1925, 23 July 1925, 24 July 1925, 25 July 1925, 17 Sept. 1925, 19 Sept. 1925, and 1 Dec. 1925; *Detroit News,* 23 June 1925; and *Detroit Free Press,* 30 June 1925 and 11 July 1925.

26. Alderman Charles R. Tuson also maintained that a "tunnel terminates abruptly at either end and does not mar the district as does a bridge." *Detroit Free Press,* 7 July 1925.

27. *Border Cities Star,* 8 Aug. 1925 and 1 Dec. 1925.

28. *Border Cities Star,* 1 Dec. 1925.

29. *Border Cities Star,* 27 Nov. 1925.

30. *Detroit Evening Times,* 9 July 1925; *Border Cities Star,* 8 July 1925.

31. *Detroiter,* 4 May 1925.

32. *Border Cities Star,* 13 June 1925 and 11 July 1925.

33. Ibid.

34. Mayor Mitchell denied that he was opposed to the Bower plan and favored only a "municipally controlled bridge." He claimed that it was Mayor John Smith of Detroit "who pressed for such a scheme." *Border Cities Star,* 8 July 1925.

35. *Border Cities Star,* 13 June 1925.

36. *Detroit Times,* 21 July 1925; *Detroit Free Press,* 22 July 1925; *Detroit News,* 22 July 1925; and *Border Cities Star,* 23 July 1925. In addition to Mayor Mitchell, the delegation to New York City included Warden W. H. Ferriss of Essex County, Mayor Vital Benot of LaSalle, Mayor Alex McKee of Sandwich, Mayor Mousseau of Ford City, Mayor St. Louis of Riverside, counsellor Louis LeBoeuf representing the mayor of Tecumseh, and counsellor Paulter of Riverside. Only Walkerville sent no representative. A copy of the statement which Bower presented to the delegation is in Publicity File, D.I.B. Archives; *Detroit Evening Times,* 9 July 1925.

37. For a copy of Bower's response to the Windsor City Council's resolution requesting further information on the bridge plan, see *Detroit Free Press,* 8 Sept. 1925.

38. *Border Cities Star,* 6 Aug. 1925.

39. *Detroit News,* 11 Aug. 1925; *Border Cities Star,* 11 Aug. 1925.

40. Other municipalities endorsing the Bower plan were Sandwich, Riverside, and LaSalle.

41. For a report of the Coverdale and Colpitts survey, see "Reports of Joseph A. Bower," 8 Oct. 1925 and 13 Oct. 1925, *Traffic Surveys,* D.I.B. Archives.

42. *Border Cities Star,* 8 Sept. 1925; *Detroit Free Press,* 8 Sept. 1925.

43. *Border Cities Star,* 16 Oct. 1925.

44. *Toronto Financial Post,* 18 Sept. 1925.

45. Colonel C. N. Monsarrat endorsed the findings of Coverdale and Colpitts. C. N. Monsarrat, *Report . . . on Proposed Detroit River Bridge* (Windsor: Better Transportation Comm. of Essex County, 1925), 7–9.

46. *Border Cities Star,* 17 Sept. 1925 and 19 Sept. 1925; Monsarrat, *Report,* 5–6.

47. *Border Cities Star,* 23 Sept. 1925 and 29 Sept. 1925; *Detroit News,* 27 Sept. 1925.

48. *Detroit International Bridge: The Ambassador Bridge* (New York: McClintic-Marshall Co., 1929), 9; Monsarrat, *Report,* 9–10; and *Border Cities Star,* 11 Nov. 1925.

49. See David Steinman, *A Practical Treatise on Suspension Bridges* (New York: John Wiley and Sons, 1922); Billington, *The Tower and the Bridge,* 72–146; David Steinman, *Famous Bridges of the World* (New York: Random House, 1953), 42–60.

50. *Detroit International Bridge,* 9; Monsarrat, *Report,* 5–6.

51. *Detroit International Bridge,* 9.

52. Joseph A. Bower, "Report," 15 Oct. 1925, 2, Publicity File, D.I.B. Archives; Monsarrat, *Report,* 5, 7–89.

53. Monsarrat, *Report,* 5, 7–89.

54. Ibid.

55. Ibid.; Joseph A. Bower, "Statement," 27 Dec. 1925, 5, Publicity File, D.I.B. Archives.

56. Bower, "Statement," 5.

57. Monsarrat, *Report,* 7, 9–11.

58. *Border Cities Star,* 20 Oct. 1925 and 26 Nov. 1925.

59. *Border Cities Star,* 20 Oct. 1925; information on Col. Monsarrat provided by Hugh Pratley, 10 July 1986.

60. *Border Cities Star,* 11 Nov. 1925. For accounts of action taken on the plebescite by local city councils, see Riverside City Council, Minutes, 23 Nov. 1925; Town of Sandwich Council, Minutes, 16 Nov. 1925; Walkerville Town Council, Minutes, 23 Nov. 1925; all in Municipal Archives, Windsor Public Library, Windsor, Ontario.

61. *Border Cities Star,* 10 Nov. 1925; Monsarrat, *Report,* 10.

62. The Monsarrat report was published in the *Border Cities Star,* 11 Nov. 1925.

63. Bower, "Statement," 27 Dec. 1925, 1–8. Bower, usually accompanied by DeWitt Smith, his engineering consultant for New York City, Wallace Campbell, Charles McTague, and A. F. Healy, addressed city councils, service clubs, church groups, and other community organizations in Windsor, Sandwich, Walkerville, Ford, Tecumseh, Amherstburg, Belle River, Essex, Kingsville, Comber, Stony Point, St. Joachim, Malden, and Riverside.

64. *Border Cities Star,* 13 June 1925 and 2 Dec. 1925.

65. *Border Cities Star,* 6 Jan. 1926.

66. *Border Cities Star,* 13 Mar. 1926 and 14 Apr. 1926.

67. *Border Cities Star,* 13 Mar. 1926.

68. *Border Cities Star,* 23 Aug. 1926.

69. *Detroit Free Press,* 18 Jan. 1927 and 19 Jan. 1927.

70. *Border Cities Star,* 1 Mar. 1927.

71. *Border Cities Star,* 14 Mar. 1927.

Chapter 4

1. For copies of the application of the American Transit Company to the various government agencies see Legal File, D.I.B. Archives.

2. Joseph C. Grew, undersecretary of state, to Cook, Nathan and Lehman, 6 Apr. 1927, D.I.B. Archives. The Dominion Railway Board approved the plan one month later. *Border Cities Star,* 6 Apr. 1927.

3. The official public notice of the hearing is in the Legal File, D.I.B. Archives.

4. *Border Cities Star,* 15 Mar. 1927 and 29 Mar. 1927; *Detroit Free Press,* 26 Mar. 1927.

5. *Detroit Free Press,* 26 Mar. 1927; *Border Cities Star,* 29 Mar. 1927.

6. A copy of the depositions of Jonathan Jones, T. M. Stephens, and others supporting the American Transit Company's position in the controversy is in the Legal File, D.I.B. Archives.

7. *Detroit Free Press,* 26 Mar. 1927.

8. *Border Cities Star,* 6 May 1927.

9. Lake Carriers Association, *Annual Report, 1927,* 167–68; *Detroit Free Press,* 7 May 1927.

10. According to a newspaper account, Lodge was quoted as being "convinced that the permission sought by Bower would be granted and other members were of the same opinion." *Detroit Free Press,* 9 Mar. 1927.

11. *Border Cities Star,* 2 Apr. 1927 and 13 Apr. 1927. During the election campaign, J. W. Austin, who represented the American Transit Company in numerous debates and public appearances, announced that "on the American side of the bridge only American labor will be employed at the prevailing rate of pay," an obvious response to the criticism of Frank X. Martel.

12. *Border Cities Star,* 11 Mar. 1927.

13. *Border Cities Star,* 2 Apr. 1927.

14. *Detroit News,* 19 Apr. 1927 and 20 Apr. 1927; *Detroit Times,* 20 Apr. 1927; and *Border Cities Star,* 6 May, 1927.

15. Detroit Common Council, *Journal, 1926–1927,* 19 Apr. 1927, 1041–1043. See also "Statement of Detroit Corporation Counsel, Charles P. O'Neill," Detroit Common Council, *Journal, 1926–1927,* 1053–1064. The Mayor's veto message was published in the *Detroit Free Press,* 20 Apr. 1927. See also *Detroit News,* 20 Apr. 1927, and *Border Cities Star,* 6 May 1927.

16. *Detroit News,* 20 Apr. 1927 and 22 Apr. 1927. For Lodge's evaluation of Mayor Smith and his stand on the Ambassador Bridge, see John C. Lodge and Milo M. Quaife, *I Remember Detroit* (Detroit: Wayne State Univ. Press, 1949), 106–10.

17. *Detroit News,* 21 Apr. 1927; *Detroit Free Press,* 26 Apr. 1927.

18. *Detroit News,* 20 Apr. 1927.

19. Ibid.

20. Ibid.; *Detroit Free Press,* 20 Apr. 1927. Mayor Smith admitted to reporters that he had been ignored, but "he had not permitted the fact to influence his judgment." *Border Cities Star,* 20 Apr. 1927.

21. *Detroit News,* 20 Apr. 1927.

22. *Detroit News,* 22 Apr. 1927.

23. Ibid.

24. Detroit Common Council, *Journal, 1926–1927,* 26 Apr. 1927, 1144. See also the opinion of Charles P. O'Neill, Detroit corporation counsel, in Detroit Common Council, *Journal, 1926–1927,* 1143–1144.

25. *Detroit Free Press,* 26 Apr. 1927; *Border Cities Star,* 6 May 1927; and *Detroit News,* 6 May 1927.

26. *Detroit Free Press,* 7 May 1927.

27. *Detroit News,* 12 May 1927, 13 May 1927, and 25 May 1927; *Border Cities Star,* 13 May 1927 and 19 May 1927; and *Detroit Times,* 14 May 1927.

28. Detroit Common Council, *Journal, 1926–1927,* 24 May 1927, 1141–1143; and *Detroit News,* 25 May 1927.

29. *Detroit Free Press,* 6 May 1927, 7 May 1927, and 13 May 1927; *Detroit News,* 6 May 1927, 7 May 1927, and 8 May 1927; *Border Cities Star,* 6 May 1927, 7 May 1927, 9 May 1927, and 25 May 1927.

30. For a detailed account of the test borings, see "Diary of W. A. Halle," D.I.B. Archives; and *Detroit Free Press,* 13 May 1927.

31. *Border Cities Star,* 23 June 1927; *Detroit News,* 23 June 1927; *Detroit Free Press,* 24 June 1927.

32. *Border Cities Star,* 25 June, 1927.

33. *Border Cities Star,* 13 May 1927.

34. "Johnny Smith, A Fighter Who Knows How to Make Friends," *Detroit Saturday Night,* 16 Sept. 1922; *Detroit Saturday Night,* 27 Sept. 1924 and 2 July 1927; *Civic Searchlight,* Oct. 1925; *Who's Who In Detroit, 1935–1936,* (Detroit: Walter Romig Co., 1935), 296; and E. G. Pipp, *Men Who Have Made Michigan* (Detroit: Pipp's Magazine, 1927), 13. See also E and M Files, Burton Historical Collection, Detroit Public Library; and Lodge and Quaife, *I Remember Detroit,* 107–8 and 116–17.

35. See, for example, *Detroit News,* 22 June 1927; and *Detroit Times,* 23 June 1927.

36. Detroit Historical Society, *Bulletin,* 12 (Feb. 1956): 13; Pipp, *Men Who Have Made Michigan,* 16. See also E and M Files, Burton Historical Collection, Detroit Public Library; and Lodge and Quaife, *I Remember Detroit,* 116–17.

37. *Detroit News,* 26 June 1927; and *Detroit Times,* 19 June 1927.

38. *Detroit Times,* 19 June 1927.

39. *Border Cities Star,* 14 June 1927.

40. *Detroit Times,* 19 June 1927.

41. *Detroit Times,* 19 Dec. 1927. Oakman also denounced the *Detroit Free Press* for its endorsement of Bower's proposal. *Detroit Times,* 25 June 1927.

42. *Border Cities Star,* 18 June 1927.

43. *Detroit Times,* 29 May 1927. Governor Green recommended that the Jay Treaty of 1794 be "abrogated before the bridge is built in order to prevent an influx of Canadian workers into Detroit and Michigan."

44. *Detroit Times,* 19 June 1927 and 21 June 1927; *Detroit News,* 20 June 1927; *Detroit Free Press,* 17 June 1927 and 21 June 1927; and *Border Cities Star,* 17 June 1927, 21 June 1927, and 24 June 1927. Campbell stressed that he favored a bridge but he predicted that the bridge referendum would be defeated if it were before the voters in June. *Border Cities Star,* 17 June 1927.

45. *Border Cities Star,* 24 June 1924.

46. Ibid.

47. *Detroit Times,* 25 June 1927.

48. *Detroit Times,* 27 June 1927.

49. *Border Cities Star,* 24 June 1927. According to John C. Lodge, Oakman's opposition to the bridge was based upon his view that its "financial structure was three times what it was worth." Lodge and Quaife, *I Remember Detroit,* 108.

50. *Border Cities Star,* 18 June 1927 and 29 June 1927.

51. *Detroit Free Press,* 18 June 1927.

52. In defending his opposition to a privately owned toll bridge, Mayor Smith often quoted Senator James Couzens: "Government should have supervision and operation of toll bridges, as well as the power to acquire a bridge at cost." *Detroit Times,* 24 June 1927; and *Border Cities Star,* 8 July 1927.

53. McMechan, "How Mr. Bower Built the Ambassador

Bridge," 65. Another probable explanation is that Smith and Judge Brennan were longtime enemies. *Border Cities Star*, 29 June 1927.

54. *Border Cities Star*, 23 June 1927. Bower's statements about his motives for building a bridge across the Detroit River are not consistent with his earlier account in which he stated that he was not a philanthropist but had "gone into the bridge scheme because he believed it offers an excellent opportunity to make money." *Border Cities Star*, 2 Dec. 1925.

55. *Border Cities Star*, 23 June 1927.

56. *Border Cities Star*, 27 June 1927.

57. *Detroit Free Press*, 22 June 1927, 26 June 1927, and 27 June 1927; *Border Cities Star*, 18 June 1927, 24 June 1927, 25 June 1927, 26 June 1927, and 29 June 1927; *Detroit Times*, 23 June 1927 and 28 June 1927; and *Detroit News*, 22 June 1927 and 26 June 1927. The strong endorsement of Detroit real estate interests, consisting of 20,000 salesmen, was considered a major force behind the bridge; *Border Cities Star*, 21 June 1927.

Robert Oakman and the Citizens Bridge Committee also placed advertisements explaining their stand against the bridge. See, for example, "Facts Concerning the Bridge Ordinance," *Detroit News*, 26 June 1927; *Detroit Times*, 26 June 1927; and "An Open Letter to Joseph A. Bower," signed by "John W. Smith, Mayor," *Detroit News*, 26 June 1927.

58. *The Chronicle*, 6 Aug. 1927; and *Detroit Free Press*, 26 June 1927.

59. *Detroit Free Press*, 24 June, 1927; and *Detroit News*, 24 June 1927.

60. *Border Cities Star*, 24 June 1927.

61. *Border Cities Star*, 24 June 1927; *Detroit News*, 27 June 1927; and *Detroit Free Press*, 15 June 1927 and 24 June 1927. *Detroit Saturday Night* refused to take a stand on the bridge proposal; *Border Cities Star*, 25 June 1927. The editors of the *Border Cities Star* not only endorsed the bridge proposal, but also urged their readers to contact friends and relatives in Detroit and urge them to vote in favor the bridge; *Border Cities Star*, 21 June 1927.

62. *Detroit News*, 28 June 1927 and 30 June 1927; *Detroit Times*, 28 June 1927; *Detroit Free Press*, 28 June 1927 and 29 June 1927; and *Border Cities Star*, 28 June 1927.

63. *Border Cities Star*, 28 June 1927. For a copy of Esselstyn's statement, see the Publicity File, D.I.B. Archives.

64. *Border Cities Star*, 28 June 1927 and 29 June 1927; *Detroit Free Press*, 29 June 1927; and *Detroit Times*, 29 June 1927.

65. *Detroit Free Press*, 29 June 1927; *Detroit News*, 29 June 1927; *Detroit Times*, 29 June 1927; and *Border Cities Star*, 29 June 1927.

66. *Detroit Free Press*, 29 June 1927.

67. *Border Cities Star*, 29 June 1927.

68. Ibid. On June 30, 1927, Bower entertained 250 of his supporters at dinner at the Barlum Hotel in Detroit. For a list of those invited and in attendance, see "Dinner for Helpers" File, D.I.B. Archives.

Chapter 5

1. See the Legal File, D.I.B. Archives; and A. A. Jakkula, "A History of Suspension Bridges in Bibliographical Form," Public Works Administration Publication reprinted in *Bulletin of the Agricultural and National College of Texas*, 1 July 1927, 302.

2. *Border Cities Star*, 30 June 1927.

3. For a copy of the agreement, see the Legal File, D.I.B. Archives.

4. See "Contract between Detroit Bridge Corporation and American Transit Company," dated 30 July 1927, in the Legal File, D.I.B. Archives.

5. See "Bill of Sale, Detroit Bridge Corporation to Detroit International Bridge Company," dated 12 Aug. 1927, in the Legal File, D.I.B. Archives.

6. Ibid., 1.

7. Ibid., 1–3.

8. For letters during Aug. 1927 from Austin, Becker, Fozard, Hanrahan, Healy, McTague, Reaume, Smith, and Walker, see D.I.B. Archives.

9. See Legal File and *Minute Books*, D.I.B. Archives.

10. *Detroit International Bridge*, 5.

11. See "Agreement between Detroit International Bridge Company and Detroit Union Railroad Depot Company," dated 20 Sept. 1927, D.I.B. Archives. See also Alfred Cook to Joseph A. Bower, 23 Aug. 1928; H. A. Cassel, P. R. Howard, and B. N. Sommerville to McClintic-Marshall Co., 10 Dec. 1924; and Frank H. Alfred to McClintic-Marshall, 3 Feb. 1925; all in the D.I.B. Archives.

12. See clipping and photographs from *Border Cities Star* in Scrapbook IV, D.I.B. Archives, 120–21.

13. Receipts for $20 million for bonds and debentures, Legal File, D.I.B. Archives. In an interview with the editor of the *Border Cities Star* in June, 1927, Bower stated, "Don't worry about our financing. We made our arrangements before we started. The bonds are underwritten and they will be put on the market immediately." *Border Cities Star*, 29 June 1927.

14. C. D. Marshall to Bower, 11 June 1927, archives of Modjeski and Masters Consulting Engineers, Mechanicsburg, Pa. As consultant to Joseph Bower, Ralph Modjeski received copies of most key documents relating to the financing and construction of the bridge. See also Jonathan Jones to C. N. Monsarrat, 22 Oct. 1925, files of Hugh Pratley, Montreal, Quebec.

15. C. D. Marshall to Bower, 11 June 1927.

16. "Contract between Detroit International Bridge Company Canadian Transit Company and McClintic-Marshall Company," 19 July 1927, Legal File, D.I.B. Archives, 3.

17. Ibid., 5.

18. Ibid., 12.

19. Ibid., 19.

20. *The Detroit River Bridge: An Engineering Record* (Pittsburgh: McClintic-Marshall Co., 1930), 9.

21. Ibid.

22. Ibid., 9, 11.

23. For an account of the development of the McClintic-Marshall Co., see "Data Relative to the Fair Market Value of McClintic-Marshall Co. in 1913," Schwab Information Center, Bethlehem Steel Co., Bethlehem, Pa; and H. H. McClintic and C. D. Marshall, *Highway and Railroad Bridges* (Pittsburgh: McClintic-Marshall Co., 1928).

24. For an account of the construction of the Golden Gate Bridge, see Richard Dillon, *High Steel: Building Bridges across San Francisco Bay* (Millbrae, Calif.: Celestial Arts, 1979).

25. McClintic-Marshall was sold to Bethlehem Steel in 1931. McClintic-Marshall File, Schwab Information Center, Bethlehem Steel Co., Bethlehem, Pa.

Chapter 6

1. For a general description of the Ambassador Bridge, see *Detroit River Bridge: An Engineering Record.* This oversized volume also contains magnificent photographs of the various stages of construction and a number of bridge design drawings. One thousand of these booklets were published by the McClintic-Marshall Company and were distributed specifically to the major university engineering libraries in the United States.

See also *Detroit International Bridge;* G. M. Bolton, "The Ambassador Bridge," *Michigan Engineer,* 46 (Sept. 1928): 4–7; Jonathan Jones, "Design of the Great International Suspension Bridge over the Detroit River," *Engineering News-Record,* 101 (27 Sept. 1928): 460–66; and *Ambassador Bridge, A Review of the Construction* (Pittsburgh: McClintic-Marshall Co., 1929).

2. *Ambassador Bridge, A Review of the Construction,* 26.

3. A complete set of the contracts are located at the D.I.B. Archives; the personal files of Hugh Pratley; and the archives of Modjeski and Masters.

4. *Detroit River Bridge,* 13.

5. Jonathan Jones, "Detroit River Bridge," Monthly Report No. 1, 31 Aug. 1927, in Detroit International Bridge Co., *Minutes Book,* 8 Sept. 1927, D.I.B. Archives.

6. For a biographical sketch of Jones, see "Deposition of Jonathan Jones, April, 1927," Acts, Resolutions File, D.I.B. Archives.

7. Jones, "Detroit River Bridge."

8. Ibid.

9. Ibid.; *Who's Who in Engineering,* 1467.

10. Leon Moisseiff to Jonathan Jones, 7 Dec. 1927, D.I.B. Archives. See also "Report from Moisseiff," Schwab Information Center, Bethlehem Steel Co., Bethlehem, Pa.

11. *Bridging the Straits* (Detroit: Michigan State Fair, 1928), 12–13; Jones, "Design of the Great International Suspension Bridge over the Detroit River," 464–65; and Jones, "Detroit River Bridge," 10.

12. Jones, "Detroit River Bridge," 10.

13. Institute of Civil Engineers, *Minutes of Proceedings* (1959), 569–70. See also the Philip Pratley Papers (Mar. 1958), Engineering Institute of Canada. Files of Hugh Pratley, Montreal. Copies of the Annual Inspection Reports of Philip L. Pratley and Hugh Pratley are in the D.I.B. Archives.

14. Jones, "Detroit River Bridge."

15. Fowler, *The Detroit-Windsor Bridge,* 11–12; Coverdale and Colpitts, *Traffic Surveys,* D.I.B. Archives. For Philip L. Pratley's analysis of Coverdale and Colpitts' survey of 1925, see files of Hugh Pratley.

16. "The Washington Award Presentation," *Journal of the Western Society of Engineers,* 36 (Apr. 1931): 69–79; Jonathan Jones to Hemphill, Noyes and Co., 30 Apr. 1926, archives of Modjeski and Masters.

17. W. F. Durand, "Biographical Memoir of Ralph Modjeski," *National Academy of Biographical Memoirs,* 23 (1944): 243–61.

18. "Agreement, Detroit International Bridge Company and Canadian Transit Co. with Ralph Modjeski and Clement E. Chase," 16 Aug. 1927, Legal File, D.I.B. Archives; and *Detroit Free Press,* 10 Nov. 1929.

19. Ratigan, *Highways over Broad Waters,* 184–87. J. Jones,

"Design of the Great International Suspension Bridge over the Detroit River," *Engineering News-Record,* 101 (27 Sept. 1928): 466.

20. Jones, "Design of the Great International Suspension Bridge over the Detroit River," 465–66.

21. Ibid.

22. *Detroit Free Press,* 30 June 1927, 15 Apr. 1928, and 13 May 1928; *Border Cities Star,* 29 June 1927, 26 June 1928, and 9 Nov. 1929.

23. *Detroit Free Press,* 21 Oct. 1928.

24. Jones, "Detroit River Bridge"; *Detroit Free Press,* 13 May 1927.

25. Jones, "Detroit River Bridge."

26. E. A. Proctor, "Foundation Construction for the Detroit River Suspension Bridge," *Engineering News-Record,* 101 (6 Dec. 1928): 830–35; *Detroit River Bridge,* 13–14; and *Detroit News,* 26 Feb. 1928.

27. Proctor, "Foundation Construction for the Detroit River Suspension Bridge," 830–35; and *Detroit News,* 26 Feb. 1928.

28. *Detroit News,* 26 Feb. 1928.

29. *Detroit News,* 26 Feb. 1928; *Border Cities Star,* 28 Sept. 1929; and *Chatham [Ontario] News,* 28 Sept. 1929.

30. *Detroit News,* 26 Feb. 1928.

31. L. L. Martin, "Suspension Bridge Tower Erection at Detroit by Creeper Traveler," *Engineering News-Record,* 102 (31 Jan. 1929): 186–89; *Detroit River Bridge,* 19–20; and Steinman, *Suspension Bridges,* 165.

32. *Detroit River Bridge,* 17–21.

33. Ibid., 15–16.

34. McMechan, "How Mr. Bower Built the Ambassador Bridge," 70.

35. Steinman, *Suspension Bridges,* 165–67.

36. *Detroit Times,* 7 Aug. 1928, and 8 Aug. 1928; *Detroit Free Press,* 8 Aug. 1928; *Detroit News,* 7 Aug. 1928 and 8 Aug. 1928; and *Border Cities Star,* 1 Aug. 1928.

37. *Border Cities Star,* 8 Aug. 1928 and 9 Aug. 1928; *Detroit News,* 7 Aug. 1928 and 8 Aug. 1928; *Detroit Free Press,* 8 Aug. 1928 and 9 Aug. 1928; *Michigan Manufacturer and Financial Record,* 11 Aug. 1928, 5; and *Detroit Saturday Night,* 10 Aug. 1928.

38. *Detroit Saturday Night,* 10 Aug. 1928.

39. *Border Cities Star,* 9 Aug. 1928; *Detroit Free Press,* 9 Aug. 1928.

40. *Border Cities Star,* 9 Aug. 1928. This issue of the *Star* also contained a full page of photographs of the event.

41. Ibid.

42. *Detroit Free Press,* 9 Aug. 1928.

43. Ibid., 6.

44. Ibid.

45. Ibid.

46. Howard Hayes, "Hazards of Work Far above Busy River Have No Terrors for Veteran Craftsmen, but They Avoid Jinxes," *Detroit Free Press,* 21 Oct. 1928.

47. Ibid.

48. Ibid.

49. George Bowers was the first person to walk across the footwalks, on Aug. 31, 1928. He was also the first to cross both Bear Mountain and Delaware River bridges. *Border Cities Star,* 31 Aug. 1928.

50. *Detroit Free Press,* 16 Sept. 1928.

51. Helen Austin Sumner, interview with author, 12 March 1983.

52. Ibid. For photographs of Miss Austin's historic walk, see *Border Cities Star,* 16 Sept. 1928; and *Detroit Free Press,* 16 Sept. 1928.

53. *Detroit River Bridge,* 23–25.

54. Ibid. For a sectional view of the cables, see Jones, "Design of the Great International Suspension Bridge over the Detroit River," 462; "Squeezing Cables," *Associated Technical Societies Review of Detroit,* 8 (Feb. 1929).

55. "Squeezing Cables"; and Steinman, *Suspension Bridges,* 177.

56. *Detroit River Bridge,* 21–22; "New Cables for Ambassador Bridge," *The Canadian Engineer,* 56 (30 Apr. 1929): 475; Jonathan Jones, "Problems of Design," *Detroit Free Press,* 10 Nov. 1929; and Jones, "Design of the Great International Suspension Bridge over the Detroit River," 465.

57. Jonathan Jones to Ralph Modjeski and Clement Chase, 15 Nov. 1927; Jones to Col. Monsarrat and Philip Pratley, 15 Nov. 1927; Jones to Philip Pratley, 26 November 1927; Jones to Moisseiff, 30 Nov. 1927; and Jones to Modjeski and Chase, 7 Dec. 1927; all in the files of Hugh Pratley.

58. Ralph Modjeski to Jones, 15 Nov. 1927, Hugh Pratley Files.

59. Philip Pratley and Col. Monsarrat to Modjeski and Chase, 9 Dec. 1927, archives of Modjeski and Masters.

60. Many years later, Steinman claimed that he was adamantly opposed to the substitution of heat-treated wire but that he finally relented because of "his partner's superior experience in cable construction, dating back to 1887." Steinman, *Highways Over Broad Waters,* 186–87. Also opposed to the use of heat-treated wire was Bradley Stoughton, prominent metallurgist. See Bradley Stoughton et al. to W. A. Anderson, vice-president, John Roebling's Sons, 30 Sept. 1927, files of Hugh Pratley.

61. *Detroit River Bridge,* 25.

62. Jones, "Problems of Design," 6; Jones, "Design of the Great International Suspension Bridge over the Detroit River," 464–65; *Detroit International Bridge,* 16–18; *Bridging the Straits,* 12–13.

63. *Detroit River Bridge,* 24; Jones, "Design of the Great International Suspension Bridge over the Detroit River," 464–65.

64. *Detroit River Bridge,* 25–27.

65. Jones, "Problems of Design," 25–27.

66. *Detroit River Bridge,* 27–29. See also from D.I.B. Archives: Bower to Jones, 21 Sept. 1927; Jones to Bower, 5 Mar. 1928; Cook to Jones, 6 Mar. 1928; Jones to Bower, 28 July 1928.

67. *Detroit River Bridge,* 29–31; Jones, "Design of the Great International Suspension Bridge over the Detroit River," 465.

68. *Detroit River Bridge,* 28–29.

69. *Detroit River Bridge,* 32; and *Border Cities Star,* 9 Nov. 1929.

70. *Detroit River Bridge,* 35; Jones, "Problems of Design." See also in the archives of Modjeski and Masters: Jones to Modjeski and Chase, 12 Sept. 1928; John Neehan and Son to Jones, 14 Sept. 1928; Neehan to Jones, 22 Sept. 1928; Jones to Modjeski and Chase, 26 Sept. 1928.

71. Jones, "Problems of Design."

72. *Detroit River Bridge,* 31.

73. Ibid.

74. *Detroit River Bridge,* 35, 43; *Michigan Manufacturers and Financial Record,* 29 Mar. 1929, 18.

Chapter 7

1. *New York Herald Tribune,* 2 Dec. 1928; *Detroit Free Press,* 2 Dec. 1928; *Literary Digest,* 15 Dec. 1928, 23; and *Michigan Manufacturers and Financial Record,* 8 Dec. 1928.

2. *Border Cities Star,* 5 Mar. 1929; *Detroit News,* 6 Mar. 1929; *Detroit Free Press,* 6 Mar. 1929; and *Detroit Times,* 6 Mar. 1929.

3. Ratigan, *Highways over Broad Waters,* 185–90.

4. Ibid., 188.

5. Ibid., 188–89. Steinman also released the information to the *Engineering News-Record.*

6. Ratigan, *Highways over Broad Waters,* 187.

7. Robert MacMinn, resident engineer for McClintic-Marshall Co. in Detroit, advised Col. Monsarrat and Philip Pratley on Mar. 12, 1929 that "considerable trouble has developed in the wire on the Mt. Hope Bridge," and although only two broken wires had been found on the Detroit River bridge, he encouraged them to visit the Mt. Hope Bridge. MacMinn to Monsarrat and Pratley, files of Hugh Pratley.

See also in files of Hugh Pratley: Jones to Monsarrat and Philip Pratley, 23 Mar. 1929; P. Pratley to Monsarrat, 25 Mar. 1929; P. Pratley to Jones, 25 Mar. 1929; Monsarrat to P. Pratley, 25 Mar. 1929; P. Pratley to Jones, 25 Mar. 1929; P. Pratley to David Steinman and Holton Robinson, 25 Mar. 1929; Robinson and Steinman to Monsarrat and Pratley, 27 Mar. 1929; James L. Fozard to Monsarrat, 28 Mar. 1929.

8. The action of McClintic-Marshall was applauded in the press. See, for example, an editorial in the *Vancouver Journal of Commerce,* 5 June 1929: "The example of professional honesty is exceptionally cheering in this age when so many doubt the sincerity of business methods or industrial ethics."

9. McMechan, "How Mr. Bower Built the Ambassador Bridge," 66–67.

10. For a copy of the press release, see Publicity File, 1928, D.I.B. Archives; *Detroit News,* 28 Mar. 1929; *Detroit Times,* 29 Mar. 1929; and *Border Cities Star,* 28 Mar. 1929. For other accounts of the cable breakage and removal, see "Technical Aspects of Cable Wire Breakages on the Mount Hope Suspension Bridge," *Engineering News-Record,* 102 (11 Apr. 1929): 602–5; "Cable on Detroit River Suspension Bridge to be Replaced," *Engineering News-Record,* 102 (4 Apr. 1929): 564, 567; "The Ambassador Bridge over the Detroit River," *Engineer,* 147 (12 Apr. 1929); "New Cables for Ambassador Bridge," *Canadian Engineer,* 56 (30 Apr. 1929): 475.

11. *Detroit Free Press,* 7 Apr. 1929; and *Border Cities Star,* 3 Apr. 1929, 13 Apr. 1929, and 16 Apr. 1929.

12. "Find Breaks in Detroit Cables," *Engineering News-Record,* 102 (16 May 1929): 808.

13. R. G. Cone, "The Ambassador Bridge," *Associated Technical Societies Review of Detroit,* 8 (Sept. 1929): 6, 19–20.

For a photograph of the removal process, see also *Border Cities Star,* 16 Apr. 1929 and 17 May 1929.

14. One of the last firms which purchased the dismantled wire cables was the Keywell Industries of Detroit. Barney

Keywell, interview with author, 19 Sept. 1984, Detroit, Mich., D.I.B. Archives.

15. *Detroit News*, 13 Apr. 1929; *Detroit Times*, 13 Apr. 1929; *Detroit Free Press*, 13 Apr. 1929, and *Border Cities Star*, 13 Apr. 1929.

16. *Border Cities Star*, 13 Apr. 1929.

17. The files of Modjeski and Masters, as well as those of Hugh Pratley, contain the reports of the various engineering tests. See, for example, Jones to Monsarrat and P. Pratley, 28 June 1929, 27 July 1929, 9 Aug. 1929, and 15 Aug. 1929, files of Hugh Pratley; and from the archives of Modjeski and Masters the following: Jones to Robinson and Steinman, 14 May 1949; Sterling Johnston to Jones, 14 May 1929; Moisseiff to Chase, 18 May 1929; A. F. Howry to Robinson and Steinman, 27 July 1929; and Jones to Modjeski and Chase, 31 July 1929.

See also *Detroit River Bridge*, 21–23, and Appendix A, 37–39; F. D. McHugh, "The Detroit River is Spanned," *Scientific American*, 142 (Feb. 1930): 122–23; Leon Moisseiff, "Reliability of Cold-Drawn Bridge Wire Assured by Recent Test," *Engineering News-Record*, 105 (17 Feb. 1930): 93–95; and Jonathan Jones, "The Ambassador Bridge," *Military Engineer*, 22 (Sept.-Oct., 1930): 401–4.

18. *Border Cities Star*, 10 Sept. 1929; and Jones, "Detroit River Bridge," 7, 23–25. *The Detroit News* recorded the completion of the final truss span with an aerial photograph, 17 Sept. 1929.

Chapter 8

1. *Sandwich Courier*, 11 Jan. 1929; *Border Cities Star*, 3 Jan. 1929; *Detroit Free Press*, 29 Dec. 1928; and *Detroit News*, 13 Jan. 1929.

2. *Border Cities Star*, 25 Apr. 1929.

3. *London [Ontario] Advertiser*, 27 June 1929; *Lansing Capital News*, 17 May 1929; *Detroit Free Press*, 15 May 1928; and Lake Carriers Association, *Annual Report, 1928*, 160.

4. *Detroit Times*, 10 Nov. 1929; *New York Times*, 10 Nov. 1929; *Detroit Free Press*, 8 Nov. 1929; *Detroit News*, 8 Nov. 1929; and *Border Cities Star*, 4 Nov. 1929. The *Border Cities Star* devoted a special edition to the Ambassador Bridge on Saturday, Nov. 9. Bower secured several hundred copies to send to "his closest personal friends, who I know will not feel that I am proud, but will understand that I am only bringing the tributes to their attention . . . to show them the wonderful Special Edition you have put out." Bower to Ellison Young, editor, *Border Cities Star*, W. F. Herman Collection, Windsor Municipal Archives, Windsor Public Library, Windsor, Ontario.

5. The invitation list is located in "Opening Day Ceremonies," *Border Cities Star*, 7 Nov. 1929, D.I.B. Archives.

6. *Border Cities Star*, 9 Nov. 1929. For reactions to the train trip and ceremony, see "Opening Day Ceremonies," D.I.B. Archives.

7. *Detroit Free Press*, 12 Nov. 1929 and 17 Nov. 1929; *Detroit News*, 12 Nov. 1929; *Detroit Times*, 12 Nov. 1929; *Border Cities Star*, 12 Nov. 1929; and *Christian Science Monitor*, 11 Nov. 1929.

8. Photographs of the crowds stampeding towards the center of the Ambassador Bridge were run in all Detroit and Windsor area newspapers and distributed by the wire services. See, for example, *Montreal La Presse*, 14 Nov. 1929.

9. *Detroit Times*, 12 Nov. 1929; *Detroit Free Press*, 12 Nov. 1929; *Detroit News*, 12 Nov. 1929; and *Border Cities Star*, 12 Nov. 1929.

10. Jack Sumner, interview with author, 12 Mar. 1983, Lake San Marcos, California.

11. *Detroit Times*, 12 Nov. 1929. McRae's speech was reprinted in *Border Cities Star*, 12 Nov. 1929.

12. *Detroit Times*, 12 Nov. 1929.

13. H. M. Morden, "Race Past Police to Boundary Gate as Span is Opened," *Border Cities Star*, 12 Nov. 1929.

14. *Border Cities Star*, 12 Nov. 1929; *Detroit News*, 12 Nov. 1929; *Detroit Free Press*, 17 Nov. 1929. Elmer Paquette, who was on safety patrol at the center of the bridge on Nov. 11, 1929, recalled vividly the huge masses of people rushing suddenly toward the center of the bridge. Elmer Paquette, interview with author, 12 Sept. 1984, Detroit, Michigan.

15. *Detroit Free Press*, 12 Nov. 1929. According to Hans Cruikshank, reporter for the *Border Cities Star*, "Some of the more daring boys could be seen climbing the cables to the tips of the towers," 12 Nov. 1929.

16. *Border Cities Star*, 12 Nov. 1929.

17. *Detroit Free Press*, 15 Nov. 1929.

18. *Detroit Free Press*, 16 Nov. 1929; *Border Cities Star*, 16 Nov. 1929.

19. *Detroit Free Press*, 16 Nov. 1929 and 24 Nov. 1929. The bridge company ordered 1,000 bronze plaquettes at a total cost of $3,535 for distribution to selected dignitaries and guests. Detroit International Bridge Co., *Minutes Book*, 6 Mar. 1929.

20. *Detroit Free Press*, 16 Nov. 1929; and *Canadian Motorist*, Dec. 1929, 543.

21. *Detroit Free Press*, 16 Nov. 1929; and *Border Cities Star*, 15 Nov. 1929.

22. *Border Cities Star*, 15 Nov. 1929.

23. *Detroit Times*, 18 Nov. 1929; *Detroit News*, 24 Nov. 1929; and *Michigan Manufacturers and Financial Record*, 21 Dec. 1929. For photographs of the bottleneck of automobiles on Sunday, Nov. 17, see *Detroit News*, 18 Nov. 1929; *Border Cities Star*, 16 Nov. 1929 and 28 Nov. 1929.

24. *Border Cities Star*, 18 Nov. 1929.

25. *Border Cities Star*, 18 Nov. 1929 and 20 Nov. 1929. Identification cards for daily commuters facilitated travel between Detroit and Windsor; *Border Cities Star*, 29 Nov. 1929.

26. *Detroit News*, 12 Nov. 1929.

27. "Agreement between Detroit International Bridge Company and McClintic-Marshall Company," D.I.B. Archives; and *Detroit River Bridge*, 9–10.

28. *Detroit River Bridge*, 11. For accounts of the engineering features of the bridge, see "Ambassador Bridge Between Windsor, Ontario and Detroit, Michigan Completed Last Week," *Contract Record*, 43 (20 Nov. 1929): 1355–1362; Jonathan Jones, "The Ambassador Bridge," *The Cornell Civil Engineer*, 38 (Dec. 1929): 57–59, 71–74; Cone, "Construction of the Ambassador Bridge," 785–88; "Some Bridges of 1929," *Engineer*, 149 (3 Jan. 1930): 22; S. G. Roberts, "Ambassador Bridge, A Steel Link Uniting Two Countries," *Dunn's International Review*, 54 (Jan. 1930): 35–37; and McHugh, "The Detroit River is Spanned," 122–23.

29. *Border Cities Star*, 28 June 1927.

30. Ratigan, *Highways Over Broad Waters*, 223.

Chapter 9

1. Paul Studenski and Herman E. Krooss, *Financial History of the U.S.* (New York: McGraw, Hill, 1952), 353; Morrison, *Garden Gateway to Canada*, 297; Woodford and Woodford, *All Our Yesterdays*, 310–13; F. Clever Bald, *Michigan in Four Centuries* (New York: Harper & Bros., 1954), 404–10.

2. Morrison, *Garden Gateway to Canada*, 297.

3. *Annual Report*, 1932, D.I.B. Archives.

4. For lists of directors and changes in board membership, see *Annual Report* for years 1930 to 1939, D.I.B. Archives.

5. The resignations of Austin and Graham were required by the Debenture Holders and Bond Holders committees. *Minutes Book*, 17 Sept. 1931 and 15 Oct. 1931, D.I.B. Archives.

6. *Minutes Book*, 16 Feb. 1928, D.I.B. Archives.

7. *Minutes Book*, 14 Nov. 1928 and 18 Sept. 1930, D.I.B. Archives.

8. *Border Cities Star*, 9 Nov. 1929; *Detroit Free Press*, 10 Nov. 1929.

9. *Detroit Daily*, 11 Nov. 1929.

10. For biographical data on Paquette, see Elmer Paquette, interview with author, 12 Sept. 1984, D.I.B. Archives; and *Detroit News Pictorial Magazine*, 12 July 1953, p. 7.

11. "Customs Facilities at Ambassador Bridge," *The National Revenue Review* (May 1930), 8; *Border Cities Star*, 1 Oct. 1929, 15 Nov. 1929, 21 Nov. 1929, 25 Nov. 1929, and 13 Dec. 1929; *Detroit Free Press*, 10 Nov. 1929.

12. Robert A. Bower, interview with author, 12 Mar. 1983, D.I.B. Archives; McMechan, "How Mr. Bower Built the Ambassador Bridge," 70.

13. Jonathan Jones to James L. Fozard, 3 May 1929; W. A. Halle to R. B. McDougald, 16 Mar. 1931; memorandum to McDougald, 12 June 1931; Clement E. Chase to McDougald, 22 May 1931 and 25 May 1931; and Chase to Detroit International Bridge Co., 25 June 1930.

14. "Memorandum of Agreement between Detroit International Bridge Company, Canadian Transit Company and McClintic-Marshall Company," 26 June 1930, Legal File, D.I.B. Archives.

15. Ibid.

16. Ibid.

17. Ibid. "Guaranty Agreement between McClintic-Marshall Co. and Detroit International Bridge Co.," 26 June 1930, Legal File, D.I.B. Archives.

18. For reports on the condition of the paint on steel and cables, see Walter Halle to R. B. McDougald, "Report," 16 Mar. 1931 and 12 Nov. 1931; Chase to McDougald, 22 May 1931, 25 May 1931, and 12 June 1931; G. A. Coffall to McDougald, 27 Aug. 1931, 1 Sept. 1931, 8 Oct. 1931, 21 Oct. 1931, 16 Nov. 1931, and 21 Dec. 1931; and McDougald to Coffall, 28 Aug. 1931. See also the detailed "Report on Condition of Paint Main Structural Steel," 15 June 1931, and "Report on Condition of Paint on Canadian Truss Span Steel," 28 June 1931, both in Maintenance File, D.I.B. Archives.

19. *Minutes Book*, 22 Mar. 1934, D.I.B. Archives; and "Final Inspection, Ambassador Bridge, May 15 to 23, 1933," Legal File, D.I.B. Archives.

20. "Traffic Statistics," D.I.B. Archives.

21. Ibid; *Annual Report*, 1934, D.I.B. Archives.

22. "Traffic Statistics," D.I.B. Archives; *Annual Report*, 1935, 1, D.I.B. Archives, and *Annual Report*, 1939, D.I.B. Archives.

23. Woodford and Woodford, *All Our Yesterdays*, 313. The Bridge refused to accept Detroit script for payment of tolls. *Minutes Book*, 25 May 1933, D.I.B. Archives.

24. *London Free Press*, 4 Apr. 1930; Coverdale and Colpitts to J. A. Bower, 23 Sept. 1930, D.I.B. Archives; and "Traffic Surveys," in *Annual Report*, 1930, D.I.B. Archives.

25. *Minutes Book*, 15 May 1930; and *Annual Report*, 1931, both in D.I.B. Archives.

26. *Minutes Book*, 16 July 1931, D.I.B. Archives.

27. Coverdale and Colpitts to J. A. Bower, 23 Sept. 1930, D.I.B. Archives; and "Traffic Surveys," D.I.B. Archives.

28. Coverdale and Colpitts to J. A. Bower, 23 Sept. 1930.

29. Ibid.

30. "Traffic Statistics," D.I.B. Archives. See also Detroit and Canada Tunnel Co., *Consolidated Balance Sheet, 1930–1939*, Detroit-Canada Tunnel File, D.I.B. Archives.

31. *Annual Report*, 1930, D.I.B. Archives.

32. Ibid.

33. Ibid.

34. *Annual Report*, 1931, D.I.B. Archives.

35. McDougald to C. B. Hibbard, 9 Dec. 1937, D.I.B. Archives.

36. *Audit Reports, 1930–1939*, and "Annual Audits," both in D.I.B. Archives.

37. Detroit and Canada Tunnel Co., *Consolidated Balance Sheet, Ending Dec. 31, 1932*, D.I.B. Archives.

38. Morrison, *Garden Gateway to Canada*, 305.

39. *Annual Report*, 1931, 1932, 1933, 1934, 1935, 1936, and 1937, D.I.B. Archives.

40. McDougald to J. A. Bower, 26 Oct. 1933, Tax File, D.I.B. Archives. For an account of the taxes levied by the town of Sandwich, Ontario, see McDougald to Frank D. Eamon, 6 Apr. 1934, Tax File, D.I.B. Archives.

41. *Annual Report*, 1933 and 1934, D.I.B. Archives.

41. "Complaint and Petition for Review of Detroit International Bridge Company to Board of State Tax Commission from Assessment of County of Wayne and State of Michigan for the Year 1934," Legal File, D.I.B. Archives.

43. *Annual Report*, 1937, D.I.B. Archives, p. 3; Stevenson, Butzel, Eamon and Long to Cook, Nathan and Lehman, 3 May 1934, Tax File, D.I.B. Archives; and Detroit and Canada Tunnel Co., *Consolidated Balance Sheet, 1934, 1935, 1936, and 1937*, D.I.B. Archives.

44. James Burns, Detroit Board of Assessors, to Detroit International Bridge Co., 2 May 1938; and McDougald to J. A. Bower, 3 May 1938, both in D.I.B. Archives.

45. McDougald to J. A. Bower, 20 Jan. 1939, Tax File, D.I.B. Archives; and *Annual Report*, 1938, 1939, D.I.B. Archives.

46. "Plan of Reorganization of Detroit International Bridge Co. and Canadian Transit Co.," 1 July 1938, pp. 7, 12–13, D.I.B. Archives.

47. *Annual Report*, 1931, 1932, 1933, 1934, 1935, 1936 and 1937, D.I.B. Archives.

48. *Minutes Book*, 15 Jan. 1931, D.I.B. Archives.

49. *Annual Report*, 1934, 1935 and 1936, D.I.B. Archives.

50. *Minutes Book*, 19 Oct. 1934, D.I.B. Archives. The Essex County Tourist Association also assisted in publicizing the Ambassador Bridge. Morrison, *Garden Gateway to Canada*, 308–9.

51. McDougald to H. H. Bowden, 7 Mar. 1934, Board of Directors File, D.I.B. Archives; and *Minutes Book,* 19 Oct. 1934, D.I.B. Archives.

52. J. A. Bower to McDougald, 19 Apr. 1934, Port Authority File, D.I.B. Archives.

53. Order-in-Council, P.C. 1601 of Aug. 1927.

54. See copies of Pratley's annual Ambassador Bridge inspection reports in D.I.B. Archives.

55. Pratley, "Report on Inspection of Ambassador Bridge between Windsor and Detroit," 12 Aug. 1948, D.I.B. Archives.

56. *Annual Report,* 1934 and 1937, D.I.B. Archives.

57. *Annual Report,* 1937, D.I.B. Archives.

58. *Detroit Free Press,* 21 Mar. 1953; and *Detroit News,* 21 Mar. 1953.

59. McDougald to J. W. Austin, 27 June 1934, Directors File, D.I.B. Archives.

60. *Border Cities Star,* 7 Dec. 1929; *Detroit Free Press,* 7 Dec. 1929; and *Waxachachie [Texas] Light,* 27 May 1930.

61. *Toronto Daily Star,* 8 Apr. 1930 and 10 Apr. 1930; *London [Ontario] Evening Free Press,* 11 Apr. 1930; and *St. Thomas Times Journal,* 14 Apr. 1930.

62. *London Evening Free Press,* 11 Apr. 1930; and *Montreal Gazette,* 10 Apr. 1930.

63. *Detroit News,* 30 June 1951; and *Detroit Free Press,* 1 Nov. 1959.

64. *Manistee [Michigan] News Advocate,* 27 Apr. 1939.

65. "Plan of Reorganization," 3; and "Report of the Securities and Exchange Commission on Proposed Plan of Reorganization, Filed Mar. 14, 1939 in U.S. District Court, Eastern District of Michigan," Reorganization File, D.I.B. Archives.

66. "Report of the Securities and Exchange Commission," D.I.B. Archives.

67. J. A. Bower to McDougald, 4 May 1980, Reorganization File, D.I.B. Archives.

68. *Minutes Book,* 20 May 1938.

69. U.S. District Court, Eastern District of Michigan, "In the Matter of Detroit International Bridge Co., No. 24131, Filed Mar. 14, 1939," Legal File, D.I.B. Archives.

70. "Plan of Reorganization," 3.

71. "Plan of Reorganization," 3; and "Report of the Securities and Exchange Commission," 4; both in D.I.B. Archives.

72. "Report of the Securities and Exchange Commission," 4; "Joint Operating Agreement between Detroit International Bridge Co. and Canadian Transit Co.," D.I.B. Archives; U.S. District Court, Eastern District of Michigan, Southern Division, "Order Approving Joint Operating Agreement, Bankruptcy Action No. 24131," D.I.B. Archives.

73. *Annual Report,* 1938 and 1939.

Chapter 10

1. *Annual Report,* 1940, D.I.B. Archives.

2. Ibid.

3. *Minutes Book,* 20 Mar. 1942, D.I.B. Archives.

4. "Traffic Statistics," D.I.B. Archives.

5. Truck crossings increased steadily from 37,262 in 1939,

44,754 in 1940, 46,232 in 1941, 51,756 in 1942, 53,325 in 1943, to 57,927 in 1945. "Traffic Statistics," D.I.B. Archives.

6. Ibid.

7. Ibid.; *Annual Report,* 1946; *Minutes Book,* 2 Nov. 1945, all in D.I.B. Archives.

8. *Annual Report,* 1946, D.I.B. Archives.

9. "Traffic Statistics," D.I.B. Archives; and Detroit and Canada Tunnel Corp., *Report,* 31 Oct. 1947.

10. McDougald to J. A. Bower, 5 Dec. 1939, World War II File, D.I.B. Archives.

11. McDougald to J. A. Bower, 5 Dec. 1939; and *Annual Report,* 1940, D.I.B. Archives.

12. Woodford and Woodford, *All Our Yesterdays,* 333.

13. Elmer Paquette, interview with author, 12 Sept. 1984, D.I.B. Archives.

14. Woodford and Woodford, *All Our Yesterdays,* 377.

15. Woodford and Woodford, *All Our Yesterdays,* 335. The Countess Von Moltke, wife of a Wayne State University German professor, was arrested, tried, and pleaded guilty to charges of espionage activities against the United States government. *New York Times,* 25 Aug. 1943, 10 Feb. 1944, and 26 Mar. 1944; *Houghton Gazette,* 18 Jan. 1953; *Detroit Free Press,* 9 May 1963; *Detroit News,* 24 Aug. 1943 and 3 Nov. 1943; and Arthur Neef, provost, to David Henry, president, Wayne State University, 26 Sept. 1945, Files of President David Henry, Wayne State University Archives.

16. *Annual Report,* 1940, 1941, 1942, 1944, and 1947, D.I.B. Archives.

17. *Annual Report,* 1951, D.I.B. Archives.

18. "Brief submitted to the U.S. Dept. of State by American Trucking Association to Authorize Transit in Bond Across Ontario Highways," 1948, In Bond File, D.I.B. Archives.

19. Ibid.; McDougald to E. B. Ryckman, 6 Nov. 1938, In Bond File, D.I.B. Archives.

20. *Minutes Book,* 28 Nov. 1941, D.I.B. Archives.

21. Ibid. See S. L. Springsteen to C. Clinton Campbell, 14 Aug. 1952, 3 Sept. 1952, and 5 Sept. 1952; C. Clinton Campbell to J. A. Bower, 10 Sept. 1952; C. Clinton Campbell to Charles McTague, 10 Sept. 1952; all in the In Bond File, D.I.B. Archives.

The Detroit Board of Commerce, led by Harvey Campbell, also played a significant role in the campaign to pressure the Canadian government to allow U.S. trucks to travel through Ontario "in bond." With the aid of the U.S. Chamber of Commerce, they also persuaded the State Dept. and Congress to negotiate with Canadian officials. See *Detroiter,* 23 Dec. 1940, 3; *Detroiter,* 5 May 1941, 4; *Detroiter,* 19 May 1941, 5; *Detroiter,* 26 May 1941, 3; *Detroiter,* 20 Oct. 1941, 3; *Detroiter,* 1 Dec. 1941, 3; and *Detroiter,* 8 Dec. 1941, 18.

22. Order-in-Council, P.C. 6129 of 16 July 1942; "Brief, American Trucking Assoc.," Appendix A; *Detroit News,* 24 Mar. 1942 and 21 July 1942; and *Detroiter,* 7 July 1942, 5; *Detroiter,* 10 Aug. 1942, 6.

23. "Brief, American Trucking Assoc.," 2; and *Detroiter,* 14 Sept. 1942, 6.

24. "Still Stymied Across Canada," *Detroiter,* 2 Aug. 1943.

25. "Brief, American Trucking Assoc.," 5.

26. "Brief, American Trucking Assoc.," 4.

27. "Brief, American Trucking Assoc.," 5. E. W. Lancaster of the Lancaster Trucking firm urged the continuation of the

wartime provision for in-bond transit across Ontario. "I don't see why we can't cooperate with each other in this matter," he stated. "I know this firm has always received cooperation from American officials." *Border Cities Star*, 2 Dec. 1945.

28. "Brief, American Trucking Assoc.," 5.

29. "Brief, American Trucking Assoc.," 6.

30. *Detroit News*, 15 Dec. 1948.

31. Springsteen to C. Clinton Campbell, 14 Aug. 1952, 3 Sept. 1952, and 5 Sept. 1952; *Annual Report*, 1952, D.I.B. Archives.

32. "Traffic Statistics," D.I.B. Archives.

33. The correspondence files of the Detroit International Bridge Co., as well as the minutes books of board of directors meetings, reveal Bower's active role in the administration of the bridge.

34. *Minutes Book*, 26 Jan. 1942, D.I.B. Archives.

35. *Minutes Book*, 16 Feb. 1943 and 12 Sept. 1960; *Annual Report*, 1942, 1943, 1945; all in D.I.B. Archives.

36. *Annual Report*, 1942–1949, D.I.B. Archives.

37. *Annual Report*, 1948, D.I.B. Archives.

38. *Detroit Free Press*, 1 Nov. 1959; and *Annual Report*, 1949, D.I.B. Archives.

39. *Annual Report*, 1949, D.I.B. Archives.

40. *Annual Report*, 1948, D.I.B. Archives.

41. *Annual Report*, 1934, D.I.B. Archives.

42. *Minutes Book*, 16 May 1941; and *Annual Report*, 1942, both in D.I.B. Archives.

43. *Annual Report*, 1941, D.I.B. Archives.

44. *Annual Report*, 1943; and *Minutes Book*, 15 Sept. 1944, both in D.I.B. Archives.

45. *Minutes Book*, 16 May 1941 and 3 Nov. 1944; and *Annual Report*, 1944, D.I.B. Archives.

46. *Annual Report*, 1949, 4–6; *Annual Audits*, 1940, 1945, and 1949; all in D.I.B. Archives.

47. *Windsor Star*, 10 Sept. 1940 and 2 Dec. 1940; Springsteen to J. A. Bower, 5 Dec. 1940, D.I.B. Archives. See also "Application, City of Windsor to Board of Transportation Commissioners for Canada," Tolls File, D.I.B. Archives, which requested disallowance of proposed toll increases.

48. *Annual Report*, 1940, 1942, 1945, and 1946, D.I.B. Archives.

49. *Minutes Book*, 11 Nov. 1945, D.I.B. Archives; *Annual Report*, 1949, D.I.B. Archives.

50. Pratley, "Report on Inspection of Ambassador Bridge between Windsor and Detroit," 28 Oct. 1949, 1, D.I.B. Archives.

51. Pratley, "Report on Inspection of Ambassador Bridge between Windsor and Detroit," 28 Oct. 1949, 1.

52. Pratley, "Report on Inspection of Ambassador Bridge between Windsor and Detroit," 12 Aug. 1948, 2.

53. *Annual Report*, 1949, 4, D.I.B. Archives.

Chapter 11

1. Woodford and Woodford, *All Our Yesterdays*, 356–57; Morrison, *Garden Gateway to Canada*, 300–308.

2. Coverdale and Colpitts, "Ambassador Bridge Passenger Car Tolls Study, Dec. 14, 1956," D.I.B. Archives.

3. Ibid.; *Annual Report*, 1952, 10, D.I.B. Archives.

4. "Advertisements," D.I.B. Archives.

5. *Annual Report*, 1956, D.I.B. Archives.

6. See, for example, the advertisement, "Motorists Who Know the Ropes Use the Ambassador Bridge to Canada," reprinted in *Annual Report*, 1952, 12, D.I.B. Archives; *Annual Report*, 1956; and *Minutes Book*, 5 Apr. 1957, both in D.I.B. Archives.

7. *Detroit News*, 21 Mar. 1953; *Detroit Free Press*, 21 Mar. 1953 and 1 Nov. 1959. In 1954, a German immigrant couple were married at the center of the span. *Annual Report*, 1954, D.I.B. Archives.

8. *Detroit News*, 30 June 1951; and Elmer Paquette, interview with author, 12 Sept. 1984, D.I.B. Archives.

9. *Detroit Free Press*, 1 Nov. 1959.

10. Ibid.

11. Ibid.

12. *Windsor Daily Star*, 1 Sept. 1954; and *Annual Report*, 1954, D.I.B. Archives.

13. *Annual Report*, 1954, D.I.B. Archives.

14. A photograph of the ceremony is on the cover of the *Annual Report*, 1954, D.I.B. Archives.

15. "Traffic Compilations," D.I.B. Archives; and *Annual Reports*, 1950–1959, D.I.B. Archives.

16. *Annual Report*, 1952, 10–11, D.I.B. Archives.

17. See C. Clinton Campbell to D.I.B. board of directors, 13 Feb. 1952 and 20 Feb. 1956; and *Annual Report*, 1959; both in D.I.B. Archives.

18. Memorandum, C. Clinton Campbell to D.I.B. board of directors, 20 Feb. 1956, D.I.B. Archives.

19. *Annual Report*, 1955, D.I.B. Archives.

20. *Annual Report*, 1950, 1958, 1959, D.I.B. Archives.

21. Memorandum, C. Clinton Campbell to D.I.B. board of directors, 13 Feb. 1952; Victor W. Klein to Campbell, 8 Nov. 1951; J. A. Bower to Campbell, 23 July 1952; Campbell to J. A. Bower, 28 July 1952; all in Toll Rates File, D.I.B. Archives.

22. Coverdale and Colpitts, "Ambassador Bridge: Passenger Car Tolls Study, Dec. 14, 1956," D.I.B. Archives.

23. Ibid.; Coverdale and Colpitts to Campbell, 14 Dec. 1956., D.I.B. Archives.

24. Coverdale and Colpitts to Campbell, 14 Dec. 1956.

25. Campbell and Robert A. Bower to J. A. Bower, 7 Jan. 1957; Campbell to J. A. Bower, "Report on Toll Schedule, Jan. 1957," both in Toll Rates File, D.I.B. Archives.

26. Campbell to Bower, "Report on Toll Rates Schedule, Jan. 1957."

27. Campbell to J. A. Bower, 14 Feb. 1957 and 27 Mar. 1957, D.I.B. Archives.

28. J. A. Bower to Campbell, 26 Jan. 1957, D.I.B. Archives.

29. *Minutes Book*, 5 Apr. 1957, D.I.B. Archives; Campbell to J. A. Bower, 27 Mar. 1927, D.I.B. Archives; *Annual Report*, 1947, D.I.B. Archives; and *Windsor Daily Star*, 22 May 1957.

30. Campbell to J. A. Bower, 9 Feb. 1959, Toll Rates File, D.I.B. Archives.

31. See Pratley, annual inspection reports, 1950–1959, D.I.B. Archives.

32. Pratley, "Inspection Report, 1959," D.I.B. Archives, 4.

33. *Annual Report*, 1952, 1953, 1955, D.I.B. Archives.

34. *Annual Report*, 1954, D.I.B. Archives.

35. Hugh Pratley, interview with author, 12 Nov. 1984, D.I.B. Archives; *Detroit News Pictorial Magazine*, 31 July 1960.

36. Robert A. Bower, interview with author, 12 Mar. 1983. See also J. A. Bower to Harry N. Bawden, 5 May 1949; J. A. Bower to Campbell, 5 May 1949; both in D.I.B. Archives; *Annual Report*, 1950, 1955, D.I.B. Archives; and *Toledo Blade Sunday Magazine*, 16 June 1974.

37. *Annual Report*, 1959, D.I.B. Archives.

38. J. A. Bower to Campbell, 18 June 1953, 25th Anniversary File, D.I.B. Archives.

Chapter 12

1. *Annual Report*, 1960, D.I.B. Archives. Although the first official reference to Campbell's retirement plans was at the board meeting of 12 Sept. 1960, he had notified Bower and other board members earlier. *Minutes Book*, 12 Sept. 1960, D.I.B. Archives.

2. *Minutes Book*, 12 Sept. 1960 and 29 Nov. 1960, D.I.B. Archives.

3. Charles McTague, a longtime friend of Joseph Bower and a D.I.B. board member, strongly recommended Lancaster. Robert C. Bower, interview with author, 12 Mar. 1983, D.I.B. Archives.

4. Roy Lancaster, interview with author, 1 Nov. 1984 and 24 Jan. 1985; Robert C. Bower, interview; and *Minutes Book*, 29 Nov. 1960; all in D.I.B. Archives.

5. *Minutes Book*, 29 Nov. 1960; and Roy Lancaster, interview, 1 Nov. 1984, both in D.I.B. Archives.

6. Roy Lancaster, "Biographical File," Windsor Daily Star Library; *Spanning a Half Century*, 13.

7. *Spanning a Half Century*, 13; "Ambassador Bridge Celebrates Fiftieth Birthday in 1979," *Michigan Trucking Today*, 24 (Nov.-Dec., 1979): 6–7; and Roy Lancaster, interview, D.I.B. Archives.

8. Lancaster, interview, D.I.B. Archives.

9. Arthur Shewman retired in August 1963 after thirty-three years of service. *Annual Report*, 1963, D.I.B. Archives.

10. Lancaster, interview, D.I.B. Archives.

11. *Annual Report*, 1962, 1963, D.I.B. Archives.

12. Lancaster, interview, D.I.B. Archives. See also Detroit-Canada Tunnel Corp. File, D.I.B. Archives. Lancaster and Burton were active together also on the U.S.–Canada Bridge, Tunnel Operators Association.

13. "Traffic Statistics," D.I.B. Archives.

14. *Annual Report*, 1956, 1960, 1961, D.I.B. Archives.

15. See Chapter 10, note 2; "Traffic Statistics," D.I.B. Archives.

16. Lancaster, interview, D.I.B. Archives.

17. Lancaster, interview, D.I.B. Archives.

18. *Annual Report*, 1964, 1966, 1967, D.I.B. Archives.

19. Bob Naylor, "The Bridge," *Renaissance City*, 1 (1980): 11; *Detroit Free Press*, 1 Nov. 1959; and *Detroit News*, 30 Sept. 1973.

20. *Annual Report*, 1964–1969, D.I.B. Archives; United Automobile Workers Union, *Solidarity* (Jan. 1965), 15, and (June 1965), 3–5.

For definitive accounts of the auto pact, see Carl Beigie, *The Canada–U.S. Automotive Agreement: An Evaluation* (Montreal: Canadian-American Committee, 1970); Ronald J. Wonnacott and Paul Wonnacott, *Free Trade between the United States and Canada: The Potential Economic Effects* (Cambridge, Mass: Harvard University Press, 1967), ch. 17; Henrik O. Helmers, *United States-Canadian Automobile Agreement: A Study in Industry Adjustment* (Ann Arbor, Mich.: University of Michigan Institute, 1967); and Ralph Cowan, "Effects of the United States–Canadian Automotive Agreement on Canada's Manufacturing, Trade and Price Posture," Ph.D. dissertation, University of Michigan, 1972.

See also U.S. Congress, Senate, Committee on Finance, *U.S. Canada Automotive Agreement of 1965*, 89th Cong., 1st sess., Sept. 14–21, 1965; and U.S. Executive Dept., *Annual Report of the President of the United States to the Congress on the Operation of the Automotive Products Trade Act of 1965*, printed for the Committee on Finance, U.S. Senate, 1967. One source of controversy was the provision that American-made automobiles had to be shipped directly to Canadian dealerships, rather than to individual consumers. Canada-built automobiles could be purchased by U.S. consumers.

21. *Windsor Star*, 15 Jan 1969, 4 Sept. 1969, 24 Oct. 1969, and 13 Nov. 1969; *Detroit Free Press*, 26 June 1969.

22. *Windsor Star*, 4 Sept. 1969.

23. *Windsor Star*, 13 Nov. 1969, 26 June 1969, and 25 Mar. 1970.

24. "Traffic Statistics"; *Annual Report*, 1965–1969; both in D.I.B. Archives. See also *Traffic Engineering Study: Interstate Highway Connections to Ambassador Bridge to Detroit* (Southfield, Mich.: Reid, Cool and Michalski, 1970), 5.

25. Lancaster, interview, D.I.B. Archives; and *Annual Report*, 1962, D.I.B. Archives. The St. Lawrence Seaway was completed in 1959.

26. Lancaster, interview, D.I.B. Archives; and *Annual Report*, 1965, D.I.B. Archives.

27. *Annual Report*, 1965, D.I.B. Archives.

28. *Annual Report*, 1966, D.I.B. Archives; *Traffic Engineering Study*, 1–3.

29. *Annual Report*, 1967, D.I.B. Archives; *Ambassador Bridge Detroit Plaza Exit Problems* (Southfield, Mich.: Reid, Cool and Michalski, 1970), 1–8.

30. *Annual Report*, 1967, D.I.B. Archives.

31. Lancaster, interview; and Robert A. Bower, interview; both in D.I.B. Archives.

32. Lancaster, interview, D.I.B. Archives; *Traffic Engineering Study*, 6–12.

33. *Traffic Engineering Study*, 8–12, and *Ambassador Bridge Detroit Plaza Exit Problems*, 1–8.

34. *Traffic Engineering Study*, 9–10.

35. Lancaster, interview, D.I.B. Archives.

36. *Annual Report*, 1962, D.I.B. Archives.

37. Woodford and Woodford, *All Our Yesterdays*, 350–55; *Annual Report*, 1967, and Lancaster, interview, D.I.B. Archives.

38. *Annual Report*, 1962, D.I.B. Archives.

39. *Annual Report*, 1956; and *Minutes Book*, 12 Mar. 1956; both

in D.I.B. Archives. See also Unions: Canadian Teamsters Local 880, and Unions: U.S. Teamsters Local 299, both files in D.I.B. Archives.

40. *Annual Report*, 1962; and Unions Files; both in D.I.B. Archives.

41. *Annual Report*, 1968; "Traffic Statistics"; and Union Files; all in D.I.B. Archives.

42. *Annual Report*, 1960; "Traffic Statistics"; both in D.I.B. Archives.

43. *Annual Report*, 1960, 1961; and Pratley, "Annual Inspection Report," 15 July 1960, 24 Nov. 1960; all in D.I.B. Archives.

44. *Annual Report*, 1969, D.I.B. Archives.

45. *Detroit News*, 20 Sept. 1973; Lancaster to Coleman A. Young, mayor of Detroit, 8 Feb. 1982, Necklace of Lights File, D.I.B. Archives. Lancaster got the idea for lighting the bridge after an earlier tour of the bridges in New York City. Lancaster, interview, D.I.B. Archives.

46. *Annual Report*, 1963, D.I.B. Archives. See subsequent annual reports for revenue received from the Ammex operation.

47. *Traffic Engineering Study*, 8.

48. *Traffic Engineering Study*, 8–10, and *Ambassador Bridge Detroit Plaza Exit Problems*, 1–8.

49. For a summary of this problem, see Lancaster to Myles J. Ambrose, Commission of U.S. Customs, 24 Sept. 1971, D.I.B. Archives.

50. Ibid.

51. *Annual Report*, 1965, D.I.B. Archives.

52. Lancaster, interview, D.I.B. Archives.

53. *Annual Report*, 1970, D.I.B. Archives.

54. Lancaster summarized the frustrations of the Detroit International Bridge Co. in dealing with U.S. Customs in a letter to members of the U.S. Senate Committee of Public Works and U.S. House Committee on Public Works and Transportation, 21 Sept. 1979, D.I.B. Archives.

55. *Customs Clearance Center, Port of Detroit, Michigan* (Detroit: Smith, Hinchman and Grylls, Inc., 29 May 1969), 1.

56. Ibid.

57. *Annual Report*, 1964, D.I.B. Archives. See also Detroit International Bridge Co., "Plan of Merger of Canadian Transit Co. with the Detroit International Bridge Co., 1963," and "Agreement of Merger of Canadian Transit Co. with the Detroit International Bridge Co., 1963," both in D.I.B. Archives.

58. *Minutes Book*, 29 Nov. 1960; and Lancaster, interview; both in D.I.B. Archives.

59. *Annual Report*, 1962, 1963, D.I.B. Archives.

60. *Annual Report*, 1966, D.I.B. Archives.

61. *Annual Report*, 1966, 1967, D.I.B. Archives; and *Valuation Report* (Chicago: Duff and Phelps, 1978). 8. See also Kefalas, Biographical File, D.I.B. Archives.

62. John Hannon, interview with author, 4 June 1985; and Lancaster, interview; both in D.I.B. Archives.

63. J. A. Bower to Campbell, 27 Mar. 1969, C. C. Campbell File, D.I.B. Archives.

64. "Traffic Statistics"; and *Annual Report*, 1960–1969; both in D.I.B. Archives.

65. For an account of the net earnings for the period 1960–

1969, see *Annual Report*, 1969, D.I.B. Archives. See also "Consolidated Financial Statements" for years 1959–1969, D.I.B. Archives. From 1959 to 1965 the annual audits were made by Lybrand, Ross Bros. and Montgomery; from 1966 to 1969 they were made by Touche, Ross, Bailey and Smart; from Audits File, D.I.B. Archives.

Chapter 13

1. "Traffic Statistics," D.I.B. Archives.

2. *Annual Report*, 1970, D.I.B. Archives.

3. Ibid.; Hugh Pratley to author, 23 July 1986.

4. Lancaster, interview, D.I.B. Archives; and *Spanning Half a Century*, 15.

5. *Annual Report*, 1971, 1973; and Pratley, "Annual Inspection Report," 1971 and 1973; all in D.I.B. Archives.

6. *Annual Report*, 1973; and *Windsor Star*, 16 Oct. 1973; both in D.I.B. Archives.

7. *Annual Report*, 1972, 1973, D.I.B. Archives.

8. *Annual Report*, 1972, D.I.B. Archives. This report contains photographs of the new toll facilities, truck scales, and renovated entrance plaza.

9. *Annual Report*, 1976, D.I.B. Archives.

10. *Annual Report*, 1973, 1974, 1975, D.I.B. Archives.

11. *Annual Report*, 1979, D.I.B. Archives.

12. *Annual Report*, 1974, 1975, D.I.B. Archives; Duff and Phelps, *Valuation Report, Ambassador Bridge*, 3.

13. Pratley, "Supplementary Inspection Report, Nov. 14, 1975," and "Annual Inspection Report, Aug. 1976," both in D.I.B. Archives.

14. Lancaster, interview, D.I.B. Archives.

15. *Annual Report*, 1975, and Howard, Needles, Tammen and Bergendoff, *Ambassador Bridge: In-Depth Inspection Report, May, 1975*, both in D.I.B. Archives.

16. *Annual Report*, 1975, D.I.B. Archives.

17. *Annual Report*, 1976, D.I.B. Archives. For Pratley's views on the HNTB Report, see Pratley to R. A. Bower and Lancaster, 2 Sept. 1975, Pratley File, D.I.B. Archives.

18. *Annual Report*, 1976, D.I.B. Archives.

19. *Annual Report*, 1975, 1976, 1977.

20. As early as 1957, Pratley reported the slippage of one of the cable bands on the east side of the Canadian tower. Pratley, "Annual Inspection Report," 1977, D.I.B. Archives. Pratley to author, 23 July 1986.

21. *Annual Report*, 1971, D.I.B. Archives.

22. *Ambassador Bridge Detroit Plaza Exit Problems*, 2, and *Traffic Engineering Study*, 8.

23. *Traffic Engineering Study*, 8.

24. *Customs Clearance Center*, 7. According to Robert Bower, the city of Detroit killed the plan. In a public statement, Bower charged that "bureaucratic agencies of the Detroit city government . . . strangled a long planned project to develop the American approach to the Bridge." *Detroit News*, 29 Mar. 1969; and *Windsor Star*, 29 Mar. 1969, 27 Dec. 1973, and 28 Dec. 1973.

25. Lancaster to Myles J. Ambrose, 24 Sept 1971, Customs Clearance Center File, D.I.B. Archives; WJBK-radio editorial, "A Crisis at the Bridge," 13 Feb. 1973; "International Traffic Jam," *Detroit News*, 27 Aug. 1978; *Annual Report*, 1972,

1973, D.I.B. Archives; *Customs Clearance Center,* 1; and *Spanning a Half a Century,* 17.

26. Eugene T. Rossides to David W. Kendall, 16 July 1969; and Kendall to Lancaster, 22 July 1969; both in Customs Clearance Center File, D.I.B. Archives.

27. Rossides to Kendall, 22 July 1969, D.I.B. Archives.

28. Edwin F. Ravis to Lancaster, 15 Nov. 1969. The Bureau also charged that the main cause of congestion at the tunnel and the bridge was "outdated facilities" which impeded the flow of traffic, created a serious safety hazard and did not "allow the inspectional agencies to fully utilize their manpower." Noting that federal funds could not be "allocated for the construction or improvement of non-governmental premises," the Customs Bureau put the blame on bridge and tunnel authorities. Rossides to Kendall, 16 July 1969; G. N. Keidbrede to Dwight Havens, 27 Feb. 1973; and Kendall to Lancaster, 22 July 1969; D.I.B. Archives.

Lancaster responded that these charges were without foundation and constituted an attempt to cloud the real issue. It is significant that the charges were not repeated by the bureau in further negotiations. Lancaster, interview, 9 July 1986.

29. For the policy statement adopted by the Greater Detroit Chamber of Commerce on Feb. 6, 1973, urging the employment of additional customs personnel, see "Greater Detroit Chamber of Commerce Official Policy on U.S. Customs Staffing at the Ambassador Bridge, 6 Feb. 1973," Customs Clearance Center File, D.I.B. Archives.

30. Lancaster to Detroit Housing Commission, 4 Dec. 1968, D.I.B. Archives.

31. Lancaster to U.S. Customs, Chicago, Ill., 8 Aug. 1968, 9 Aug. 1968, 2 Oct. 1968, 4 Oct. 1968, and 10 Oct. 1968; and Lancaster to U.S. Customs, Detroit, Mich., 26 Dec., 1968, D.I.B. Archives.

32. The minutes and reports of these meetings, along with the lists of attendees are in the Customs Clearance Center File, D.I.B. Archives. See, for example, reports of meetings of 12 Dec. 1968, 17 Jan. 1969, 3 Mar. 1969, 10 Mar. 1969, 11 Mar. 1969, 18 Mar. 1969, 27 Mar. 1969, 1 Apr. 1969, 2 Apr. 1969, and 10 Apr. 1969.

33. John V. Sheoris to Lancaster, 21 Mar. 1969, D.I.B. Archives. Reid, Cool and Michalski and Smith, Hinchman and Grylls conducted engineering studies for the bridge. *Annual Report,* 1973, D.I.B. Archives.

34. *Detroit News,* 5 July 1970; Customs Clearance Terminal Committee, "Minutes of Meeting, Aug. 2, 1973," p. 4; John V. Sheoris to Lancaster, 21 Mar. 1969; Al Begter, "Notes on Phone Call Relating to Detroit City Planning Commission and Hubbard-Richard Community Council," 13 Mar. 1969; *Customs Clearance Center,* 7; John Kanters to Detroit Common Council, 15 June 1973; all in Customs Clearance Center File, D.I.B. Archives.

35. "Notes of Phone Call," Walter Sahli to Lancaster, 7 Oct. 1969, Customs Clearance Center File, D.I.B. Archives. It is significant that in 1977 U.S. Customs changed its position for an off-site examination warehouse and approved the location recommended by Lancaster for a large trucking terminal. An off-site terminal had been successfully utilized by U.S. Customs during the Teamster strike in 1968. *Customs Clearance Center,* 1.

36. Lancaster to Kendall, 7 Oct. 1970, Customs Clearance Center File, D.I.B. Archives.

37. Samuel B. Simon to Joseph P. Veakes, U.S. General Ser-

vices Administration, 5 Apr. 1971; "Notes of Meetings," Lancaster and J. Trainor, Mayor's Committee for Industrial Development, Detroit, 7 Apr. 1971 and 27 Apr. 1971; D.I.B. Archives.

38. "Report of Meeting Between Samuel Simon and G.S.A. officials, 24 May 1971," D.I.B. Archives.

39. *Annual Report,* 1973, D.I.B. Archives; Detroit International Bridge Co., "Agreement: Offer to Purchase," 26 Oct. 1973, D.I.B. Archives.

40. Dennis Keilman, GSA, to Lancaster, 12 Dec. 1973; Lancaster to GSA, Chicago, 10 Apr. 1974; both in Customs Clearance Center File, D.I.B. Archives.

41. *Annual Report,* 1974, D.I.B. Archives. The bridge company offered to extend the agreement for ninety days but Overland Western refused because of the "downturn in the economy." memorandum, 31 Dec. 1974, Customs Clearance Center File, D.I.B. Archives.

42. The minutes of the meetings of this committee are in the Customs Clearance Center File, D.I.B. Archives.

43. Thirty-five thousand dollars was raised from local business groups, custom brokers, trucking companies, and the Detroit International Bridge Co. The firm of Lenton, Mields and Coston was hired to produce the report, *Developing a New Customs Clearance Terminal Facility* (Sept. 1973); and "Proposal for Study," 11 May 1973; both in Customs Clearance Center File, D.I.B. Archives.

44. For a report of the visit of Lancaster and the representatives of the Greater Detroit Chamber of Commerce with senators Griffin and Hart, congressmen Dingell and Diggs, and congresswoman Griffith, see D.I.B. *Report,* 12 Sept. 1973, Customs Clearance Center File, D.I.B. Archives.

45. Of the six potential locations considered by Lenton et al., the Overland Western site was rated the most desirable. Lenton, Mields and Coston, "Proposal for Study," 26–34.

46. D.I.B. *Report,* 4 Apr. 1975, Customs Clearance Center File; Lancaster, interview; both in D.I.B. Archives.

47. Gerald Finn, GSA, to Lancaster, 30 Dec. 1975, Customs Clearance Center File, D.I.B. Archives.

48. GSA to John Dingell, 5 Feb. 1976; GSA, "Purchase Prospectus No. PMI 76011 to U.S. House Committee on Public Works and Transportation and U.S. Senate Committee on Public Works," 4 June 1976; both in Customs Clearance Center File, D.I.B. Archives.

49. Detroit International Bridge Co., "Offer to Purchase Overland Western, Ltd. Site," 30 Nov. 1976, Customs Clearance Center File, D.I.B. Archives; Lancaster, interview, D.I.B. Archives.

50. Lancaster to Donald H. Lee, 22 Dec. 1976; Detroit Chamber of Commerce to John Dingell, 27 Dec. 1976; notes of telephone conversation between Lancaster and GSA, Chicago office, 12 Dec. 1976; all in D.I.B. Archives.

51. Jerry Cohen, GSA, to Lancaster, 2 Aug. 1977, Customs Clearance Center File, D.I.B. Archives.

52. Lancaster to Jerry Cohen, 5 Aug. 1977; Lancaster to Kenneth Knight, 10 Aug. 1977; Customs Clearance Center File, D.I.B. Archives.

53. Jerry Cohen to Lancaster, 17 Aug. 1977, Customs Clearance Center File, D.I.B. Archives.

54. GSA to Lancaster, 8 Aug. 1978; Lancaster to GSA, 8 Aug. 1978; Customs Clearance Center File, D.I.B. Archives.

55. Butzel to GSA, 16 Feb. 1979, Customs Clearance Center File, D.I.B. Archives.

56. GSA to Lancaster, 8 June 1979, Customs Clearance Center File, D.I.B. Archives.

57. Lancaster to U.S. Senate Committee on Public Works and U.S. House of Representatives Committee on Public Works and Transportation, 21 Sept. 1979, Customs Clearance Center File, D.I.B. Archives.

58. *Detroit News*, 27 Aug. 1978.

59. U.S. District Court, Eastern District of Michigan, Southern Division, "Order of Immediate Possession," 14 Jan. 1980, Legal File, D.I.B. Archives.

60. Lancaster, interview, D.I.B. Archives.

61. United States–Canada Bridge-Tunnel Operators Association, "A Brief on Accommodation Practices Submitted to Canada Customs and Canada Immigration," Dec. 1974, Legal File, D.I.B. Archives. Lancaster was president of the association in 1974 and in1986.

62. Ibid.

63. See "Traffic Statistics," 1929–1984, and *Annual Report*, 1970, 1971, 1975, 1976, 1978, D.I.B. Archives.

64. *Annual Report*, 1970, D.I.B. Archives.

65. Labor Relations File, 1972, D.I.B. Archives.

66. Labor Relations File, Teamsters Local 880 and Teamsters Local 229; Detroit-Canada Tunnel Corp., *Annual Report*, 1979; D.I.B. Archives.

67. *Annual Report*, 1978, D.I.B. Archives. See also Lancaster to D.I.B. board of directors, 6 Apr. 1978, 17 May 1978, 21 July 1978, and 31 July 1978, D.I.B. Archives.

68. *Annual Report*, 1972, D.I.B. Archives.

69. *Annual Report*, 1970, D.I.B. Archives.

70. *Annual Report*, 1970, 1971, D.I.B. Archives.

71. *Detroit Free Press*, 4 Nov. 1971; *Windsor Star*, 4 Nov. 1971; and *Detroit News*, 4 Nov. 1971.

72. *Annual Report*, 1973, 1974, D.I.B. Archives.

73. *Annual Report*, 1976, D.I.B. Archives.

74. *Windsor Star*, 23 May 1970, 9 June 1970, 14 Jan. 1972, 17 Feb. 1972, 3 May 1972, 8 May 1972, 30 May 1972, 16 June 1972, 21 July 1972 and 14 Oct. 1972; and *Detroit News*, 16 June 1972.

75. *Detroit News*, 3 June 1973.

76. *Windsor Star*, 17 Feb. 1972 and 21 July 1972; and *Detroit News*, 3 June 1973.

77. *Windsor Star*, 17 Feb. 1972, 3 May 1972, 8 May 1972, 16 June 1972 and 14 Oct. 1972.

78. Other interest groups supported the major automobile companies in their lobbying efforts on behalf of the U.S.–Canada auto pact. The United Automobile Workers International Union, for example, was very active in its support for the pact in the United States and in Canada. Indeed, George Burt in Canada and Leonard Woodcock in the United States campaigned in their respective federal government legislative halls in support of the auto pact. Sen. Philip A. Hart Papers, Bentley Library, University of Michigan, Box 433; UAW Region 7 Collection, Boxes 8 and 9, Walter Reuther Collection, Box 49, Archives of Labor and Urban Affairs, Wayne State University; UAW *Solidarity*, Canada ed., Dec. 1975–Jan. 1976.

79. *Windsor Star*, 27 Jan. 1976.

80. "Traffic Statistics," D.I.B. Archives.

81. Ibid.

82. Ibid.

83. Traffic Statistics File, D.I.B. Archives. See also, Duff and Phelps, *Valuation Report*, 6.

84. Duff and Phelps, *Valuation Report*, 15.

85. Duff and Phelps, *Valuation Report*, 10–15; *Annual Report*, 1969–1978; and "Audit Report," 1969–1978; all in D.I.B. Archives.

86. *Annual Report*, 1971, D.I.B. Archives; *Windsor Star*, 29 May 1971; *Detroit News*, 30 May 1971; and *Detroit Free Press*, 29 May 1971.

87. See press release, "Toll Adjustment," 28 Nov. 1980, Toll Rates File, D.I.B. Archives.

88. *Annual Report*, 1975, D.I.B. Archives.

89. *Annual Report*, 1977, D.I.B. Archives. To the end, the Ambassador Bridge was always one of Joseph Bower's major accomplishments, according to his son, Robert. "He dreamt about it; he financed it; he owned it; he lost it; and he regained control of it after its reorganization." R. A. Bower, interview, D.I.B. Archives.

90. *Annual Report*, 1976, 1977, D.I.B. Archives.

91. On retiring, Joseph Bower wrote to Lancaster as follows: "Mr. Chairman you were a big help to me in the conduct of my duties. As chief operating officer and President, you ran a good operation which is most satisfying." Bower to Lancaster, 16 Apr. 1969, D.I.B. Archives.

92. *Minutes Book*, 29 Nov. 1960, D.I.B. Archives.

93. *Annual Report*, 1971, 1972, D.I.B. Archives; *Detroit News*, 5 Sept. 1971.

94. *Annual Report*, 1972; IPEX Corp. File; both in D.I.B. Archives; *Detroit News*, 1 Mar. 1972; *Detroit Free Press*, 2 Mar. 1972; *Wall Street Journal*, 2 Mar. 1972; and *Windsor Star*, 2 Mar. 1972.

95. D.I.B. Stockholders Meeting, *Minutes Book*, 12 June 1972; *Annual Report*, 1972; both in D.I.B. Archives; *Detroit Free Press*, 7 June 1972, 17 July 1972; and *Detroit News*, 7 June 1972 and 17 July 1972; *Wall Street Journal*, 18 July 1972; *Windsor Star*, 17 July 1972; and Duff and Phelps, *Valuation Report*, 7.

96. *Annual Report*, 1972, D.I.B. Archives.

97. Ibid.

98. Duff and Phelps, *Valuation Report*, 7; *Detroit Free Press*, 16 Oct. 1973; *Detroit News*, 19 Oct. 1975. The long-range impact of this decision, based on the "white paper" of the FIRA is still a source of legal controversy and has yet to be resolved.

99. *Annual Report*, 1977, 1978; Lancaster to shareholders of D.I.B., 14 Mar. 1979; both in D.I.B. Archives.

100. D.I.B. "News Release," 19 Mar. 1979, 23 Mar. 1979, 20 Apr. 1979, and 8 June 1979; *Detroit Free Press*, 14 Mar. 1979; *Wall Street Journal*, 13 Mar. 1979; and *Windsor Star*, 24 Mar. 1979, 26 Mar. 1979, and 27 Mar. 1979.

101. D.I.B. "News Release," 31 July 1979; "Agreement of Sale of Certain Assets and Merger between DIB and Fallbridge Holdings, Ltd. and AMBRI"; both in D.I.B. Archives.

102. D.I.B. "News Release," 23 Mar. 1979, D.I.B. Archives.

Chapter 14

1. See Lloyd McLachlan, "Ambassador Bridge No Longer the Novelty It Was Fifty Years Ago," *Windsor Star*, 15 Nov. 1979; WXYZ-TV, "50th Anniversary Celebration," 12 Nov. 1979; and "Ambassador Bridge Celebrates Fiftieth Birthday in 1979," *Michigan Trucking Today*, 24 (Nov.–Dec., 1979): 6–7.

Television text and other news stories are located in Fiftieth Anniversary File, D.I.B. Archives.

2. For the program and addresses, see Fiftieth Anniversary File, D.I.B. Archives.

3. Lancaster, interview, Fiftieth Anniversary File, D.I.B. Archives.

4. *Windsor Star*, 24 Mar. 1979.

5. Lancaster, interview; Lancaster to M. J. Moroun, 7 Oct. 1981; and Lancaster to Coleman A. Young, mayor of Detroit, 8 Feb. 1982, Necklace of Lights File; all in D.I.B. Archives.

In 1981, the bridge underwent rehabilitation under the direction of Hugh Pratley. This included the removal of asphalt from all the Canadian approach surfaces and from the main span, replacement of the deck slab on the approach except for portions that had been rebuilt ten years previously, entirely new expansion joints, and complete repaving with asphalt. In 1982 the U.S. contract provided for total reconstruction of the entire deck on the U.S. approach, including curbs and sidewalks, new expansion joists, and asphalt paving. Pratley to the author, 23 July 1986.

6. *Windsor Star*, 10 Sept. 1981; and *Detroit News*, 20 Oct. 1981.

7. Lancaster to M. J. Moroun, 7 Oct. 1981, D.I.B. Archives. Fred Somes was also given credit for originating the necklace of lights proposal, *Detroit News*, 22 Nov. 1981.

8. For a list of contributors, see Necklace of Lights File, D.I.B. Archives.

9. *Detroit News*, 20 Oct. 1981; and *Windsor Star*, 7 Nov. 1981.

10. *Detroit Free Press*, 24 Nov. 1981; and "Detroit Aglow" Program, D.I.B. Archives.

11. "Traffic Statistics," D.I.B. Archives.

12. Ibid.

13. *Windsor Star*, 26 Apr. 1983, 2 June 1984, 18 June 1984, and 15 Dec. 1984; *Detroit Free Press*, 13 July 1984; and *Wall Street Journal*, 17 Dec. 1984.

14. Bradford Wernle, "Detroit Could Become Major U.S. Rail Gateway," *Crain's Detroit Business*, 1 (June 3–9, 1985): 1.

15. Ibid., 26.

16. The Ambassador Bridge has recently [1985] commissioned William Walsh Associates of Birmingham, Michigan, to study the impact of such competition.

17. "Engineering Report No. 1921, A Location Design Study Report for the Improvement of I-94, Blue Water Bridge and Plaza in Port Huron, St. Clair County," Nov. 1982, D.I.B. Archives.

Although the Blue Water Bridge, opened in 1938, is located considerably north of Detroit, its strategic position is evident from an examination of the freeway system in Michigan and Ontario. Port Huron is now easily accessible from western Michigan, Indiana, Illinois, and other midwestern states via interstates 94 and 69 and Route 21. From the Canadian plaza of the Blue Water Bridge, Ontario's freeway 402, makes a direct connection with MacDonald-Cartier 401 west of London, Ontario. The Blue Water Bridge thus provides an excellent transportation link between the Midwest

and Toronto, Buffalo, and Montreal. With additional plaza facilities and eventually a second span, the Blue Water Bridge may become an attractive alternative to commercial trucking firms, especially if the Ambassador Bridge is unsuccessful in overcoming the truck inspection delays caused by inadequate U.S. government facilities.

18. "Traffic Statistics," D.I.B. Archives. Truck crossings in 1985 numbered 1,554,000; in 1986, 1,575,000.

19. Carl E. Beigie, *The Canada–U.S. Automotive Agreement: An Evaluation* (U.S. Planning Assoc. and Private Planning Assoc. of Canada, 1970), 124.

20. Ibid. See also Henrik O. Helmers, *The United States–Canadian Automotive Agreement* (Ann Arbor, Mich.: University of Michigan Institute for International Commerce, 1967); and Ronald J. and Paul Wonnacott, *Free Trade Between the U.S. and Canada: The Potential Economic Effects* (Cambridge, Mass.: Harvard University Press, 1967), chapter 7.

21. James Dow, "Auto Pact: Tune Up or Trade On?", *Windsor Star*, 19 Jan. 1985; and *Journal of Commerce*, 363 (1 Feb. 1985).

22. For information on containerized cargo, intermodal freight shipment, and recent changes in shipment of goods from East Coast ports, see: "Symposium to Focus on St. Lawrence River," *Journal of Commerce*, 363 (6 Feb. 1985): 12A; "Need Stressed to Boost St. Lawrence River Trade," *Journal of Commerce*, 363 (12 Feb. 1985): 1B; Tim Neale, "Steamship Group Targets Intermodal Costs," *Journal of Commerce*, 363 (1 Mar. 1985); "Speculation Abounds with Introduction of Host of New Big Ships," *Journal of Commerce*, 363 (11 Mar. 1985): 12C; "'Shippers in Driver's Seat' as Huge Containerships, Load Centers Proliferate," *Journal of Commerce*, 363 (11 Mar. 1985): 13C, 23C; Craig Dunlap, "Intermodalism Urged for Seaports to Retain Competitive Edge," *Journal of Commerce*, 363 (11 Mar. 1985): 14C; "Double Stacked Containers Receive Success Rating," *Journal of Commerce*, 363 (27 Mar. 1985): 1B; and "Trucks, Trains and Ships Grow Larger, Producing Savings and Problems," Business Bulletin in *Wall Street Journal* (1 Nov. 1984).

23. See "Air Commerce," magazine supplement, *Journal of Commerce*, 363 (29 Apr. 1985); Bradford Wernele, "Metro Draws Cargo Warehouses," *Crain's Detroit Business*, 1 (18–24 Mar. 1985): 1.

24. Michigan Department of Transportation, *Detroit Travel Information Center* (1983), p. 1.

25. Ibid.

In an earlier study, the tunnel was recommended for the site of the information center. M. Sharif Shakrane, *Detroit Travel Information Center Study* (Lansing: Michigan Dept. of State Highways and Transportation, 1974).

26. Ibid., 1.

27. Ibid.

28. Ibid., 2.

29. Ibid. See also Federal Highway Administration, *Detroit Travel Information Center and Associated Roadways Near I–75 and the Ambassador Bridge* (1983).

30. Lancaster, interview, D.I.B. Archives.

INDEX

Philip P. Mason is professor of history and director of the Archives of Labor History and Urban Affairs at Wayne State University. He received his M.A. and Ph.D. from the University of Michigan. Dr. Mason is the author of numerous scholarly articles and several historical studies, including A History of American Roads.

The manuscript was edited by Kathryn Wildfong. The book was designed by Don Ross. The typeface for the text is Palatino. The display face is Uptight Neon. The book is printed on 70-lb. Sterling Litho Matte and bound in Joanna Arrestox black vellum.

Manufactured in the United States of America.